Hidden Heretic of the Renaissance: Leonardo da Vinci

By Andrew Linnell

Threefold Publishing

Seattle, WA.

Copyright © 2019 Andrew Linnell.

All rights reserved. No part of this publication may be reproduced, distributed, or transmitted in any form or by any means, including photocopying, recording, or other electronic or mechanical methods, without the prior written permission of the publisher, except in the case of brief quotations embodied in critical reviews and certain other noncommercial uses permitted by copyright law. For permission requests, write to the publisher, addressed "Attention: Permissions Coordinator," at the address below.

ISBN: 978-0-578-66387-6 (paperback)

Front cover image by Andrew Linnell.
Book design by Andrew Linnell.

Published by Threefold Publishing, in the United States of America.

First published edition November, 2019, updated 5/27/2020.

Threefold Publishing
P.O. Box 251
Mountlake Terrace, WA 98043

www.cfae.us/threefold-publishing

Table of Contents

Table of Contents 3
Acknowledgements 6
Preface 8
Introduction 12
    What Will Be Covered 17
    A Brief Recap of Leonardo's Platonic Studies 21
    Early Christian Understanding of the Christ 29
    Theological Underpinnings 31
    Leonardo and the Church 40
1. Grooming the Renaissance Man 44
2. A Tale of Two Paintings 62
    The Start of a Deep Investigation 63
    Which Painting is the Original? 64
    Exploring the History Surrounding These Two Paintings 68
    Restoration by the National Gallery 70
    How Did Each Painting Get to Their Respective Museum? 72
3. Debating the Depictions 82
    Common Interpretations of the Paintings 82
    Religious Belief Expressed in Art 97
    Why Were the Paintings Not Identical? 105
    Depiction of a Heretical Mystery 114
    Theological Basis for the Painting's Mystery 128
    The Heretics 130
4. Fusing the Fragments of a Mystery 153

    Holy Infants Embracing...154

    Haloes 167

    How the Two Children Were Merged............................175

    Summary of the Role of Leonardo's Students...........188

5. Lifting the Veil of Isis 189

    Secrets of the Background..189

    Sacred geometry..196

    Hand Gestures 205

    Gnostic Esotericism: Androgyne, Cain, and Abel 215

    Ancient Expectations of Two Messiahs 225

    Applying Our Insights...232

    Participation of Florentine Artists 235

    The Archangel 241

    Conclusion 243

6. The Emergence of a Mystery......................................249

    Understanding Why Leonardo Choose Two Infants.................251

    Renaissance 2.0 260

    Final Thoughts 262

Appendix A 264

    Exploring the History Surrounding the Two Paintings 264

Appendix B 271

    Merging of Zarathustra and Gautama Buddha 271

Appendix C..274

    Initiation in the New Testament..................................274

Appendix D 276

Modern Mysticism 276

List of Figures 281

Bibliography 286

Index 292

Acknowledgements

Many come to mind to whom I would like to express my sincere gratitude. As I write this before publication, I am sure to have forgotten some whose contributions were important.

Author and friend Neill Reilly became my most prolific reviewer finding numerous awkward sentences and frequently challenging my explanations for my intended audience. Supporting my efforts to compose this has been my dear wife Natasha who has been my first reader for each section, my most listened to critic, and my principle cheerleader. Her unflinching support for me and this project persisted over these past four years. While I closed my office door to keep out the cats, she prepared sustenance and insights that kept this effort rolling along.

In aid of my research, I wish to thank Norwegian scholar and philosopher Trond Skaftnesmo whom I have never met. Despite this, I feel we've been colleagues. His book *Verdensordet*, supports the conclusions of this book. Our emails have had a deep effect on the outcome of this book. And another scholar who I've never met but has had great influence on this book is Andrew Welburn and his two books: *The Beginnings of Christianity* and *The Mysteries*.

In 2005, I was invited by Tom Raines, the editor of the magazine *New View*, to present to a conference in London on Technology and the Human Future. While staying at his house, our conversations drifted away from technology only to come to the subject of the *Virgin of the Rocks*. I had been working on a paper discussing the painting's depictions that his magazine would later publish. Thankfully, as a result of our discussion, I found errors and impediments to my thought flow. Tom gave me a book by a David Ovason (penname) entitled *The Two Children*. While I found this book to be sprinkled with errors, I also found some valuable nuggets.

I am deeply indebted to the work of Rudolf Steiner who was, for me, the first to unveil this Christian Mystery regarding the two different boys of Matthew and Luke.

I am grateful to my paternal grandfather who as a Presbyterian pastor and homesteader was also a 33-degree Mason. Some of his interests in Christian mysteries must have rubbed off onto me.

Special mention goes to Marek Majorek whose insights into Christianity helped awaken my interest in Christology. We met at Emerson College, Forest Row, England in 1978 and been friends since. There I attended evening lectures by William Mann on Art History and in the spring of 1979 joined a group led by Julian Pook that toured various Italian and French sites with Renaissance artwork.

Lastly, I give thanks for all the encouragement by the members of the Seven Bridges writer's group with whom I've shared much of this book as it was being written. The group met in the Thayer Public Library, Lancaster, MA.

Preface

As the son of a professor of Astronomy, I grew up with an inherited deference for the academic. My older brother, however, was already a gifted artist as a child. Through him, I experienced that art too had a significant role in our human culture, albeit, in those years, a role secondary to science. Whenever I visited a home with those large coffee table art books on Renaissance art, I always found myself engrossed in them.

Tests in high school on my reading level revealed that because of my double vision, I would likely flunk out of a college liberal arts program. At the age of two, a sharpened stick had pierced the skin of my right eye, injuring muscles near the base of the nose. Although the eye healed, it never again aligned with the left eye. As I read, I could not sweep my eyes from right to left to find the next line. Thus, my reading speed and comprehension suffered greatly. I thereby sought a science or engineering degree.

In my college years in the School of Engineering at the University of Michigan, I would sit in on art history classes and often wished that a career there could be viable for me. My cousin must have had the same art history 'bug' as me, but she had more courage and determination. Her career led to her appointment as curator of Northern European painting at NYC's Met.

My fire for art history smoldered until IBM granted me a sabbatical in 1978 to attend one year at Emerson College in Forest Row, England. There I attended evening classes by William Mann whose introduction to Renaissance art stoked that fire whose flame has not diminished in these past 40 years! William brought my awareness to the usual compositional features of this art but also ventured deeply into the biographies, historical contexts, and meaning to these masterpieces. William certainly had been inspired through his studies of Rudolf Steiner, but he spoke out of his wisdom he had won through his own remarkable work.

As a result of William's class, I toured northern Italy to experience much of the area's art treasures with a group of students from Emerson College. We traveled through Colmar, the Alps, Orvieto, and Assisi, before spending a week in Florence followed by additional days in Milan. At the time, I was initially drawn to the works of Raphael and Botticelli but the call to Leonardo was already sounding.

Later, a trip to Paris afforded me a day in the Louvre where I spent most of my time with Leonardo's *Mona Lisa* and the first of his two *Virgin of the Rocks* paintings. Then, a 1979 springtime trip to London allowed me to spend a day in the National Gallery. Much of that glorious day was spent in front of (and to the side of) Leonardo's second *Virgin of the Rocks*.

Figure 1 Virgin of the Rocks, LdV, Nat'l Gallery, London, close-up of child

This book comes as a result of what I saw that spring day in 1979, namely that the version at the National Gallery had objects painted on top of the finishing varnish! It shocked me but I could not find any indications that art historians were even aware of this (this was before the Era of the Internet). This enigma led me to investigate the known history of this painting. That historical exploration raised far more questions than answers. The most perplexing part of this mystery for me later became my quest to resolve what Leonardo had intended to portray in this painting.

Figure 2 shows the wood panel upon which a white base would be applied and on top of this base the oil paints would be applied. When the painting was complete, a coat of varnish would be applied. But this painting in the National Gallery had more paint on top of the varnish! This extra paint depicted the haloes and the staff in the painting *Virgin of the Rocks*.

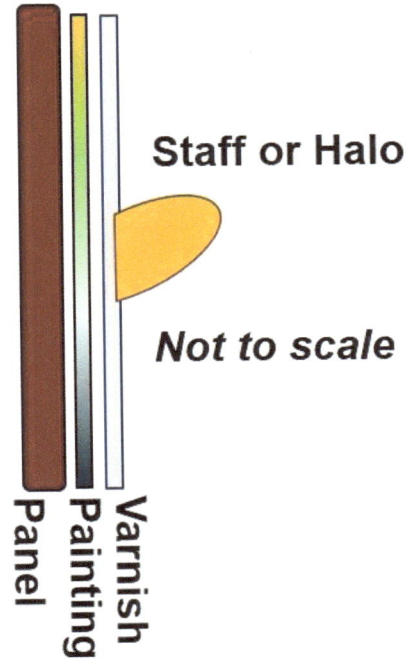

Figure 2 Sideview of painting

This book cycles through several themes gradually deepening them with each cycle. While employing the rigors of an academic book, I have intended the subject matter to be approachable by a layperson.

Lastly, when noting dates, I have used the common nomenclature of academic works using the modern terms "BCE" and "CE" that replaced "BC" and "AD" for dates less than year 1000. All dates larger than 1000 should be assumed to be "CE".

Introduction

Figure 3 Virgin of the Rocks with frame, LdV, National Gallery London

As mentioned in the Preface, this book comes as a result of a special day in the spring of 1979 when I was fortunate to tour the National Gallery in London. There I wanted to see the second of Leonardo da Vinci's two paintings, the *Virgin of the Rocks*.

Figure 4 Virgin of the Rocks, LdV, Nat'l Gallery, London

Because of how this painting was displayed, I was able to stand at its edge to look across its surface. I witnessed how this painting had objects, namely the three haloes and the staff of John, that had been painted on top of the finishing varnish! It shocked me but in the years of subsequent research, I could not find any indications of why.

This research revealed details about a legal dispute Leonardo and his painting partner had against their customer, the Confraternity of the Immaculate Conception. As I continued this research, I came to the inner feeling that I had found the reason for why the paint was on top of the varnish.

But this raised a far more puzzling question, why were these objects not included in both paintings when the varnish had been applied? Was the answer intentional technique or had the painters finished their work, sealed the painting with varnish only to find that the Confraternity would not accept it without changes? If so, then what Leonardo had intended to portray in this painting became obscured. What happened and why?

I discovered clues in Andrew Welburn's book *The Beginnings of Christianity*.[1] His book pointed to the works of Rudolf Steiner whose New Testament exegesis had clearly distinguished differences in the two gospel stories regarding the birth of Jesus.

The insight from Rudolf Steiner, given in a lecture in 1909[2] opened the door for me to reveal what Leonardo was intending to portray and why. Leonardo's portrayals could have, in those times, led to an Inquisition declaring him to be a heretic. Steiner repeated this revelation multiple times thereafter in numerous theological lectures.[3]

---

[1] Andrew Welburn, *The Beginnings of Christianity*, Floris Books, 1991
[2] Rudolf Steiner, *The Gospel of St. Luke*, lecture 7, 21Sep1909, Basel, GA 114
[3] Rudolf Steiner, (listing included in Bibliography)

Figure 5 Virgin of the Rocks, LdV, Louvre, Paris

This insight from Rudolf Steiner shed light on the Christmas stories of Luke and Matthew. Steiner argued that these two stories are so different because there are indeed different babies and different families in each story. With this insight, one can understand what is being depicted in these paintings. The *Virgin of the Rocks* has baffled art historians for centuries as to the characters portrayed. The far-reaching implications of this revelation urged me to publish the results of my research.

I believe strongly that I have uncovered the truth of why there are two[4] *Virgin of the Rocks* paintings and that its story must be told, not only for Leonardo but also for Christianity. While I am not, by profession, an art historian nor a theologian, I hope that you will find the research as convincing as I have found it. I am excited to share with you my thirty years of research.

But in sharing this, I realize that most readers will be unaccustomed to the philosophies prevalent during the Renaissance and even less so with their roots that take us back to Hellenistic and Early Christian times. In order to lead the reader, I have chosen to "peal the onion" in explaining these concepts and philosophies as they relate to my research. Themes will be introduced and returned to several times in the forthcoming chapters so that the reader has a chance to assimilate the concepts and weave these into one's understanding of the unfolding mystery revealed by this book.

I have been encouraged to write this book by the Belgian scholar and author Jos Verhulst. Our conversations led to his academic article *The Esoteric Content of Leonardo da Vinci's 'Virgin of the Rocks'* (Louvre; 1483/86)[5] where Jos explores the chronology and

---

[4] An exhibition in Ancona, Italy displayed a third *Virgin of the Rocks* that had been in private collection. Some art historians believe this painting has been done mostly by students but in part by Leonardo.
[5] Jos Verhulst, *The Esoteric Content of Leonardo da Vinci's 'Virgin Of The Rocks'* (Louvre; 1483/86) can be found on Academia.edu here:

horoscope of each of the birth stories from the Gospels of Luke and Matthew. While Jos and I came to the subject with different intentions, our brief sharing of ideas led to great enthusiasm by me to persevere to complete this book.

Some of the key findings from my research include:

- Leonardo da Vinci disguised a theme in his painting *Virgin of the Rocks* that would have been considered heretical in his times
- One of his students, Pinturicchio, portrayed the next important step in this heretical tale when in the Temple in Jerusalem the two Jesus boys are, in a mysterious way, merged. Each boy possessed highly evolved spiritual elements. The result would be that one boy continued on to be the one who becomes known as Jesus of Nazareth while the other, without its spiritual members, would soon die.
- Leonardo's students corroborate in their paintings entitled *Holy Infants Embracing*
- Finally, Bernardino de Conti, another student, proves who the characters of *Virgin of the Rocks* must be by adding to the above clues with his painting, *The Three Holy Infants*.

What Will Be Covered

We begin our journey by tracing the history of at least two paintings known as the *Virgin of the Rocks*. This history will lead us to conclude that the painting at the Louvre was the original while the painting with the same name found in London's National Gallery was its replacement. Leonardo's own life story and goals will be shown to be intimately connected with the history of these

---

https://www.academia.edu/19773794/The_esoteric_content_of_Leonardo_Da_Vincis_Virgin_of_the_Rocks

paintings. This history cannot be properly appreciated without also delving into the evolution of Western or Roman Christian theology up to the time that the Renaissance began to blossom. That task falls to the related book, *The Uncomfortable History of Christianity*. Since the time of Augustine (354 – 430 CE), Knowledge had taken a back seat to Faith. Leonardo, as we'll see, was the hidden heretic of the Renaissance who sought to restore Knowledge to its former prominence. This book will explore Leonardo's disposition towards Science, Art, and the Church of his day. This will help to color our understanding of his motivation for this painting.

Leonardo had a highly developed capacity for observation. He brought his perceptive exactitude into scientific and engineering insight as well as into his painting. Through his training and insights, he became free of existing dogmas, teachings, stereotypes, and biases – he became the Renaissance Man. Yet, as a philosopher and a scientist, Leonardo was fenced in by the on-going Inquisition. He was able to steer clear of accusations of heresy by holding up his privilege as a master painter who was revered by the politically powerful.

Leonardo found a path to reveal theological foundations from early Christian times through his art. From the Inquisitors, he hid these revelations in plain sight. Only a genius like Leonardo could dismember[6] an esoteric Christian insight, reveal it in its scattered parts that consisted of multiple works by himself and his students,

---

[6] In the Ancient Egyptian Mysteries of Osiris, as told by Plutarch, Osiris is murdered by his brother Set who dismembers his body. Isis, his wife, searches for and finds the parts to properly bury them together. This enabled Osiris, in a ray of light, to impregnate her. Her son Horus becomes a model, some claim, for Christian theology. See E. A. Wallis Budge, *Osiris and the Egyptian Resurrection*, P. L. Warner, 1911, pp. 19-21.

and finally have it reconstituted to its wholeness. This book puts the parts together to reveal the whole mystery.

Figure 6 Three Holy Children, Bernardino de Conti, private

One of Leonardo's students, Bernardino de Conti, played a major role in providing clues to piece together this Christian mystery. Figure 6 shows a painting that remains in a private collection. Carlos Pedretti was able to include it in an exhibit in 2005 entitled *The Genius and Vision in the Marche*. The exhibit was held in Ancona, Italy. The painting shows three holy children with the center one being John the Baptist. It provides convincing proof that neither boy in the original *Virgin of the Rocks* can be John the Baptist! De Conti painted the same two boys as seen in *Virgin of the Rocks* and he placed John the Baptist between the boys to prove that neither of them should be considered to be John the Baptist. The other two holy children are replicas from other paintings by Leonardo's students who participated in this scheme to reveal this mystery. Leonardo involved his own students to help reveal what would have been deemed a heretical theological view if the inquisitors could have put together what this book has.

Both the original *Virgin of the Rocks* and its copy depicted two innocent infants. Ancient texts as well as the Gospels of Luke and Matthew support the conclusion that Leonardo was depicting the Jesus of these two gospels as separate individuals. Among documents of the Dead Sea Scrolls, two messiahs, one kingly and one priestly, were expected by the Essenes.[7] The expectation of both a kingly and a priestly messiah shows up in several ancient texts.

---

[7] The Essenes were an ancient Jewish ascetic sect in Palestine from the second century BC. They avoided impure food, impure thoughts, and impure acts including sex. Along with the Sadducees and Pharisees, they comprised the three main Jewish religious groups in the two centuries leading to the time of Christ. The Essenes communities were highly organized with property held in common. They are most likely the authors of the Dead Sea Scrolls.

A Brief Recap of Leonardo's Platonic Studies

Dartmouth College offers an excellent brief biography of Leonardo.[8] It claims, "Legend has it that Leonardo was Raphael's model for Plato in the School of Athens, and he would probably have been appalled if he knew of this, for the scientific and artistic Leonardo apparently had little sympathy for the lofty [unscientific] poetic Neoplatonism of the Medici court." Leonardo certainly had deep respect for the original Neoplatonic philosophers but not for those in his time that dominated over its serious implications for the emerging sciences.

The article points out that Leonardo was aware that dilettantes saw him as an *omo sanza lettere*, an unlettered and uneducated man. His scientific knowledge was perhaps without equal in his time. But, like Shakespeare who also knew little Latin and less Greek, Leonardo's lack of these languages of the learned kept him estranged from the inner circles of the intellects of his time who looked down upon those not well versed in Greek and Latin.

The article concludes that he "shunned their ideas about the *route* to wisdom, preferring observation, experience, and experiment to [vain] contemplation. In his notebooks he wrote, 'I am fully conscious that, not being a literary man, certain presumptuous persons will think that they may reasonably blame me; alleging that I am not a man of letters. Foolish folks! Do they not know that I might retort ... that they, who deck themselves out in the labors of others will not allow me my own ... they do not know that my subjects are to be dealt with by experience rather than words, and experience has been the mistress of those who wrote well.'"[9]

---

[8] https://www.dartmouth.edu/~matc/math5.geometry/unit14/unit14.html accessed 21May2018
[9] IBID

The Dartmouth author concludes, "the phrase ... they who deck themselves out in the labors of others must certainly be a jab at the Neoplatonists, decking themselves out in the labors of Plato."[10] Leonardo's retort is that he drinks from the fountain of wisdom itself rather than through the works of these learned men. Keep in mind this drinking from the "fountain of wisdom." This is the same fountain of wisdom had previously flowed into the Hellenistic mind that flourished before and during the first two centuries following the Christ Event. How did Leonardo rediscover this fountain of wisdom? Was it through the new way of thinking that was born in Leonardo's time, namely the Scientific Method? Like the Scientific Method, Leonardo emphasized accurate and objective observation, not only of nature but of thinking and art as well. But was the fountain of wisdom something more than this?

The Dartmouth article continues with, "Most humanists of the Renaissance had a reverence for Plato, and Cosimo de Medici (Lorenzo's grandfather) resolved to make Florence the center of Neoplatonic learning."[11]

The "Plato Four" and Their Academy

Leonardo's adult education was connected with the Platonic Academy and other institutions in Florence that were greatly influenced by George Gemistus Plethon who had a key role in awakening the Florentine philosophers through lectures begun in 1438 on Greek philosophy, mysticism, and mythology. Before returning to the Byzantine lands in 1441, Plethon offered a trunk full of esoteric books for translation. The de facto ruler of Florence, Cosimo de Medici, full of enthusiasm from Plethon's lectures, commissioned Marsilio Ficino to translate these into Latin. For

---

[10] IBID
[11] IBID

Ficino to perform this work, Cosimo built a villa for him in nearby Careggi. There, in Plato's honor, Ficino burned an eternal lamp beside a statue of Plato. Ficino could recite the entire Plato *Dialogues*, but, according to his nieces, he couldn't remember where he put his slippers! Perhaps he was the model for the absent-minded professor. By 1463, when Leonardo was an eleven-year old boy studying at Verrocchio's studio, the Platonic Academy was in operation. It would draw scholars from across Italy as well as Europe.

Figure 7 from Zachariah in the Temple: Marsilio Ficino, Cristoforo Landino, Angelo Poliziano & Demetrios Chalkondyles, Domenico Ghirlandaio, Santa Maria Novella, Cappella Tornabuoni, Florence

Why did Plethon leave Florence? To found a mystery center in his home near Sparta! He could only do this if he knew how to select and initiate students as a hierophant. Likely Plethon had initiated some of those who traveled with him and remained behind to teach in Florence. For a school with initiation to have survived, it would need to have been hidden from watch of the Inquisitors of the Catholic Church. Thus, no records exist of what this hidden academy accomplished as its activities remained secret.

This author suggests that someone who had been trained by George Gemistus Plethon and was associated with the Platonic Academy of Florence initiated Leonardo around 1481. Plethon himself must have been capable of this because after leaving Florence, Plethon returned home to found a Greek mystery school in Mystra or Mistra. He died either just before or just after the fall of Constantinople in 1453. This premise that Plethon was a hierophant is supported by the fact that in 1466, some of his Italian disciples, risked their lives to gather his remains from Mystra to inter them in the Tempio Malatestiano in Rimini, the port city of Florence. They undertook this mission "so that the great Teacher may be among free men". His plaque reads, "The remains of Gemistos the Byzantine, Prince of Philosophers in his time."

Another source for the eminent Greek Philosophers was a collection of ten books by Diogenes Laërtius called the *Lives and Opinions of Eminent Philosophers.* Laërtius lived in the third century CE but little is known about his life. His books were translated from Greek to Latin by Ambrogio Traversari who presented his manuscript to Cosimo de' Medici on February 8, 1433, just five years before the arrival of Plethon. The books were printed in 1472 when Leonardo was twenty years old.

Figure 8 Bust of Ficino by A.F. da Fiesole, Duomo, Florence

Marsilio Ficino, the first of the Plato Four, was selected for his role by Cosimo de Medici following the lectures by Gemistus Plethon. Ficino's influential humanist philosophy escorted early Italian Renaissance thought. In 1492 Ficino summed up the birth of the Renaissance this way, "This century, like a golden age, has restored to light the liberal arts, which were almost extinct: grammar, poetry, rhetoric, painting, sculpture, architecture, music ... this century appears to have perfected astrology." But, as an example to his student Leonardo, Ficino's enthusiastic pursuit of knowledge led to an accusation of heresy. In 1489, he was accused of magic! Pope Innocent VIII presided over his trial. A strong defense coupled with Medici support led to his acquittal. In addition to being a philosopher and an astrologer, his alchemy work was very highly regarded. Perhaps his greatest contribution to Renaissance thought came through his translations into Latin of all of Plato's existing works.

The second member was Pico della Mirandola. Pico was a bold and brilliant young philosopher. He could read and write in 22 languages. It is said that because the totality of human learning was ponderable, he aspired to hold all of it in his mind. As a young man, he challenged any and all to a knowledge contest. His great ambition was to reconcile all religions. As a first step, he attempted to reconcile the creation stories in the *Timaeus* with *Genesis*. Similar attempts at reconciliation of Greek mythology with Christian themes were undertaken by many contemporary Florentine artists. Pico also sought to connect the Jewish kabbalah with Christian themes. Don Karr, in his *Esotericism and Christian Kabbalah: 1480-1520* writes, "If a definition of kabbalah within a Jewish context is limited to the movement begun among certain Jewish mystics and esotericists of the late twelfth and early thirteenth centuries, then, in one respect, so-called Christian kabbalists had too broad a concept of what kabbalah was, while, in another respect, they developed only a portion of the contemporary kabbalistic doctrine. Our early Christian kabbalists assumed that (Jewish) kabbalah was as ancient as the Torah, if not more so (certainly Mosaic—if not Adamic), even as they had assumed the remote antiquity of the Hermetic writings. With all this, they considered kabbalah to be the Oral Law in its entirety according to the legend of its inception as proffered in the account of 4 Ezra (II Esdras) 14:42-48; this would include the Talmud, various Midrashim, and other rabbinic writings. For Pico, this Oral Tradition, or cabala, even included Jewish philosophers such as Maimonides."[12] Pico's interest in reconciling Christianity with the Kabbala and other pre-Christian philosophical traditions was later

---

[12] Don Karr, *Esotericism and Christian Kabbalah: 1480-1520*, L'Époque de la Renaissance, Benjamins B. V., 2017

taken up by the German humanist, Johannes Reuchlin (1445–1522).

The third of the Four was Cristoforo Landino. He published philosophical dialogues: *De anima* (1453), *De vera nobilitate* (1469), and the *Disputationes Camaldulenses* (1474). When he joined Ficino at the Academy, Cristoforo was already a well-known author and commentator on Virgil, Dante, and Horace. Lorenzo's patronage of the arts fueled the Renaissance and Landino prospered as a Platonic professor and tutor to Medici offspring. He saw in Cosimo's son, Lorenzo, Plato's "Ideal ruler."

The fourth member was Angelo Poliziano (figure 7 shows Demetrios Chalkondyles instead. Chalkondyles taught Greek literature at the great universities of the Italian Renaissance). Poliziano, as a wonder boy, began publishing in Latin at age 10. By 16, he had translated Homer's *Iliad*. Like Landino, he also served as a tutor for the Medici children and taught at the Platonic Academy. His many students held him in the highest esteem. "It is likely that Poliziano was homosexual, or at least had male lovers, and he never married."[13] Poliziano was interred in the Church of San Marco in Florence in 1494. Persistent question about the cause of his death led to forensic tests in 2007 that showed that both Poliziano and Pico died of arsenic poisoning, likely on the order of Piero de Medici whose rule of Florence was collapsing to the monk Girolamo Savonarola. Following Lorenzo de Medici's death, the 20-year-old Piero became the maestro of Florence in 1492. But he soon was so unpopular that he was exiled in 1494, right after the deaths of Poliziano and Pico. In the years 1492 to 1494, Piero was in great fear of Savonarola's political strength and followers who

---

[13] Paul Strathern, *The Medici: Godfathers of the Renaissance*. London: Random House, 1993

found the teachings of the Platonic Academy to be heretical. Piero ensured the closing of the Plethon-inspired Academy by poisoning its prominent professors.

The so-called Plato Four were the main but not the only teachers at the Academy. These four attracted the most brilliant minds in Italy to come for study with them. They would often meet in a studio at Lorenzo de Medici's estate and invite students residing in the Medici household such as Leonardo and Michelangelo to participate.

Figure 9 Bible Moralisee, 1220 AD, Osterreichische National Biblioteck, Vienna

Geometrician

Over the entrance to Leonardo's Academy in Milan were the words, "Let no one enter here who is not a geometrician".

An article from Dartmouth university speaks about Leonardo's love for mathematics and geometry, "Recall Plato's inscription over his academy door, "Let no one enter who is lacking in geometry!" This phrase taken from Leonardo's notebooks gives some idea of the importance he placed on mathematics. He also wrote, "There is no certainty in sciences where one of the mathematical sciences cannot be applied."[14]

This delightful Dartmouth article points out common misconceptions about Leonardo and theology. Most want to assume that Leonardo, like the image of modern scientists, must have been a reductionist, a materialist, indeed an atheist underneath the personality veneer. But Leonardo, to the contrary, wove together Science, Art, and Religion seeing these three as a whole.

The article points out that Leonardo was aware that dilettante saw him as an *omo sanza lettere*, an unlettered and uneducated man. His scientific knowledge was perhaps without equal in his time, but his ignorance of Latin and Greek kept him estranged from the inner circles of the learned men of his time who looked down on those not well versed in Greek and Latin letters and grammar. Despite this, Leonardo was recognized as a genius in all other fields.

The article concludes that he "shunned their ideas about the *route* to wisdom, preferring observation, experience, and experiment to [vain] contemplation. In his notebooks he wrote, 'I am fully

---

[14] https://www.dartmouth.edu/~matc/math5.geometry/unit14/unit14.html accessed 21May2018

conscious that, not being a literary man, certain presumptuous persons will think that they may reasonable blame me; alleging that I am not a man of letters. Foolish folks! do they not know that I might retort ... that they, who deck themselves out in the labors of others will not allow me my own ... they do not know that my subjects are to be dealt with by experience rather than words, and experience has been the mistress of those who wrote well.'"[15]

Early Christian Understanding of the Christ

Those of the first two centuries understood that what the Christ had performed was an act of Divine Love. They regarded Christ's decision to work upon earth in a human body as a decision for which there was no compulsion. No human feeling could match the magnitude of love that was needed for this God to make and carry out this decision. Through this act of love, they felt, the most important event in human evolution had occurred for their benefit.

These Early Christians sought to be present and to experience, through their imagination, what took place on Golgotha where Christ died on the cross. In trying to meditate on what happened upon Golgotha, these early Christians were overwhelmed by the feeling for the Divine Love that was needed to suffer through an ignominious death. It was already astounding that God would enter a human body. But to then go through the humiliation followed by the crucifixion left such meditators in awe of the extent and depth of love thus expressed.

For them, a new Mystery had been enacted on Golgotha. Christ, by becoming a human, had become the new and last Adam. Thus St. Paul wrote, "as in Adam all die, so in Christ all will be made alive,"[16]

---

[15] IBID
[16] 1 Corinthians 15:22

and then adds that Christ-Jesus was the last, the final Adam.[17] Every person was now capable of going this new path because its archetype now existed. A new initiation arose that followed Christ's steps from the Washing of the Feet to the Resurrection. They found an echo and a fulfillment of the ancient mystery initiations in these new steps.

Theological Underpinnings

In order to understand the action depicted in the scene of *Virgin of the Rocks*, this book will explore the theological foundations to Christianity and to the constitution of the human being. We will find that Early Christians believed that spirit, soul, and body composed the human being. The merging of the two boys, both named Jesus and mentioned above, can only be understood with a concept of the human being such as this.

We will explore Christian theological roots in Greek and Neoplatonic philosophies. We will come to the same conclusion regarding Christian theology that one of the foremost scholars of Early Christianity, Walter Bauer, reached in his book of 1971, *Orthodoxy and Heresy in Earliest Christianity*. He concluded that in the early centuries there were numerous forms of Christianity. What became known as Orthodoxy was just one of them. The supremacy of Orthodoxy began with the conversion to Christianity of the Roman Emperor Constantine I. Thereafter, the emperor used his resources to establish one Christianity that would be centered in the eastern Roman empire capital Constantinople. Bauer pointed out that this history was revised to justify the conflicts and to make it appear that the Orthodox view had always been the majority and the correct one. The historical records and

---

[17] 1 Corinthians 15:45, So it is written, "The first man Adam became a living being"; the last Adam, a life-giving spirit.

theologies of other views were systematically destroyed. What was retained was misrepresented as described in Walter Bauer's book, *Orthodoxy and Heresy in Earliest Christianity*.[18]

Helmut Koester (1926 – 2016) a scholar of the New Testament and early Christianity at Harvard Divinity School, wrote in 1982 in his *Introduction to the New Testament*, "the expansion of Christianity in the first years and decades after the death of Jesus was a phenomenon that utterly lacked unity. On the contrary, great variety resulted from these early missions."[19]

More recently, Bart Ehrman has also supported this view with his courseware *Lost Chritianities: Christian Scriptures and the Battles over Authenticity*.[20]

It will be shown that Leonardo became aware, through the Platonic Academy and other sources, of this early Christian theological variety. His drive for knowledge led him to explore what he could of these heretical theologies. And through his study and his teachers, he found a wealth of knowledge that he longed to reveal for the sake of the Goddess of Wisdom, Sophia, and for the sake of human evolution.

It will be shown that Christianity evolved out of the Ancient Mysteries and how St. Augustine referred to these Mysteries as being Christian before the name Christian was used. Bearing that in mind, one can see how the great philosophers of Plato, Philo, and Plotinus played significant roles in the philosophy used to understand nascent Christianity. These philosophers claimed that

---

[18] Walter Bauer, *Orthodoxy and Heresy in Earliest Christianity*, Fortress, 1971
[19] Helmut Koester, *Introduction to the New Testament*, Vol. 1, 1982, de Gruyter 2nd Ed, 1995
[20] Bart Ehrman, *Lost Chritianities: Christian Scriptures and the Battles over Authenticity*, lesson 19, The Great Course, 2002

human reasoning was replacing the fading role played once by the Mysteries. Reason had become a conscious path to experience God. Such a path was the path of the Gnostic Christians. Philo wrote of the old form of initiation, "But even if we voluntarily close the eye of our soul and take no care to understand such mysteries, or if we are unable to look up to them, the hierophant himself stands by and prompts us. And do not thou ever cease through weariness to anoint thy eyes until you have introduced those who are duly initiated to the secret light of the sacred scriptures, and have displayed to them the hidden things therein contained, and their reality, which is invisible to those who are uninitiated. (1.165)"[21]

During Early Christianity, a period existed where both the path of reason or knowledge and the path of initiation co-existed. In this light, such a passage as this from 1 Corinthians can be understood, "We do, however, speak a message of wisdom among the mature, but not the wisdom of this age or of the rulers of this age, who are coming to nothing. No, we declare God's wisdom, a mystery that has been hidden and that God destined for our glory before time began."[22]

But, these first few centuries experienced the growth of the intellect that distinguished between "I" and "Thou" or "That." Thus, grew individualism and egoism. On the one hand, this led to human freedom but on the other to the closing of the door to the spirit. Into this transitional drama came Augustine. He struggled to find a way to settle this contention. Augustine reasoned that each human has different intellectual capacities but each one can go

---

[21] Philo, *On Dreams, That They Are God-Sent*, Book 1:165, paragraph 26, *The Works of Philo Judæus: The Contemporary of Josephus*, Volume 2, transl. C. D. Yonge, George Bell & Sons, 1894
[22] 1 Corinthians 2:6-7

only so far within the ponderable realm. To go further, one would need faith. He reasoned that what the Apostles had given first to Christian Initiates and then had been written down so that posterity could continue to find the truth. For him, Faith in the Truth of these scriptures served to carry the human onwards to the experience of God.

Theological Debates Regarding the Trinity
The Early Christians saw the Father God as the God who brought about the transition from the super-sensible to the material, thus came the expression *Ex Deo Nascimur* or 'Out of God we are born.' They saw the Son God as the God who brings about the transition from the material to the super-sensible, thus 'In Christ we die' (*in Christo morimur*). And they discovered a third Principle. For some, they saw this Principle as proceeding from and being co-equal with both the Divine Father and the Divine Son. That third God is what Christianity calls the Holy Spirit who transcends both birth and death (*per spiritum revivisimus*). "And the Principle which knows neither birth nor death is the Spirit. Through the Holy Spirit we shall be awakened."[23] The Trinity debate during the Middle Ages was about how the Holy Spirit came into being – was it through just the Father or through both the Father and the Son. Arian Christianity that flowed through the Gothic peoples to be embodied in the Franks believed in the Filioque[24] that claimed the Holy Spirit had originated through *both* the Father and the Son. Theological stubbornness in this slight difference helped to lead to the Great Schism.

---

[23] Rudolf Steiner, *The Revelation of the Cosmic Christ*, lecture 7, Basle, 26Dec1921, GA 209

[24] Joseph F. Kelly, *The Ecumenical Councils of the Catholic Church: a history*, Liturgical Press, 2009

Foundations to Christianity

The connection four great philosophers, Plato, Philo, Plutarch, and Plotinus had to Early Christianity will be explored. They supported an understanding of Platonic Ideas as beings that live in a spiritual world. The Greek philosophers had been preceded by their Ancient Mystery cults each with their own oral traditions.

Christianity arrived during a time of transition from these Ancient Mysteries to Individualism. As the intellectual capabilities of each person grew, philosophy arose. For Plotinus, what Plato called the world of Ideas was above human concepts. There, in the World of Ideas (Nous), the Logos could be found creating. Then above Ideas and the Logos existed the One. For Plotinus, everything was spirit. For him, sensory things did not exist. What seems to be material was for him only the lowest manifestation of the spirit. He would say if we penetrated deeply enough into things, we would find everything is a manifestation of spirit.

It will be shown that by the close of the fourth century, the attainment of clairvoyance via the Mysteries had ceased. Such capabilities were soon thought of as mere legend. The still-existent longing for the grandeur of the Mysteries became seen by Christian leaders as a hindrance to the seeking of the new Mysteries of Christianity. Thus, Emperor Justinian I (527-565 CE) felt justified in branding the great Church Father Origen (185-~254 CE) who had respected the Mysteries as a heretic in 553 CE. For the first time, an Emperor had decided a theological matter at this level of importance.

There arose in the fourth century the desire to merge the many varieties of Christianity into one so as to form a Catholic Church for all of Christianity. But to accomplish this, those in power used the declaration of heresy to convert others and then to destroy their theological heritage. What is known today of these so-called heretics is little and it is based on what their conquerors wrote.

In the three centuries that followed the fourth, of the various heretics, the Manichaeans suffered the most. Their slaughter within Christendom made a mockery of "love thy neighbor."[25] Augustine had come to Manichaeism searching for initiation and wisdom. Augustine sought for the source of the human being. Was it a divine source? And what will one become? Because of how deeply materialism had pervaded his thinking, he could not find an answer in Manichaeism. But later, he felt he found it in Orthodox Christianity.

Augustine expected to find a spiritual that is above the material. He had been taught that the spiritual would be free of anything sense-perceptible. In the prior Greek era, one did not yet differentiate between thinking and sense perception. The Greek considered the sense-perceptible as derived from the spiritual and the spiritual as something manifesting in the sense-perceptible. A Greek soul from before the fifth century BC still experienced the spirit together with sense-perceptions.

Today, one understands the physical world through sense perception and their extensions through instruments such as the microscope. From these sense perceptions one abstracts concepts. One then weaves these concepts into one's own thought fabric. One retains these concepts as an inner soul experience. One is aware, more or less, that he or she has made these abstractions. Our ideas result from the sum of our concepts which have arisen from our sensory experiences. It is thus not surprising that our ideas today are steeped in materialism. Even our concepts of the spiritual, such as thinking itself, must find a material basis. As Gus

---

[25] See Matthew 22:39 and Mark 12:31, "Thou shalt love thy neighbor as thyself"

Speth said, "materialism is toxic to happiness, and we are losing our connection to the natural world."[26]

Augustine tried to grasp the spiritual world from which Christ-Jesus had come with the concepts of these four philosophers, Plato, Philo, Plutarch, and especially Plotinus. Augustine believed that there was a spiritual world above the human beings from whence Christ came. He then arrived at his concept of a tripartition, a trinity of Father, Son, and Spirit. Augustine's Trinity concept appears in the works of John Scotus Eriugena, (815 – 877 CE) who wrote a book about the division of nature (*De divisione naturae*) that describes a similar trinity. Eriugena would come to teach at the Palace School in France, and this greatly influenced European Scholasticism and carried Christian mysticism into the Renaissance.

St. Augustine: Completing Christianity's Transition

Augustine realized that since the Christ event new conditions existed. For souls seeking the spirit, the old ways would no longer be fruitful. Christ had banished the fruit found under the fig tree.[27] For him it was firmly established that in Christ Jesus there had been revealed in the outer historical world what the mystic had sought through preparation in the Mysteries. The new path from Augustine consisted in going with learning to a certain point and from there receiving the ideas connected with the Christ event from written accounts and oral traditions out of Faith. In pre-Christian times when one wished to seek the spiritual foundations of existence it was only possible through the way of the Mysteries. When that path closed, Augustine opened a new one: Go as far as

---

[26] James Gustave Speth, https://www.azquotes.com/author/54497-James_Gustave_Speth, accessed 19Oct2018
[27] Matthew 21:19. Christ said to a fig tree, "May you never bear fruit again!" Immediately the tree withered.

you can on the path of cognition with your human powers and then let faith carry you up into the higher spiritual regions.

Thomas Aquinas (1224–1274 CE) verified Augustine. He argued that human perception can only attain to self-knowledge. The nature of the divine and its relation to the world must come from revealed theology. One perceived his or her inability to penetrate by means of cognition past a certain limit. Thus, from one's limit he or she ascended further via faith. By this, Christianity brought the *content* of the Mysteries out of the darkness of the temple into the clear light of day.

Theology in Leonardo's Era
When Leonardo was a youth in school, religious indoctrination would have been his fate but because he was an illegitimate son, his loving father had enrolled him in an art school in nearby Florence. Freed from the yoke of becoming a notary like his father and somewhat freed from the catechisms of his day, Leonardo learned church history from the many scholars who had been drawn to Florence. He learned of the recent Albigensian Crusade, the destruction of the Knights Templar, the failings of the church during the Black Plague, the corruption of church leaders and the corruption from monarchs and money. He learned of the Western Schism, of three popes, of puppet popes, of council decrees intended to silence and destroy rivals. He learned of the Great Schism and the failed attempts to heal it. What kind of Christianity was this? That question must have arisen for Leonardo as a young man as it did for many who could feel the coming of the Protestant Reformation. The Battle between Faith and Knowledge had begun anew with the Renaissance, and we know what side Leonardo was on.

Figure 10 Adoration of the Magi, LdV, Uffizi, Florence, Italy, 1481

True to his devotion to Truth, Leonardo elected to paint a theme that had been important to Early Christianity but had been lost with the extermination of other Christian theologies that had been judged to be heretical. Also lost since the Eighth Ecumenical Council, Plethon had awakened in Florence the spiritual knowledge of the human being comprised of body, soul, and spirit. This wisdom flowed into Leonardo's *Virgin of the Rocks,* as foundation to reveal a great Christian mystery. Leonardo learned of this heresy while working on his *Adoration of the Magi*. Once awakened to the mystery of the two messiahs, the two Jesus boys, Leonardo abandoned his *Adoration* in 1481. Soon thereafter, he moves to the safety of Milan where he could reveal this heretical mystery away from the eye of the Inquisition.

Leonardo and the Church

This book will outline how corrupt the Roman Church had become, how its claims to power and lands were from a forgery, and how its Inquisition was holding back the advancement of science and the search for Knowledge. More depth is to be found in the companion book, *The Uncomfortable History of Christianity*. Historian Silvano Vinceti agrees with this author that Leonardo used iconographic language because of the fear of Pope Innocent VIII, the Borgia popes, and the Inquisition.

Mockery was expressed through this language. Vinceti concludes, "Leonardo used this painting [*Virgin of the Rocks*] to express his thought and request for a rigorous Christianity."[28]

In Leonardo's painting of *John the Baptist* (1514, Louvre, Paris), he choose Gian Giacomo Caprotti da Oreno, nicknamed Salai, as the model. Salai was known to authorities as an incorrigible delinquent whose mischief showed his lack of conscience. But Leonardo took this wayward youth under his wing.

---

[28] http://www.iitaly.org/magazine/focus/art-culture/article/experts-discover-dog-in-leonardos-virgin-rocks

Figure 11 John the Baptist, LdV, Louvre, Paris

Historians generally agree that his pupil, Salai, was the model for *John the Baptist*.[29] John points with two fingers of his left hand at his heart and with the index finger of his right hand at God. The face has a knowing smile that proclaims "I am revealing to you something you don't yet understand." Leonardo seems to be directing the Baptist's expression to the Church. This author believes that Leonardo selected Salai purposefully to ridicule the

---

[29] http://en.wikipedia.org/wiki/Leonardo_da_Vinci

pretentious piety of the corrupt Church of his day. In fact, Salai has a smirk on his countenance. And Leonardo has tied this painting to his *Virgin of the Rocks* with a repeat of the hand gesture that says "and the two became one." Leonardo is also proclaiming "here I have painted John the Baptist who was not among those painted in *Virgin of the Rocks*!

All four gospels describe the baptism. The mystery of the baptism as told in Luke 3:22 says "and the Holy Spirit descended on him in bodily form like a dove. And a voice came from heaven: "You are my Son, whom I love; with you I am well pleased."[30] Early texts of Luke, before the sixth century, have different words, namely "This is my dearly beloved son; *today* I have begotten him."[31] This change reflects the lost mystery of the baptism. It placed the entry of Christ at the birth and no longer at the baptism. By placing the birth of Christ with the birth of Jesus, the mystery of the two Jesus boys had to be obliterated.

In his paintings, Leonardo found a medium in which to embed the so-called heretical mysteries and yet retain deniability in order to avoid prosecution by the Inquisition. Many of his students

---

[30] New International Version, 2011

[31] Bart Ehrman, in his book *The Orthodox Corruption of Scripture: The Effect of Early Christological Controversies on the Text of the New Testament*, offers multiple arguments that in Luke 3:22 the words originally were "today I have begotten you." On page 63 he states, "witnesses as far-flung as Asia Minor, Palestine, Alexandria, North Africa, Rome, Gaul, and Spain" where the texts of Luke 3:22 had these words. The Church Fathers such as Clement of Alexandria, Origen, and others, used "today I have begotten you." Justin Martyr in *Dialogue with Trypho* 88, "but then the Holy Ghost, and for man's sake, as I formerly stated, lighted on Him in the form of a dove, and there came at the same instant from the heavens a voice, which was uttered also by David when he spoke [Psalm 2:7], personating Christ, what the Father would say to Him: 'You are My Son: this day have I begotten You;' [the Father] saying that His generation would take place for men, at the time when they would become acquainted with Him: 'You are My Son; this day have I begotten you.'"

participated by revealing different parts of the overall mystery. Had Leonardo painted these various works, the Inquisition would have had sufficient evidence to try him.

1. Grooming the Renaissance Man

"Leonardo da Vinci" means, literally, Leonardo from the city of Vinci. Although technically one should not use "da Vinci" as Leonardo's surname, it has long been a common practice. As is the custom, this book will also use it as his surname. Even Leonardo signed his name this way. In most of this book, he will simply be known as just Leonardo.

Figure 12 Leonardo's signature

Despite the passage of some 500 years, Leonardo never ceases to be in the news. The frequency of his name being mentioned today reveals his special place in history. New details about Leonardo's parents, especially his mother Caterina, appeared in the news in 2016. Biographer Walter Isaacson put out a best-seller entitled Leonardo da Vinci in October of 2017. He then participated in multiple talk shows to discuss his book thereby keeping Leonardo's presence in the news throughout the close of 2017. 2018-19 saw multiple publications of books about Leonardo by some of the world's best art historians including Frank Zöllner, Martin Kemp, Martin Clayton, and perhaps the foremost authority, Carmen Bambach. 2019 marked the 500th anniversary of the death of Leonardo.

Figure 13 Salvador Mundi, LdV, private

Not surprisingly, the highest price ever for a piece of art, $450 million, went to one of his paintings, *Salvador Mundi* (Savior of the World). It sold at auction in November 2017. *Salvador Mundi* is one of his few completed paintings leaving many art historians to wonder to what extent his students finished the work. It had been found, oddly, in an American's collection. The owner had no idea that it was Leonardo's lost *Salvador Mundi*. In 1625, this painting had traveled to England as part of the dowry of the French princess Henrietta Maria who was to marry King Charles I of England (1600-1649) who was, at the time, Europe's greatest painting collector. In 1685, it was given by the next king to his mistress. The painting was sold at an auction in 1763. It then disappeared for 200 years! The Cook Collection in England obtained it in 1900 with the expectation that it was merely a copy by Bernardino Luini, a student of Leonardo of whom much more will be written.

Then, in 1958, it disappeared again! Finally, an American art dealer, Alexander Parish, recognized it in the estate of businessman Basil Clovis Hendry Sr. of Baton Rouge in 2005. Later that year, it sold at an auction in New Orleans for less than $10,000 to a consortium of art dealers. A restoration began in 2007. In 2008, it was verified to be a painting by Leonardo. Doubts continued so it was reverified in 2010. Next, it was sold to an unidentified collector in May 2013 who later sold it at Christie's auction in November of 2017 to Prince Badr bin Abdullah of Saudi Arabia who allegedly purchased it on behalf of Abu Dhabi's Department of Culture and Tourism. There have been reports that the painting will eventually be put on display at the Louvre Abu Dhabi.

In 2003, NYC's Metropolitan Museum of Art hosted an exhibit entitled *Leonardo da Vinci, Master Draftsman*.[32] The exhibit was organized by the Met's curator of Renaissance Art, Carmen Bambach, and showed over 120 works from across Europe and North America. The exhibit surveyed Leonardo's amazing contribution as a scientist, an inventor, a theorist, a teacher, and

---

[32] Carmen C. Bambach, Leonardo da Vinci, Master Draftsman, Metropolitan Museum of Art, 2003, Watsonline.

especially as an artist. Carmen, also had a role in confirming that a sketch discovered in 2016 was indeed Leonardo's lost drawing of *Saint Sebastian.*

Figure 14 Erotic Lady in Red, Leonardo da Vinci, private collection

Two years later, in Ancona, Italy, Carlo Pedretti curated a special exhibit that headlined paintings probably by Leonardo that had been in private collections. In 2005, Pedretti was considered one of the foremost authorities on Leonardo. One of these paintings was surprising in its erotic quality of a bare breasted woman. Surprising because in no other paintings did Leonardo express sexuality. It depicted a woman wearing a red robe and holding up a sheer veil over her belly. Her front was exposed nearly to her crotch. Pedretti decided that this erotic painting was indeed by Leonardo although, he concedes, Leonardo's student Giampietrino may have assisted.[33] It was painted in 1515.[34] Some have claimed this was a depiction of Mary Magdalene but there is no record to prove that.

Another of the remarkable paintings in Pedretti's 2005 curated exhibit in Ancona, Italy was a third copy of *Virgin of the Rocks*! Found in 2002 in a private Swiss collection, it was likely painted in Leonardo's workshop between 1494 and 1497. Some art historians claim this one, figure 15, was painted by Leonardo with his student Giampetrino in Milan before 1508.[35] [Unfortunately, no full or higher resolution image was available]. These rarely-seen paintings had been in private collections. It was remarkable that Pedretti was able to convince their owners to include them in the exhibit. During his career, Pedretti was considered one of the foremost authorities on Leonardo da Vinci.

---

[33] Michael Haag, *The Quest of Mary Magdalene: History and Legend*, Profile Books, 2016
[34] http://news.bbc.co.uk/2/hi/entertainment/4344512.stm
[35] https://uk.reuters.com/article/uk-britain-leonardo/da-vinci-restoration-reveals-hidden-details-idUKTRE66D1B620100714, accessed 28May2019.

Figure 15 Third copy, Virgin of the Rocks, LdV et al, private collection

According to Pedretti, formerly professor of art history at UCLA and its Armand Hammer Chair of Leonardo Studies, this so-called Ceheramy Madonna "is wholly similar to the one in the Louvre."[36] Pedretti concluded, "because of the very high quality, I am inclined to believe that it is much more than a supervision of the student by the master." Pedretti, at that time, would not go so far as to declare it to be solely from the hand of Leonardo. He added that

---

[36] https://www.italymagazine.com/italy/marche/virgin-rocks-smash-hit

although it "has the character of a Giampietrino painting, it is far beyond his qualities."[37] Pedretti wanted to research it more, but, unfortunately, he died in January of 2018.

This 2005 exhibition also displayed another remarkable painting, *Three Holy Infants* (see figure 6). It was likely by Leonardo's student Bernardino de Conti whose contributions to this mystery appear in chapter 4. This painting was connected to Leonardo's school in Milan, and it reveals dramatic conclusions concerning the depictions in the *Virgin of the Rocks* paintings. As we'll see, Leonardo's students became involved in the drama of revealing Christian mysteries hidden in the *Virgin of the Rocks*. The conclusions of this book could not be supported without the inclusion of this painting in the evidence provided.

In the autumn of 2017, Walter Isaacson's biography of Leonardo was published by Simon Schuster. Already Isaacson had written several biographies of innovative individuals such as Benjamin Franklin, Albert Einstein, Henry Kissinger, and Steve Jobs. This book surpassed his other works in interest and sales, once again demonstrating our unabated interest in Leonardo. During Isaacson's appearances on talk shows throughout the late autumn of 2017, he cleverly equated Leonardo's sfumato technique of blurring lines and boundaries in his paintings with his ability to blur the boundary between art and science. This book adds religion to this list.

Many biographies preceded Isaacson including books from this century by Serge Bramly, Jay Williams, George Stanley. One notable is that by Charles Nicholl called *Leonardo da Vinci: The*

---

[37] Southern Cross Review https://southerncrossreview.org/43/leonardo-article.htm, and China Daily http://www.chinadaily.com.cn/english/doc/2005-09/22/content_480049_2.htm

Flights of the Mind. This excellent biography was published in 2004. In 2013, H. Anna Suh published Leonardo's remarkable notebooks followed by Jean Paul Richter doing the same in 2016. These notebooks take the reader into the mind of this Renaissance genius.

All of these biographers note that Leonardo was infamous for starting paintings and sculptures but often never completing the work. For all his fame, he completed less than twenty paintings![38] Adding credence to this reputation, the biographer Giorgio Vasari quotes Leonardo as stating, "Art is never finished, only abandoned."[39] Two of his (mostly) finished works, *The Last Supper* and the *Mona Lisa,* were the most endearing to Isaacson. He points to the eyes and smile of the *Mona Lisa* and the 3D perspective of the *Last Supper* as two of the greatest artworks in human history. In this book, the Louvre's version of the *Virgin of the Rocks* is elevated to this realm of excellence. Here is a courageous masterpiece that subtly reveals lost Christian theological themes. It was painted in a time when being accused of holding a heretical view could result in the forfeiture of one's life.

Isaacson calls Leonardo, "One of the most well-documented yet elusive men of the Renaissance." Although his notebooks provide an extensive paper trail, they are generally cryptic, leaving unanswerable questions such as: how did Leonardo know what he knew? This book attempts to answer this question. At a time when heretics were still burned at the stake, for Leonardo to

---

[38] A complete and annotated display of Leonardo's paintings can be found at https://en.wikipedia.org/wiki/List_of_works_by_Leonardo_da_Vinci.

[39] Thomas Cahill, *Heretics and Heroes: How Renaissance Artists and Reformation Priests Created Our World*, pg. 95, Anchor Books, 2014

theologically challenge Church dogma with his painting the *Virgin of the Rocks* took immense courage.

Born on April 15, 1452, in or near Vinci, Italy (just outside Florence), as the illegitimate son of a 25-year-old notary whose wealthy family were notaries. Leonardo was fortunate to grow up not in poverty. And the world was fortunate that he did not to become a notary. Instead, he was surrounded by educational opportunities within his grandfather's household. His grandfather, Antonio di Ser Piero da Vinci, "recorded in a memorandum that Caterina, a farmer's daughter, had on 15 April 1452 given birth to an illegitimate son fathered by his own son, Ser Piero."[40] About two years later, his mother, Caterina, was married (obviously not to Leonardo's father, Ser Piero) and moved away. His father took on full custody of the boy but his grandfather recorded in his tax declaration that the cost of infant care came from his earnings. Growing up in the da Vinci home afforded Leonardo access to scholarly texts owned by family and friends.[41]

When Leonardo reached the age of eight years, Ser Piero enrolled Leonardo in a school in Florence. Here Leonardo flourished. Four years later, his caring father, although with seventeen other children to take care of, enrolled his gifted son in Florence's best artistic workshop, the school of Andrea del Verrocchio. While still in Verrocchio's workshop, the twenty-year old Leonardo joined the painters' Confraternity of Saint Luke in 1472.[42] Soon thereafter, Leonardo's amazing talents were recognized by Florence's most powerful family, the Medicis.

---

[40] Martin Kemp and Thereza Wells, *Leonardo Da Vinci's Madonna of the Yarnwinder, A Historical & Scientific Detective Story*, Artatk ePub, 2016
[41] Museum of Science, Boston, Biography of Leonardo, https://www.mos.org/leonardo/biography
[42] https://www.nga.gov/collection/artist-info.1479.html

During the era of Lorenzo the Magnificent (1449-1492), Leonardo would join the Medici household at the age of 28. With all the traveling scholars who came to stay in the Medici household, Leonardo's boundaries to knowledge melted away. That same year, he was admitted as a member of the Garden of San Marcos whose library was the favorite meeting place for Florence's teachers and philosophers, especially those of the Platonic Academy run by Marsilio Ficino.

By being a member of the Medici household, Leonardo could attend the Platonic Academy in nearby Careggi. Ficino taught not only Plato but other Greek and Egyptian philosophers while John Argyropoulos, from Constantinople, was a renowned Aristotelian scholar and alchemist. Even though Ficino was perhaps the most respected intellectual of the Florentine district, even he ran afoul with the Inquisition because of his writings on Hermetic magic and astrology that he had learned from Gemistus Plethon. Only a strong defense acquitted him of heresy charges and a possible death sentence. Hence, much of what was taught in these schools attended by Leonardo was kept secret.

Leonardo's thirst for knowledge was broad and relentless. Anatomy became a subject of special interest to him. While other artists might be satisfied with mere measurements and proportions of the person or scene to be painted, Leonardo sought a deeper truth. One might feel moral repugnance to know that Leonardo dug up the deceased to dissect their decaying corpses in order to understand anatomy's secrets such as how the smile was affected by facial muscles. Leonardo sought not the outer truth alone, but also the inner truth.

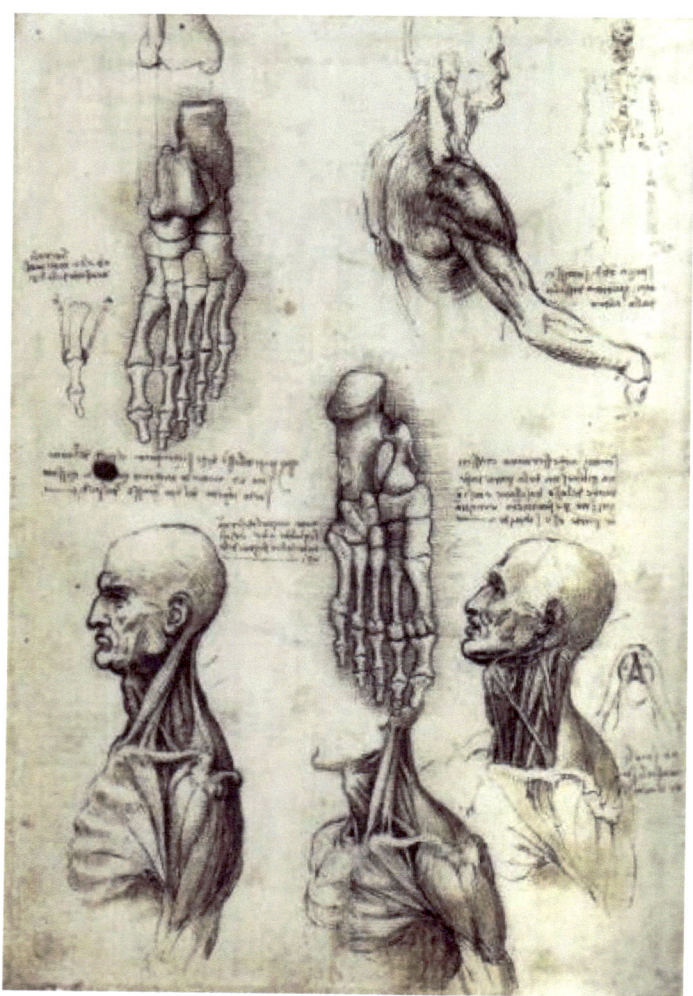

Figure 16 Anatomy Sketches from Leonardo's notebook

Leonardo was highly skilled in both painting and sculpture. As a left-handed artist, he was already unusual. But it was his genius as a self-made scientist that has given Leonardo his lasting position in history. Besides anatomy, he greatly advanced the state of knowledge in many fields such as civil engineering, medicine, optics, and hydrodynamics to name but a few.

He even sketched out a theory of plate tectonics. But his fame today perhaps rests with his far-before-his-time inventions such as a helicopter, a tank, a method to concentrate solar power, a calculator, an automated bobbin winder, a machine for testing the tensile strength of wire, and double hulled ships as sketched in his notebooks.

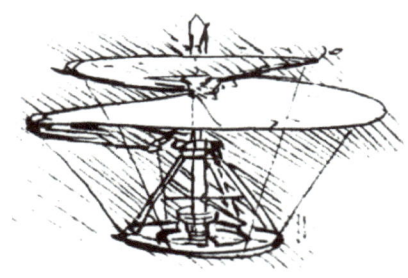

Figure 17 Human-powered helicopter, LdV

Thus, in his resume to the future Duke of Milan, Ludovico Sforza, Leonardo sought a court position by describing his many scientific and engineering talents. He had 11 paragraphs promoting such skills and only in his last paragraph did he say "I can also paint as well as anyone".[43] In addition to his artistic, scientific, and engineering talents, according to his contemporary biographer, Vasari, he was also a talented musician.[44]

Leonardo was successful in being employed by the Duke of Milan who asked Leonardo to design buildings, weapons, and new machinery. And Leonardo did this and more, extending it to include flying machines, submarines, and other armored vehicles for combat. His Milan studio expanded into a workshop not only for

---

[43] http://buffaloah.com/a/virtual/italy/milan/sforza/leo.html
[44] Emanuel Winternitz, *Leonardo Da Vinci As a Musician*. MIT Press, 1982.

painting and sculpture but also for engineering and scientific studies.

Figure 18 Baptism, Verrocchio with LdV, 1474

When Leonardo sought this court position in Milan, he was already well known to those who judged art and artists in Florence Italy. It is likely that his talents were also recognized by Ludovico Sforza when he applied for a position in his court. The biographer Vasari claimed that Verrocchio, Leonardo's teacher, was "astonished" by his talent. Verrocchio invited the teenage Leonardo to work with him on his studio paintings such as his *Baptism of Jesus* where

Leonardo painted the angels on the left bank of the River Jordan (see figure 18).

Leonardo's first two solo masterpieces, *The Annunciation* (1472-75) and *Ginevra de' Benci* (1474-77) established his reputation in Florence and beyond. These works awoke the art world to this budding adept.

But Leonardo's coming masterpieces might never have been because in 1469, at 17, young Leonardo was arrested and charged with sodomy. Normally this would have ruined his career by costing him his position in Verrocchio's school (plus the tarnish would have later prevented him, at 28, from being accepted into a position in the Medici household). But one of the four young men with whom he was accused had connections with the powerful Medici family. Soon, the case was quietly dropped. This has led many biographers, including Isaacson, to have concluded that Leonardo was gay. But perhaps Leonardo was not sexually drawn to either gender for he wrote "Whoever does not curb lustful desires puts himself on the level of beasts." Leonardo certainly learned from his close-call with disaster at 17 to keep his private life private. All claims as to Leonardo's sexuality are conjecture. His painting that some entitle *Mary Magdalene* (see figure 14), clearly showed that he fully understood sensuality and sexuality.

Leonardo was flamboyant, enjoying colorful dress and lifestyle. When the Duke of Milan, Ludovico Sforza, hired Leonardo, the duke hoped Leonardo could provide 'color' for his social affairs and court extravaganzas.

From 1490 to 1495 while in Milan, Leonardo was sketching and recording his thoughts, questions, and intentions in notebooks providing biographers like Isaacson with reliable information.

Isaacson has called Leonardo's notebooks "the greatest record of curiosity ever created."

We know from these notebooks and other letters that Leonardo's integrity and sensitivity to moral issues was his reason for being a vegetarian, for example.[45] Indeed, one can deduce much about Leonardo through his musings, quips, and even his To-Do lists that are recorded in his notebooks. There we read such insights and intentions as "Get a master of hydraulics to tell you how to repair a lock ... Observe the goose's foot ... Describe the tongue of the woodpecker."[46]

Leonardo's thirst for knowledge led him far beyond the arts and the known sciences. Of his contemporary educators and scholars, Leonardo found many to be "puffed up" because they had not worked through the knowledge received to make it their own. Rather, they relied on the ideas they had merely received from others who were considered authorities. Leonardo wrote "He who can go to the fountain does not go to the water-jar."[47] Surely Leonardo drank regularly from this fountain of wisdom.

Florence, in his day, drew students and scholars from across Europe. It was thriving with various schools. A plethora of teachers

---

[45] Jean Paul Richter, The Literary Works of Leonardo da Vinci, 1883 and Eugene Muntz, *Leonardo da Vinci Artist, Thinker, and Man of Science*,1898

[46] Walter Isaacson, *Leonardo da Vinci*, Simon and Schuster, 2017. The full text: *"The tongue of a woodpecker can extend more than three times the length of its bill. When not in use, it retracts into the skull and its cartilage-like structure continues past the jaw to wrap around the bird's head and then curve down to its nostril. In addition to digging out grubs from a tree, the long tongue protects the woodpecker's brain. When the bird smashes its beak repeatedly into tree bark, the force exerted on its head is ten times what would kill a human. But its bizarre tongue and supporting structure act as a cushion, shielding the brain from shock."*

[47] Walter Isaacson, *Leonardo da Vinci*, Simon and Schuster, 2017, from Notebook entry 490, *of Study and the Order of Study*.

offering workshops and lectures plus an abundance of libraries. With his membership in the Garden of San Marcos, Leonardo had access to these men and their vast knowledge and texts. Although these gardens were lost in the course of history, they played "a major role" according to the writings of Condivi and Vasari. Condivi tells us that the young Michelangelo, when introduced to the gardens by his friend Granacci, was so struck with the beauty of the ancient statues placed there by Lorenzo de' Medici that he never returned to Ghirlandaio's workshop but made the gardens his school. Vasari presents a far more elaborate account. He maintains that the gardens were the exclusive creation of Lorenzo who kept there not only a collection of ancient sculpture but also paintings, cartoon, drawings, and models by Donatello, Brunelleschi, Masaccio, Uccello, Fra Angelico, and Fra Filippo Lippi. With Vasari, the gardens acquire the prestige of a veritable museum of ancient and contemporary Renaissance art. Even more sensationally, he states that "Lorenzo had created the gardens in order to institute in them an art school for young artists under the supervision of Bertoldo."[48] Here, was one of the fountains of knowledge from which the young Leonardo drank frequently.

Leonardo's impressive inventory of inventions and ideas demonstrate a far-reaching creativity of this self-driven, self-taught genius. What was the extent of the knowledge available to his inquisitive mind? How far into ancient Greek wisdom did he delve? Was he able to learn about Hermeticism, Gnosticism and the theologies of the various early Christianities?

These paths of knowledge were certainly available in Florence to Leonardo the student. But, to fully appreciate this, one will need to

---

[48] Ludovico Borgo and Ann H. Sievers, *The Medici Gardens at San Marco*, Max-Planck-Institut, 1989 http://www.jstor.org/stable/27653259

grasp the mood of the Renaissance where the battle between the old way of faith and the new way of knowledge was to be waged. Corruption had stained the very fabric of the Roman Catholic Church. Failed Crusades and plagues seemed to many to be an indication of God's wrath falling upon a sinful society. A groundswell of discontent was amassing that would culminate in Luther's publication of the *Ninety-five Theses* in 1517, two years before Leonardo's death. Luther's struggles led to the Protestant Reformation.

What theological struggles existed just below the surface in this period of history? What might Leonardo have been aware of while he was painting these two (or possibly three[49]) *Virgin of the Rocks*? Did his own studies lead him to subscribe to any of the so-called Christian heresies or any of the prevailing mysticisms?

On the 19th of December 1515, when Pope Leo X met with French King Francis I in Bologna, Leonardo was a member of the Pope's delegation. Francis I subsequently invited Leonardo, early in 1516, to become his Royal Painter. Leonardo accepted and his assistant Francesco Melzi accompanied him to Clos Luce, a manor house in the Loire Valley of France. During the next three years, the French king and queen, with a summer residence nearby, became his friends. Francis was reported as saying: "There had never been another man born in the world who knew as much as Leonardo, not so much about painting, sculpture and architecture, as that he

---

[49] See figure 15 and footnote 32. Because the third painting is not verified as a Leonardo, this book will consider the known two, namely those displayed in the Louvre, Paris and the National Gallery, London.

was a very great philosopher."[50] The cause of Leonardo's death in 1519 has been deemed to be a stroke.[51]

The Renaissance, born in Florence and cultivated by Leonardo, had already spread across Italy and northward to Antwerp. Painters and scholars had come from across Europe to Florence and Milan for Renaissance-inspired trainings. Leonardo, himself, brought his talents and his creative spirit northward from Florence to Milan and finally to the heart of Europe, to the Loire Valley, to Clos Luce in France. Like blood streaming from the heart, the impulse spread. And fortunate it was for historians that when Leonardo was requested to return to Milan to complete the second *Virgin of the Rocks,* he took on the meticulous Francesco Melzi as his assistant and secretary. Melzi would accompany Leonardo to Rome and then to France. After Leonardo's death, Melzi compiled his notebooks and other works for posterity. From these notebooks, much can be learned of the inner life of the most significant and the most enigmatic of all the great Renaissance artists and scientists. To artist and scientist, perhaps the title theologian can now be added.

---

[50] Mario Lucertini, Ana Millan Gasca, and Fernando Nicolo, *Technological Concepts and Mathematical Models in the Evolution of Modern Engineering Systems*, Birkhäuser, 2004
[51] Philippe Charlier and Saudamini Deo, *Neurology*, "A physical sign of stroke sequel on the skeleton of Leonardo da Vinci?", April 4, 2107

2. A Tale of Two Paintings

There is not one painting by Leonardo da Vinci called *The Virgin of the Rocks* (or sometimes called the *Madonna of the Rocks*), but two![52] Here they are shown side-by-side. On the right is the version at the Louvre in Paris while on the one on the left hangs in the National Gallery London.

Figure 19 Comparing Virgin of the Rocks, Nat'l Gallery. London- Louvre, Paris

The physical dimensions of these two *Virgin of the Rocks* are very similar. Both paintings are about six feet (two meters) tall by four feet wide. Interestingly, the one on the right is 199 cm × 122 cm (78.3 in × 48.0 in) while the one on the left is 189.5 cm × 120 cm (74.6 in × 47.25 in) making it nearly four inches shorter. Originally, both had a poplar wood backing but the Louvre lifted their painting and transferred it to canvas. The painting at the National Gallery

---

[52] See footnote 4. There may have been a third *Virgin of the Rocks* that has been in a private collection.

remains on a poplar wood panel. One can conclude that because these two paintings have such similar sizes, both with curved tops rather than rectangular, that each was intended to fit into a specific space such as a pre-built frame or an existing altarpiece.

But why did Leonardo paint two (or three)? The relationship between these two works has remained mysterious since the passing of Leonardo who took an abundance of secrets with him into death. But, as we shall see, works of his students shed considerable light on this mystery.

The Start of a Deep Investigation

One goal is to understand what Leonardo intended to portray in the original painting. Achieving this goal will become an exciting journey through a dramatic period of the Italian Renaissance. This book will venture into the ideas and wisdom held by this period's hero, Leonardo da Vinci. This exploration began in the Introduction by asking why there are two paintings by Leonardo that are so similar. During the Renaissance, commissions drove Renaissance painters. There was no market for a copy. Thus, an artist did not make a copy of one of his masterpieces with the hope of cashing in again.

Students of a great painter, however, often practiced by making a copy of one of their teacher's paintings. They did not try to sell these classroom copies (although such practice paintings do hang in museums today). Painting the same subject, especially a religious one, was common, such as *The Crucifixion*. In such cases, a student painter might add something new or take a slightly different perspective. In the two *Virgin of the Rocks,* the layout, geometry, scene, characters, and gestures prove that one of these was intended to be a (near) copy of the other, but it is clear today that both paintings were largely done by the master, Leonardo.

Two versions of *The Madonna of the Yarnwinder* exist (both in private collections). Within Leonardo's workshop, training of students involved making copies done while the master directed and added touches. This has led to art historians debating whether or not Leonardo was the exclusive painter of several paintings attributed to him. Did Leonardo, or perhaps a student, fail to make an exact copy of the original or were the differences intentionally incorporated into the copy? If the answer is that it was intentional, then Leonardo's motivation for completing multiple paintings of the same theme needs to be examined.

What is known of the historical situation? Court records show that, of these two paintings, one was intended for a client in Milan. But which one? And, which of these paintings was the original and which was the copy? This has been debated by art historians for many decades.

Which Painting is the Original?

Both London's National Gallery and the Louvre in Paris have, at times, claimed that their painting must be the original. Then, at other times, they have concluded that the other museum has the original! This debate may have been settled when the two paintings were shown together in 2011.[53] Research leading up to that exhibit revealed sufficient facts that the art world "is now nearly universally agreed" that the Louvre's painting must be the original painting. A report from the National Gallery states that the Louvre's painting was "almost certainly finished by the mid-

---

[53] National Gallery press release, 28 July 2011. The National Gallery exhibition *Leonardo da Vinci: Painter at the Court of Milan* lasted from 9 November 2011 to 5 February 2012 and displayed both paintings. National Gallery director, Nicholas Penny, was quoted to have remarked "I am quite sure that the experience of seeing these masterpieces juxtaposed will be one that none of us will ever forget, or that will ever be repeated."

1480s"[54] when Leonardo was in Florence while the *Virgin of the Rocks* at the National Gallery was completed some twenty-five years later while Leonardo was primarily in Milan.

The former director of London's National Gallery (1968-73), Martin Davies, had argued that the painting in the Louvre is stylistically close to Leonardo's earlier Florentine works while the London painting reveals his later, more mature style. Thus, he concludes, the London painting must be a derivative of the Louvre painting. [55] Martin Davies' predecessor, Kenneth Clark, also wrote that the Louvre version was begun in Florence.[56] This author agrees with Davies and Clark that the Louvre painting was begun in Florence. This author argues that it likely was completed in Milan or perhaps even later when Leonardo moved to France.

Although, since 2011, it is generally accepted by art historians and by this book that the Louvre version is the earlier work, a few, including Tamsyn Taylor,[57] uphold the opposing view. Tamsyn, of the Colchester Gallery, finds evidence to support the argument that the National Gallery's is the original. She implores us, "If we accept the notion that the Louvre painting is the earlier of the two, then we must also believe that Leonardo began, painted and delivered a most perplexing and challenging artwork, a painting with an obscure emphasis that only dimly related to the

---

[54] Larry Keith, Ashok Roy, Rachel Morrison, Peter Schade, National Gallery Technical Bulletin, Volume 32, *Leonardo da Vinci: Pupil, Painter and Master*, Yale University Press, 2011

[55] Martin Davies, *The Earlier Italian Schools*, Volume 1, National Gallery Catalogues, London 1951, reprinted 1986.

[56] Kenneth Clark, *Leonardo da Vinci: An Account of his Development as an Artist* (1939, rev. ed. 1952 and 1967)

[57] Tamsyn Taylor, Colchester Gallery, http://www.leonardodavincithevirginoftherocks.com/, 2011 (accessed 26Jan2018)

commissioned subject."[58] Indeed, this book does make this case! The painting now at the Louvre was begun in Florence based on early Christian themes. Tamsyn concludes, "The only sensible way of viewing the existence of and the differences between the two versions of the Virgin of the Rocks is to understand the National Gallery version as being that designed to fulfil the commission of 1483." Although this may sound contradictory, this book fully agrees with this conclusion. As will be shown, it was not the first painting (Paris), but the second one (London) that was intended to fulfill the commission.

Jonathan Jones, an art journalist for the Guardian, added to the ongoing debate, "In its official statement yesterday [12Jul2010], the [National] Gallery was naturally cautious; but talking to me over several weeks in the workshop, in front of the painting [being restored], the National's experts made it clear they believe this to be a pure and unsullied painting by Leonardo's own hand. 'We now have a picture which I believe is entirely by Leonardo,' said Luke Syson, Curator of Italian Paintings and Head of Research.[59] Syson sees Leonardo's hand in 'such brilliances as the tangle of sharp thorny branches behind the angel. That bush, at once natural observation and fantastic improvisation, is obviously Leonardo. So are most of the grasses and leaves that perforate every crevice. But the key to rethinking this picture is to grasp that it is not finished. It is not a neatly executed copy made to satisfy a commissioning

---

[58] Tamsyn Taylor, Colchester Gallery, http://www.leonardodavincithevirginoftherocks.com/p/summary-of-case.html, 2011 (accessed 2Feb2018)

[59] In 2012, Luke Syson was hired by the Metropolitan Museum of Art, NYC, to the position of Curator in Charge of the Department of European Sculpture and Decorative Arts.

body.' It now seems possible that Leonardo painted all the picture himself."[60]

When both paintings were shown in London, Jonathan Jones attended the museum's gala event and wrote, "The first time I saw the cleaned picture I thought, wow, it's a true Leonardo. Then hearing someone else say it – for all Syson's expertise and eloquence – brought out the cynical journalist in me. I had to see it one last time, to look at it as objectively as possible. I started with the angel's hair, those rivers of light. Then I looked at the angelic sleeve, the grasses and leaves, the palms, the Virgin's hair, which for the first time I recognised as another riverine braid straight out of a Leonardo drawing. I looked at the tendons of her outstretched hand (think of Leonardo's anatomical studies), the profound facial expressions. Why did anyone ever doubt this was anything but a great Leonardo?"[61]

Jones reports that Syson came to the realization that it took Leonardo and Ambrogio twenty-five years to finish the London painting because both painters were often away from Milan because of war or for weddings. Syson also believed that Leonardo, true to his reputation, never completely finished the London painting. Completed parts are jewel-like while unfinished parts remained vague.

An examination of the landscape leads to the conclusion that Leonardo did not paint the rocks in London's version. It would be an insult to the botanical and geological accuracy employed by Leonardo to claim he has painted the rocks of the London painting. The version at the Louvre is indeed scientifically perfect. Geologist

---

[60] Jonathan Jones, *The Virgin of the Rocks: Da Vinci decoded*, The Guardian, 13Jul2010
[61] IBID Jonathan Jones

Ann C. Pizzorusso wrote, "The *Virgin of the Rocks* in the Louvre is a geological tour-de-force. ... An observer with some knowledge of geology would find that the rock formations represented in the National Gallery work do not correspond to nature. ... The difference in the two sets of rocks may not be immediately obvious to the layman. Yet given Leonardo's passion for geology and his genius for painting, closer evaluation suggest that the Louvre's rocks are Leonardo's while the National Gallery's are not."[62] Tamsyn Taylor dismisses these findings as misunderstandings and misinterpretations as such structures do appear in Italy's Dolomites.[63] Pizzorusso's findings align with this book's theory that Leonardo painted the four characters leaving his partner Ambrogio to paint the rocks and some of the flowers in the copy.

Exploring the History Surrounding These Two Paintings

In April 1483, the Brethren of the Immaculate Conception awarded a commission of 800 Lire to Leonardo and the De Predis brothers. They were to paint an altarpiece for their Chapel at San Francesco il Grande, in Milan. An elaborately made frame was already nearing completion by Giacomo del Maino. The artists were to complete the frame and a painting was to fit within it.

The commission had several additional parts but the main one was to be a Madonna and Child painting that was to be consistent with the new doctrine of the immaculate conception. Leonardo, never known for painting quickly, somehow met their December 1483 deadline with some composition. But it was clearly unfinished thus preventing this painting from being installed. In 1486, something

---

[62] Ann C. Pizzorusso, *Leonardo's Geology: The Authenticity of the Virgin of the Rocks*, https://www.leonardo.info/isast/articles/pizzorusso.html
[63] Tamsyn Taylor, Colchester Gallery, http://www.leonardodavincithevirginoftherocks.com/p/leonardos-geology.html, (accessed 2Feb2018)

satisfied the confraternity until their commissioned painting was ready. Perhaps there was an agreement with the confraternity for them to hold the original as a placeholder until their commissioned painting was ready.

In 1490, Leonardo's partners, the de Predis brothers, apparently were still working on the project. They appealed for additional payment. In their appeal, they say that the completion of the unfinished frame, because of its gold leafing, had cost them the entire 800 lire. The painting of the Virgin needed additional funds. If this could not be met, they requested that the "oil painting of Our Lady" (*Virgin of the Rocks*) be withdrawn. The Confraternity, believing they had bargained in good faith and upheld their end of the bargain, refused. Thus, little to no work continued. Later that year, Evangelista de Predi, the expert on gold leafing, died. A stalemate ensued. In 1499, Leonardo had to flee from Milan as war approached. In 1503, Ambrogio De Predis petitioned the Confraternity but the case was dismissed by the court. It appears that sometime between 1501 and 1506, a frustrated Ambrogio varnished the surface of the painting thereby declaring it finished.

The existing documentation is not clear what may have been in the frame that was hanging in the confraternity's chapel. It may have been the Louvre's painting. The confraternity must have had something of value because it did not sue the artists for their multi-year late fulfillment of the commission. Thus, what painting was Ambrogio de Predis working on and what painting hung in the confraternity's chapel?

A third time the artists sought legal help and this time they appealed to the King of France who had recently conquered the Milan area. This intervention did lead to a settlement in 1506. Documents from this legal settlement exist. They show that

Leonardo was required to finish the commissioned painting within two years whereupon a final 200 lire payment would be made after it was installed. For this reason, Leonardo came to Milan in 1506 to complete the requested work. Only after acceptance of a painting was the entire 200 lire given to Ambrogio de Predi. Installation occurred in 1508. The original painting was, in good faith, returned to Leonardo with the intention of making yet another copy. It is believed that this third copy is what Carlo Pedretti displayed from a private Swiss collection in the 2005 exhibit in Ancona, Italy. This so-called *Ceheramy Madonna* was the centerpiece of the exhibit called: *Leonardo, Genius and Vision in the Marche.*

If the Louvre painting had been installed in the chapel in 1486, then Leonardo received no compensation for it. His team of artists used up the entire 800 lire completing the frame. Evangelista de Predi was the likely principle for the decoration of the frame. Sometime after 1486, a second painting was underway, but it was not finished by 1499 when Leonardo left Milan. In 1506, the court agreed with the confraternity that the painting needed alterations by Leonardo before it could be deemed complete. This latter painting is the one that now hangs in the National Gallery. It was painted to replace the loaner in the confraternity's chapel.

Restoration by the National Gallery

In 2007, the National Gallery performed a cleaning of its *Virgin of the Rocks*. Evidence from this restoration does lead to the conclusion that Leonardo was the principal painter of both paintings.

Because of the similar dimensions of the two wood panels used for each painting, one can conclude that both were designed to fit the Giacomo del Maino built altarpiece. This is the position of Ottino della Chiesa.[64] She surmises that although the Louvre version is the "original," the London painting was begun in 1486 as a substitute. She argues that it is an unlikely coincidence that Leonardo painted the "original" prior to the commission and that it magically fit the dimensions of Giacomo's altarpiece frame. But the two are about four inches different in height. It is entirely plausible that the wood panel for Leonardo's unfinished original was altered to fit the frame of the altarpiece (and that the trimming of the wood panel did not fit the frame).

Despite the debates as to which painting is the earlier, most authors conclude that the Louvre painting fulfilled the commission of the Confraternity in 1483.[65] But still something does not fit. Another similar painting is worked during the subsequent sixteen years. A court case arose concerning this painting and its follow-on painting. This author proposes that the original was shown to the Confraternity in order to win the commission in 1483. But, because of theological issues, Leonardo promised the Confraternity a new, theologically acceptable version to take its place. But even in the replacement painting, Leonardo attempted to leave the depictions ambiguous. Thus, the Confraternity would not accept it until it fit their theology.

Possible students who may have participated in some way in the London *Virgin of the Rocks* include Marco d'Oggiono who later paints a similar *Madonna,* Giovanni Antonio Boltraffio, and Francesco Napoletano. Several art historians point to Francesco as the painter for one of the side panels that each portray a musical angel (see figures 21 and 22).

---

[64] Angela Ottino della Chiesa, *The Complete Paintings of Leonardo da Vinci*, Penguin Classics of World Art, 1967
[65] Martin Kemp, *Leonardo*, Oxford University Press, 2004

Not unlike Leonardo's other contractual agreements, the painter failed to deliver what the Confraternity requested. The central panel, according to the contract, was to show the Madonna and Child surrounded by a troupe of angels and two prophets. What Leonardo delivered had no angels, one archangel, and no prophets. What is presumed to be the infant John was never specified and likely Leonardo never intended to show him in the painting. The side-panels were to feature four angels each, singing or playing musical instruments, yet what was delivered had only one musical angel each. Tamsyn Taylor remarks, "Leonardo abandoned the conservative and doctrinally based subject matter prescribed by the Confraternity."[66]

How Did Each Painting Get to Their Respective Museum?

Between roughly 1500 and 1625, history cannot tell us where the version of *Virgin of the Rocks* that is now in the Louvre was. Some possible theories where this painting was "hidden" include:

1. It remained with Leonardo in his studio until he fled Milan in 1499. He took his beloved paintings, including the *Mona Lisa*, with him wherever he went. From 1499 onwards, Ambrogio had to paint the unfinished sections of the second version from memory. Eventually, these beloved paintings go with Leonardo to Clos Lucé, France, where on May 2, 1519, at age 67, Leonardo dies. Three years earlier, in 1516, Leonardo had accepted a commission from King Francois I, to be his personal chief painter, engineer, and architect. Leonardo's manor house at Clos Lucé was near the king's residence at Château d'Amboise. There he spent his last three years accompanied by his pupil Francesco

---

[66] Tamsyn Taylor, Colchester Gallery, http://www.leonardodavincithevirginoftherocks.com/p/blog-page.html, (accessed 2Feb2018)

Melzi. After Leonardo died, Melzi inherited his scientific works and manuscripts while his paintings likely became royal property upon Leonardo's death. During the legal dispute with the Confraternity, it had been the prior French King who had intervened.

Figure 20 Clos Luce manor where Leonardo died

2. It was temporarily installed at the Confraternity until the 'replacement' (National Gallery) version was completed. Then, it may have been sold to the Duke of Milan or the King of France.
3. Historian James Kettlewell agrees that the painting in the Louvre is the original. He adds that this "painting, apparently, was finished and installed in the Chapel in late 1484 or early in 1485. A final payment was made to the artists on December 28, 1484, according to a document discovered in 1999. [Marani, p. 125]. That it remained in place for some time is suggested by a later, undated document, from sometime between 1491 and 1494, in which Leonardo and Ambrogio de' Predis petitioned the Duke of Milan to assist them in receiving an additional

payment for the central panel of the work. This states that the 'the central panel with an image of the Virgin' was entirely done by Leonardo and is worth much more than was paid for it. It requests that the central panel be returned if the amount demanded by the artists cannot be paid.

A second appeal was made, this time in 1503, to the King of France, who now ruled Milan. Among other things it stated that a painting by Leonardo had been in the possession of the Confraternity for many years. This is important since, at some subsequent date, the painting was removed, and replaced by the version now in London. It is often stated that the first painting was probably never accepted by the Confraternity, or that it was removed shortly after it was installed. The documents suggest, however, that the painting was in place since as early as 1483, and that the Confraternity was satisfied that it met the original contract for an Immaculate Conception subject, in spite of its unconventional arrangement of the figures."

Kettlewell then surmises that the original "painting was removed, probably by the French king, who had taken over Milan in 1499. The Confraternity required that Leonardo and Ambrogio replace it. I think the second, London version, essentially a copy of the first, was probably begun around 1503. (However, as I discuss later, there is evidence that Leonardo, as early as 1501, may have intended to produce a different composition for the Confraternity.) The second version, still unfinished in 1506, was finally installed in the altarpiece in 1508."[67]

While this book agrees with much of what Kettlewell has written, it does not accept that the French King "stole" or removed the painting. Rather, the painting remained in place until Ambrogio de Predis completed and varnished the copy sometime before 1506. After Leonardo touched up the varnished painting, his original was then returned to him. The return of this painting would be sufficient reason for Leonardo to journey from Florence to Milan.

The original will eventually be listed by Cassiano dal Pozzo in an inventory of paintings at Château de Fontainebleau in 1625. These were considered then part of the royal collection.

Leonardo's Expression of Religious Belief in His Art

Given Leonardo's propensity for scientific accuracy and his thirst for knowledge, one can safely assume that Leonardo brought this Renaissance spirit also to theology. Undoubtedly, Leonardo would not welcome dogma nor substitute faith where knowledge could be attained. Leonardo was no materialist. But what was his theology when he painted *Virgin of the Rocks*? Did it align with his contemporary Roman Catholic theology?

Clues from Legal Documents

In many historical cases, legal documentation can greatly assist in sorting out intentions and disagreements. A number of legal documents were discovered by Signor Grazioso Sironi during the month of May of 1980 in the Archivio di Stato at Milan. This find added significantly to other known legal documents[68] pertaining to

---

[67] James Kettlewell, *Leonardo da Vinci's Virgin Of The Rocks: The Subject Matter Explained*, http://www.jameskettlewell.com/virgin.html

[68] L. Beltrami, *Documenti e Memorie riguardanti la Vita e le Opere di Leonardo da Vinci*, Milano, 1919.

the *Virgin of the Rocks*. Cecil Gould, writing in JSTOR, concludes from these legal documents that, "the work [commissioned on April 25, 1483] was not finished within the time specified in the contract [Dec. 8, 1483], but the documents do not permit the precision as regard the various delays."[69]

The Confraternity received a painting by their deadline just before December 8, 1483. But it was not finished. As patrons wanting to begin to celebrate on time the new festival of the immaculate conception, they certainly were angered by Leonardo's antics. They had pushed the Pope to institute this feast so it was of great importance to them. Further, the painting did not meet specifications in size nor in its depiction which was theologically ambiguous. The icing on this indigestible cake for the feast: no side panels were delivered.

Despite Leonardo being a master, the Confraternity felt cheated and could have sued. They felt justified in refusing to renegotiate or to offer additional payment. With no resolution, the artists could have refused to continue work. By 1485, the lingering disagreement had both parties appealing to Milan's court. Seven long years later, documents from an appeal, signed by both Leonardo and Ambrogio indicate that the artists' expenses had exceeded the agreed fee. This would explain the delay in completing the painting. Leonardo and Ambrogio de Predis then sought the help of the Duke, Ludovico Sforza, to reach a resolution with the Confraternity. Art historian, Angela Ottino della Chiesa, agrees there was an on-time delivery of some painting and believes

---

[69] Cecil Gould, *The Newly-discovered Documents Concerning Leonardo's 'Virgin of the Rocks' and their Bearing on the Problem of the Two Versions*, JSTOR, 1981

that this petition to the Duke Ludovico Sforza was "an extreme move after normal negotiations had failed."[70]

The Duke arranged for a court to hear the case. Historian Charles Nicholl summarizes the contents of the pertinent legal documents of this case, "the painting is described, with that marvellous reductiveness of the legal document, as 'la Nostra Donna facta da dicto florentino' – 'the Madonna done by the said Florentine'. We learn that they had asked for aconguaglio, or adjusted payment, of 1,200 lire, claiming that the 800 lire they had received, as per the contract, had barely paid for the work on the frame alone. The Confraternity had responded by offering them a paltry 100 lire [more]."[71]

Apparently, as an alternative to a larger payment, the artists offered to take back the painting. Charles Nicholl suggests that they had a potential purchaser for the original painting. Nicholl suggests that the interested party was Ludovico himself. His niece, Bianca Maria, was to marry Emperor Maximilian and he may have used it as a wedding-present in 1493. To support this, Nicholls points to a comment appearing in the Antonio Billi's biography of Leonardo from right after his death, that indicates 'He did an altarpiece for Lord Lodovico of Milan, which is said to be the loveliest painting you could possibly see; it was sent by this Lord into Germany, to the Emperor.' The fact that Ambrogio accompanied Bianca Maria to the imperial court in Innsbruck lends further credibility to this theory. Since there may have been as many as three *Virgin of the Rocks* paintings in Milan at this time, one may indeed have been sent as a gift to Maximilian. This interesting supposition fits best if there was a third copy because,

---

[70] Angela Ottino della Chiesa and L.D. Ettlinger, *The Complete Paintings of Leonardo*, Penguin Classics of World Art, 1967
[71] Charles Nicholl, *Leonardo da Vinci: The Flights of the Mind*, Penguin, 2005

in 1493, there was one copy being worked in Ambrogio's studio and one was installed in the altarpiece at the Confraternity. If the Confraternity had no painting in their possession, then it would have been them, rather than the artists, who petitioned for resolution. This author concludes that if a *Virgin of the Rocks* was sent as a wedding gift, it was neither the version at the Louvre nor that at the National Gallery but perhaps a third version became the wedding present.

Cecil Gould writes, "an appeal for more money from Ambrogio Preda, as late as 1503, says that he and his brother, who was dead by this time, had finished their share. Evidently, Leonardo, who had left Milan at the end of 1499 [because of war], had not yet done so. In 1506, a new contract or settlement was signed whereby more money would be forthcoming, provided Leonardo came to Milan and finished his painting."[72] Gould's conjecture that Leonardo had not finished his portion of the painting while Ambrogio had, is not consistent with their partnership as well as Leonardo' relationship with his students. Leonardo was beloved. Ambrogio would never have thrown the master under the bus. Something else, such as the Confraternity seeking depiction clarity in the painting, was holding up the completion of the contract.

When the appeal for more money that was made by Ambrogio in 1503, it was likely based on instructions given to him by Leonardo. Ambrogio felt he could do no more with the painting. The master was gone, and the client would not accept it. There is no indication that the painting was subsequently worked upon until 1506 or 1507 when Leonardo applies some legally requested finishing touches that would satisfy the Confraternity. From 1499 to 1506,

---

[72] Cecil Gould, *The Newly-discovered Documents Concerning Leonardo's 'Virgin of the Rocks' and their Bearing on the Problem of the Two Versions*, JSTOR, 1981

Ambrogio's frustration grew until he may have forced the issue by applying a varnish. This resulted in a legal settlement in 1506 that required Leonardo to return to Milan to do something that would complete the legal requirements for the painting to be accepted. The settlement specifically requested Leonardo to do this work. Because this painting already had been varnished by Ambrogio, Leonardo's task seemed hopeless.

Figure 21a Side Panel, Red Angel, A. de Predi?

Figure 21b Side Panel, Green Angel, M. d'Oggiono?

Once again, Leonardo demonstrated his genius as he spent very little time in Milan completing the painting. What did he do? In 1508, twenty-five years after the original commission, the work was finally accepted and installed. Ambrodio de Predis would finish painting the side panels and delivered them after the dispute was settled.

"When the two side panels, now in the National Gallery, London, were provided, at date unknown, they were very much inferior to the central panel. Any idea for four angels in each panel had entirely disappeared. The right panel which has an angel in red playing a lute, is presumed to be by Ambrogio de Predis. The left panel, with an angel in green playing the vielle, must be by a different artist, perhaps Marco d'Oggiono, one of Leonardo's pupils. The difference in quality explains why the conscientious Ambrogio would not have dared to work on a Leonardo masterpiece by himself.

Of the two side panels (figures 21a and 21b), only the face of green musical angel may have had Leonardo's assistance. It has similarities to the facial features of John the Evangelist in Leonardo's *Last Supper*.

The face of the angel in red bears a strong resemblance to drawings by Leonardo where the mischievous Salai had served as the model, for example, a drawing in red chalk of a youth, now in the Uffizi. While the posture of the bodies and the position of the feet plus their clothing appear to be based on the same cartoon, the angels are very different in style. The angle's heads and the musical instruments are also different. Note how the drapery of the angel in green is crisp and flowing, even flamboyant, while the red garment's drapery seems to have been rushed. Perhaps these side panels were rushed so as to be submitted within a time limit.

When the outer panels are assembled with the centerpiece, the fact that both angels are turned the same way gives a strange appearance as if both were intended to go on the right side of the central panel. One would expect that, even if a single design was used, the motif would have been reversed, as was common in early Renaissance paintings such as this Piero della Francesca's painting

Madonna del Parto."[73] Clearly, Leonardo was not involved with at least the red angel of these side panels.

Figure 22 Piero della Francesca, Madonna del Parto, Museo della Madonna del Parto of Monterchi

---

[73] Tamsyn Taylor, Colchester Gallery, http://www.leonardodavincithevirginoftherocks.com/p/blog-page.html, (accessed 2Feb2018)

3. Debating the Depictions

Common Interpretations of the Paintings

Answering what Leonardo had intended to portray in his original painting, will help us in our journey to discover why there are two or perhaps three similar paintings. Exploring the possibilities will itself become an exciting journey through Leonardo's seed-spreading during the Italian Renaissance. This book ventures into these ideas and the garnered wisdom that were available to this period's hero, Leonardo da Vinci.

Lippi and Religious Art

The generation of artists that preceded Leonardo was epitomized by the delicate beauty in the religious paintings of Fra Filippo Lippi. Born in Florence in 1406, Lippi grew up in poverty. Both of his parents died when he was a toddler. No surviving family member could afford to raise him. When he turned eight years of age, he was sent to a Florentine Carmelite convent. There he received an education. His experience drew him towards becoming a Carmelite friar. At the age of twenty-one, he attained his goal, becoming ordained as a Carmelite priest.

Besides religion, Lippi had another love - to sketch. He would observe painters, inwardly longing to be a painter himself. Giorgio Vasari, in his *Lives of the Artists*, describes Lippi's other love, "Instead of studying, he spent all his time scrawling pictures on his own books and those of others." Thus, his Carmelite brothers eventually permitted him to explore his artistic passion but they never released him from his vows.

Lippi's inherent skills eventually earned him a patronage with Cosimo de' Medici. With this support, his unique and delicate style greatly influenced the pre-Leonardo generation of painters.

Figure 23 Madonna and Child Enthroned, Filippo Lippi, 1430

Not only did Lippi's artistic style sway Early Renaissance techniques, but his focus on the Madonna and her role in Christianity must have been in the minds of the Confraternity when they envisioned their chapel.

Mary, Madonna, Virgin

As the human mother of Jesus, Mary was given special honor from the early days of Christianity onward. Throughout the centuries, Mary's esteem compounded. The Gospels indicated that Mary was present at both the birth and the death of Jesus. In John's Gospel, it is said that Jesus, while dying on the cross, gave his own mother unto the care of the only disciple with sufficient courage to be present at the crucifixion, namely John the Evangelist. John's Gospel described who was present at this scene, "his mother, his mother's sister, Mary, the wife of Clopas, and Mary Magdalene." The Gospel then says, "When Jesus therefore saw His mother, and the disciple whom He loved standing by, He said to His mother, 'Woman, behold your son!' Then He said to the disciple, 'Behold your mother!' And from that hour that disciple took her to his own home."[74]

"Behold your mother" became a tenet supporting the Cult of Mary that emerged in the Middle Ages. Earlier, in the first centuries, Christians had differed about when Jesus had become God. Was it at birth or at baptism? If at baptism, then Mary gave birth to a human baby. But if at birth, then Mary had given birth to God! The role of Mary became elevated to godliness. The Mary of Matthew from whom came siblings for Jesus was swept aside. And the mystery of the birth of Christ became lost. The "Mother of God" (Theotokos) concept at first split Christians. The Theotokos concept was approved by the Council of Ephesus in 431 CE. Henceforth, the other Christians were considered heretics.

The Second Ecumenical Council of Constantinople in 553 CE granted perpetual virginity to the Luke Mary who had become the only Mary. It described her as "ever virgin". This sanctification of

---

[74] John 19:25-27 NIV

Mary continued into Leonardo's time when the concept of the immaculate conception arose. This concept deals with how Mary, not Jesus, was conceived. It thereby frees Mary of "original sin" so that she is pure enough to give birth to God (or to a God of the Trinity). That would elevate her to be in a special place well above the human level while it obscured the coming of God into Mankind to be a human among humans and go through death. It was the brethren of the Confraternity of the Immaculate Conception that convinced the Pope to institutionalize this and make it a feast. They reasoned that Mary, to be the mother of God, must have been born without original sin, that is, not by sexual procreation. The brethren succeeded to sway the Pope and get their feast day.

Saint Paul had recognized the equality of women in the new church of Christianity. Women led some of his congregations. Although it was the women, along with John, who were present on Golgotha, all of the disciples had been men. Following the Council of Nicea in the fourth century, Western Christianity took on a decided masculine control of spirituality.

Bart Ehrman makes a strong case that proto-Orthodox proponents in the second century altered Paul's letters when making copies so as to support the prevailing view that the role of women should remain inferior to men in the nascent Christian church.[75] Thus, the Church, by the third century, only allowed men to be priests and bishops.

---

[75] Bart Ehrman, https://ehrmanblog.org/pauls-views-of-women/

Figure 24 Coronation of the Virgin, Filippo Lippi, 1468

In 1476, Pope Sixtus IV established the Feast of the Immaculate Conception by issuing the apostolic constitution *Cum Praeexcelsa*. Yet, it was not until 1854 that the doctrine of the Immaculate Conception became Church dogma via a papal bull, *Ineffabilis Deus*, by Pope Pius IX. In 1950, Mary's status was elevated further with the dogma of the Assumption of Mary defined by Pope Pius XII. This states that, at the end of her earthly life, her body and soul were lifted into heavenly glory. Note, there is no mention of her spirit which had been deemed heretical by the Eighth Ecumenical Council which declared that each human is comprised of only body and soul, not two souls, nor any other higher members.[76]

Later, Pope John Paul II spoke in his encyclical *Redemptoris Mater* about the veneration of Mary, "At the center of this mystery, in the midst of this wonderment of faith, stands Mary. As the loving Mother of the Redeemer, she was the first to experience it: 'To the wonderment of nature you bore your Creator'!" Such a venerable depiction of Mary was hoped for by the Confraternity when they opened bids for the altarpiece to reside in their new chapel.

How does the scene of the *Virgin of the Rocks* compare to the Madonna scenes of Filippo Lippi? As a Carmelite priest, Lippi artistically felt that the spiritual world had participated and rejoiced in the birth of Jesus, thus, the Madonna, Mary, should be depicted as the highest of humans. For Lippi, this meant spiritual enthronement for Mary. Figures 23 and 24 illustrate this religious portrayal.

Rather than an enthroned Madonna in her glory, Leonardo paints his central figure, apparently Mary, seated on the ground, down to earth. The term "Madonna of Humility"[77] has been applied to this more human representation of Mary. She towers over all including an archangel!

---

[76] See Canon 11, https://sourcebooks.fordham.edu/basis/const4.asp
[77] Beth Harris and Steven Zucker, *Virgin of the Rocks*, https://www.khanacademy.org/humanities/renaissance-reformation/high-ren-florence-rome/leonardo-da-vinci/a/leonardo-virgin-of-the-rocks

Figure 25 Madonna close-up, VoR, LdV, Louvre

Rather than the blue and red colors of the classic Madonna, this central figure is sheathed in dark blue and gold colors. Missing, in the original *Virgin of the Rocks*, are haloes for any of the characters. Why? Was Leonardo trying to draw our attention to the importance of grasping the mystery of what took place in the earthly element for all of humankind?

Probing for Differences

Even in the copy, the haloes are mere golden rings around the heads of the three non-angelic characters. Note that the arch-angelic being is the only one lacking a halo (see figure 26)!

Until this book, the common description of the depictions of the *Virgin of the Rocks* would be:

- Mary in the center with her right arm around the infant
- John the Baptist and her left arm above the head of her
- Christ child. John, on the left, has his hands clasped in prayer directed toward the Christ child who blesses John with his right hand,
- And an angel or archangel.

The archangel whose right-hand points to John while her left hand supports the back of the Christ child gazes into the pool of water. The figures are arranged in a rocky landscape with window-like vistas. In the distance can be seen a river that seems to lead nowhere. Throughout the rough and rocky scene are numerous plants, some with flowers.

Figure 26 Comparing Archangels, VoR, LdV, National Gallery and Louvre

What is this rough and rocky setting? What purpose would it serve Leonardo for him to use it as the setting for the Madonna or to promulgate her Immaculate Conception? The National Gallery has long claimed in its published literature [at least through 1979 when I was there] that Leonardo has painted a scene from an apocryphal book but they failed to state which book.

Art historian Luca Fiore repeats this common tale that "Leonardo chose to begin from ancient apocryphal prophecies about the life of the Baptist, which tell that, on their return from Egypt, Jesus and Our Lady went to see their cousin, John, who had taken refuge from Herod's persecution in a cave that opened miraculously thanks to the prayers of Elizabeth. In this cave, they could see out but those outside could not see them within. Fiore adds that in Leonardo's painting we get a glimpse of the countryside with the Jordan passing though. The apocryphal stories say that on that occasion, Jesus revealed to John both their destinies."[78]

Again, the claim of "apocryphal" book fails to cite which book. No such book exists that Leonardo would have considered authentic, especially with the wisdom he possessed. Further, this description cannot be believed because Jesus was already well beyond his toddler years by the time the family returned from Egypt. John would have been a young boy by this time and no longer hiding out in a cave, if he ever had. Perhaps, as the National Gallery once maintained, the apocryphal story occurred not on their return *from*, but on their *journey to Egypt.* Then they perhaps had a chance meeting in the desert along the way. Many art historians have accepted this "apocryphal" claim of the National Gallery for several decades without investigating it.

Art historian Tamsyn Taylor, who otherwise is adept at investigating such claims, disappointingly fails to question the claim of an apocryphal story writing, "The Bible tells us nothing of what happened to John the Baptist as a baby. It does not indicate that he, like Jesus, lived in the town of Bethlehem where all boys under two years were slaughtered by Herod's soldiers. There is no biblical

---

[78] Luca Fiore, Traces, n. 10, Art London, Leonardo's Version, 11Jan2011, http://archivio.traces-cl.com/2011/11/leonardosversi.html

reason to think that his life was under threat. Yet medieval tradition has it that the infant John left the Holy Land, guided and guarded by the Archangel Uriel and travelled, like Mary, Joseph and the infant Jesus, to Egypt. Tradition has it that the Holy Family met John and his Guardian Angel on the road. This is the subject which Leonardo has chosen to paint and which was also painted repeatedly by Raphael and was treated both in sculpture and painting (minus the Angel) by Michelangelo. In fact, for a time, among Florentine painters the Virgin and Child and infant John was to become the most common subject of smaller works for personal devotion. Leonardo's rendering of this subject made an indelible mark on the history of painting."[79] The "tradition" she mentions was fostered by the National Gallery, not by any apocryphal book. Again, this scene or story appears in no Biblical nor in any apocryphal book. Whenever this claim has been made, no reference has ever been given until 2011 when the Gospel of James was first mentioned as a possible for source for Leonardo's scene. Let's examine it as a possible source.

The Gospel of James
Because the Gospel of James has birth stories of Mary, John the Baptist, and Jesus, it is sometimes cited, erroneously, as the source of the painting's scene. This Gospel of James contains three equal parts, each with eight chapters. Part one tells the story of the birth and childhood of Mary up to her presentation in the temple. Part two begins when Mary is 12 years old. Because she is nearing child-bearing age, she must leave the temple. Joseph is selected to be her husband. Part three then describes the birth of Jesus, including the visit of midwives. "And he *found a cave* and led her there and

---

[79] Tamsyn Taylor, Colchester Gallery, http://www.leonardodavincithevirginoftherocks.com/p/blog-page.html, (accessed 2Feb2018)

stationed *his sons* to watch her, while he went to a find a Hebrew midwife in the land of Bethlehem."[80] Then it tells of the hiding of Jesus "in a stall of cows" during the slaughter of the innocents by Herod the Great. John the Baptist was also a babe at this time. The story tells of how his mother, Elizabeth, "looked around to find where she could hide him, but there was not any good place. Then, as Elizabeth sighed, she said with a loud voice, 'Mountain of God, take me, a mother with her child.' For Elizabeth was too afraid to go up higher. And at once, the mountain split open and received her." The scene of the *Virgin of the Rocks* might be construed to be the cave where Jesus was born or the other cave where Elizabeth and John hid. But at no time in this story do Jesus and John meet.

The Gospel of James would have been known in Florence during Leonardo's time there. In 1958, what is now the earliest known manuscript of this text was found.[81] It is a papyrus dating to the third century. Often during this era, the actual author of a text was not named because their story was told verbally for a few generations and only later, well after the author had died, was the oral tradition written down by a scribe. The text claims the author to be "James, a servant of God and of the Lord Jesus Christ." This epistle was attributed to James the Just[82] who was described by Paul as "the brother of the Lord" [Galatians 1:19]. Interestingly, in Matthew's gospel [13:55–56], Jesus did have brothers. In Luke's gospel, Jesus was an only child. Its date, the late third or early fourth century, make this text suspicious of theological forgery. Likely the Gospel of James was written to explain the stark differences between the birth stories of Luke and Matthew.

---

[80] https://www.asu.edu/courses/rel376/total-readings/james.pdf
[81] Papyrus Bodmer 5, Bodmer Library, Geneva
[82] Peter H. Davids, *New International Greek Testament Commentary: The Epistle of James,* Eerdmans, 1982

Apparently, the intended audience for the Book of James were the Jewish Christians. In James 5.10-11 it is not Jesus but Job whose suffering is cited. Norman Perrin offers this analysis of the book, [There is] "almost nothing distinctively Christian about it. Jesus Christ is mentioned only twice (1:1, 2:1), and both verses could be omitted without any harm to the flow of thought in the text. When the "coming of the Lord" is mentioned (5:7) there is nothing to denote the specifically Christian hope of the Parousia [Second Coming]. 'Faith' in this text is not specifically Christian faith but rather the acceptance of monotheism (2:19). These facts have led some scholars to suggest that the text is a Jewish homily lightly Christianized."[83]

As mentioned, in Matthew's gospel there was a brother of Jesus whose name was James. This James inherited, at the death of Jesus, a leadership role for the Jewish Christians of Jerusalem. It is not known what role he had as a disciple or if he had any exposure to Christ-Jesus after the baptism.[84] There are no references in other texts from before the third century to a Gospel of James.

The book has sometimes been called the Protoevangelium of James. Its goal seems to be attempting to tie together the four gospels by dealing with their contradictions, especially the birth

---

[83] Norman Perrin, *The New Testament: An Introduction*, Thomson Learning, p. 255, 1982

[84] James apparently had influenced Peter leading to Peter's confrontation with Paul as described in Galatians 2:11-13, "But when Peter came to Antioch, I had to oppose him to his face, for what he did was very wrong. **12** When he first arrived, he ate with the Gentile believers, who were not circumcised. But afterward, when some **friends of James** came, Peter wouldn't eat with the Gentiles anymore. He was **afraid of criticism** from these people who insisted on the necessity of circumcision. **13** As a result, other Jewish believers followed Peter's hypocrisy, and even Barnabas was led astray by their hypocrisy." This adherence to Jewish rules, shows James was not trained in the new Christianity yet he, as the brother of Jesus, wielded power even over Peter.

stories. This text was troubling for third century theologians. Many texts were written during the second century that attempted to support one theological position over another. This book seems to follow that lead. Christianity had brought about a great upheaval within theological domains. As it spread through Gnostic, Mithraic, Zoroastrian, pagan, and across the realms of multiple ancient mysteries, there was a recognition of Christianity as the fulfillment of what was expected. But its concepts that God had entered the flesh of fallen Mankind was, however, nearly impossible to grasp by even the brightest minds of the time. Many traditions that Christianized accepted some but rejected other aspects of the new religion.

The idea of a God being put to an ignoble death like a common criminal on a cross was especially difficult to grasp for those of the Roman empire. The first mention of the Gospel of James is by the church father, Origen of Alexandria, who was active from the early to mid-third century. Origen found this text, like that of a Gospel of Peter, to be of dubious authenticity. In addition, both Eusebius and St. Epiphanius had strong ecclesiastical doubts about this epistle thereby keeping it out of the eventual canon. Leonardo likely would have known about such opinions and would not base his painting upon such an unreliable text.

In all of the many books that analyze these two paintings, the one with the most credible explanation for the scene painted by Leonardo comes from James Kettlewell who explains, "An intimate relationship between Mary and John [the Baptist] pertains first of all to the fact that both served, in their own ways, as precursors of Jesus. More important for this painting, they were also related by being the only two mortals besides Jesus, to have been born cleansed of the original sin. But only the story of John appears in the Bible. The story of Mary's origins does not. In the Gospel of St.

Luke, one learns about John being free of the original sin in his mother's womb. The angel Gabriel announced to John's father Zacharias, that his wife, Elizabeth, would bear a son 'filled with the Holy Ghost, even in his mother's womb.' (Luke, 1:15) One only learns about Mary's parents, Anna and Joachim in an apocryphal text, the Protoevangelium of James. [Despite theological doubts,] this text became almost equivalent to the Bible itself, particularly in the history of art. The story of Mary in the Protoevangelium[85] became embedded in Christian legend and was a favorite subject of artists during the latter Middle Ages and the Renaissance. It is probably in the story of the origins of John in the Gospel of St. Luke that the whole idea of the Immaculate Conception of Mary originated, because John was immaculately born, so to speak, and it became the basis for a principal argument for the Immaculate Conception of Mary. This was at a time in Church history when arguments pro and con, between the Franciscan 'Immaculists' and the Dominican 'Maculists,' were being heatedly debated. So, the angel aggressively points at the infant St. John, directing our attention, in no uncertain terms, to his major role in the work The Christ child looks intently at, and blesses John. Mary holds on to John, not to her son, and looks at him with motherly affection."[86]

This explanation has merit if the "Protoevangelium of James" carried as much significance during the early Renaissance as Kettlewell claims. Likely there were some painters who used this Epistle as their inspiration, but that would not be the case for the painters of Leonardo's Academy whose themes were inspired from

---

[85] In addition to the Epistle of James, there is also Romans 16:20 "And the God of peace shall bruise Satan under your feet shortly. The grace of our Lord Jesus Christ be with you. Amen" which relates to the Fall of Man in Genesis 3:15 "it shall bruise thy head [serpent] and thou shalt bruise his heel [Man]."
[86] James Kettlewell, *Leonardo da Vinci's Virgin of the Rocks: The Subject Matter Explained*, http://www.jameskettlewell.com/virgin.html

the fountain of wisdom from where Leonardo, according to his notebooks, drank. What Leonardo learned at the Platonic academy, in the Gardens of San Marcos, and from the students of Plethon, and from his own drinking at the fountain, showed to him profound truths. These truths would reveal that the Gospel of James made a mockery of Christian theology in order to appease the new ruler in knowledge, materialism.

We can conclude that there was no apocryphal story Leonardo used as the basis for his painting. Moreover, he began the painting while still in Florence. He could only win the Confraternity's commission with a painting that was well on its way to completion if it was to be ready in the six months remaining before the first new Feast of the Immaculate Conception. His painting depicts two toddlers each about a year and a half after birth so our mystery concerning the depictions and the description of the scene remains unsolved.

Iconographical Intrigue
For a couple centuries, art historians have largely agreed that Leonardo was depicting the Madonna, Saint John, Jesus, and an angel (or archangel). This interpretation fits with Roman Christian theology, at least since the start of the second millennium.

The Louvre version lacks iconographic clues to identify its characters. Typical clues such as St. John's staff and haloes are missing. This must have been perplexing to the Confraternity. Adding to the confusion is the fact that not only is the supposed Christ Child not seated in the Virgin's lap as was customary, but she is not even touching her own son. Instead, her hand stretches to touch the back of the other child, supposedly John the Baptist who kneels in adoration toward his cousin. The supposed Christ child is seemingly blessing St. John.

Our clues have led to a potential conclusion that Leonardo painted the original with a new kind of iconography in mind, one suffused with a knowledge of the Christian Mysteries. Leonardo had learned of these Mysteries during his education in Florence, especially within the halls of the Platonic Academy. With this perspective, a different depiction will come to be realized. It is a depiction of a mystery that was intended by Leonardo in the original *Virgin of the Rocks* painting. Because such a depiction would be deemed heretical, Leonardo had to hide the true meaning. Then in his copy, he had to include iconographic symbols in order to render the characters into a theologically acceptable depiction. For the copy, Leonardo borrowed from the iconography of earlier artists who drew from the Epistle of James only when legally obligated to do so. Otherwise, he could violate in his work his sense for truth.

Religious Belief Expressed in Art

Given Leonardo's propensity for scientific accuracy and his thirst for knowledge, one can safely assume that he brought this Renaissance spirit from his work in science to his work with theological themes. He certainly would not submit to mere faith nor to dogma wherever knowledge could be attained. Leonardo was certainly not a materialist nor was he an atheist. But what was his theology? Did it align with his contemporary Roman Catholic theology? Leonardo's biographers have never ventured to answer this question. His notebooks shed no light upon it. But we will find clues in the content of his paintings plus in those of his students.

Accademia Platonica

During his formative years in Verrocchio's School, Leonardo likely attended the lectures at Ficino's Platonic Academy. The Academy had been started by Cosimo de Medici after his enthusiasm for Plato and the ancient mysteries was piqued when he heard the lectures of Gemistus Plethon. Plethon had been sent by Byzantine

Emperor, John VIII, to serve as an envoy for the 1438 Council of Florence. The goal of this council was to heal the Great Schism of 1054 that had split the Church of Rome and the Church of Constantinople.

Figure 27 Marsilio Ficino by Giovio de Como, 1520, Palazzo Volpi

Later, the exact year is not known, the Accademia Platonica becomes established with Florence's top philosopher, Marsilio Ficino as its head. No known documents describe the exact nature of this academy between the time of Plethon's lectures and Ficino's appointment but given the Platonic concepts plus those of other mystics, participants and lecturers needed to keep out of the eye and ear of the Inquisitors. Notable members of the Academy included Cristoforo Landino, Pico della Mirandola, Gentile de' Becchi, and Angelo Ambrogini, aka Poliziano. Forensic tests in 2007 showed that both Poliziano and Pico had died in 1494 of arsenic poisoning. One theory has Piero di Lorenzo de' Medici, son of Lorenzo, who was under political pressure from Savonarola, had ordered their deaths to wipe away the heretical history of the academy. Piero hoped such a "cleansing" would restore the Medici to political power.[87] Support for the academy become a religious

---

[87] Malcolm Moore (7 February 2008). "Medici philosopher's mysterious death is solved" *The Daily Telegraph*. London, plus Medici writers exhumed in Italy. BBC News, 28 February 2007.

embarrassment for the Medici family during and after the period of Savonarola-style fundamentalism.

Despite the Academy's secrecy, Christophe Poncet has shown through extant letters that the Platonic Academy did exist in Careggi, just outside of Florence. Poncet writes in his paper *Ficino's Little Academy of Careggi*,[88] "As a matter of fact, this small farm had been given him by Cosimo de' Medici as a reward for his translation of the *Corpus Hermeticum*. The donation act, dated 18 April 1463, states: «unum predium cum domo pro laboratore et hoste etterris laboratis, vineatis et olivatis [...]».[89] The plot has been identified on the side of a hill called Monte Vecchio, about halfway to the top. From this site, the superb panorama of Florence and the Medici villa of Careggi can be enjoyed. Its southern exposure provides sunlight from dawn to sunset. And, protected from the north winds by the mountain, it is a most pleasant location. It is well known that Ficino had a tendency to identify with the philosopher he so zealously translated and commented, to the point of being considered an alter Plato by some of his contemporaries. Did Ficino have his own small estate of Careggi in mind when he described Plato's Academy as a little farm?

Ficino's Gymnasium

In one of his letters, Ficino reminds three of his correspondents of a painting that they had seen in his gymnasium: «You have seen painted in my gymnasium the globe of the world and on either side Democritus and Heraclitus, but the first is laughing while the other

---

[88] Christophe Poncet, *Ficino's Little Academy of Careggi*, Bruniana & campanelliana, xix, 1, 2013
[89] Cfr. Marsilio Ficino e il ritorno di Platone, eds S. Gentile, S. Niccoli, P. Viti, Firenze, Le Lettere, 1984, p. 175.

is crying».⁹⁰ Evidently, Ficino had his own gymnasium, the walls of which were decorated like those of Plato's Academy, according to the *Vita Platonis*. We know from another letter by Ficino that Bernardo Bembo, the ambassador of Venice in Florence, had visited this gymnasium: «Five month after, on the very day I completely fulfilled my vow, and at the same hour, you came of your own will to my gymnasium, escorted by a large company».

George Gemistus Plethon
Plethon was born in Constantinople in 1355. Oddly, Plethon was not part of either the Greek or the Roman Christian church. He was renowned for his wisdom and morality. The Byzantine Empire was asking for European help against the Ottomans. Sending Plethon as an envoy was hoped to warm the Europeans leading to their acceptance of military assistance.

Plethon caused quite a stir in Florence when he offered to give some lectures on the differences between Plato and Aristotle. Cosimo de' Medici attended these lectures that became the catalyst for the ensuing Renaissance. Inspired, Cosimo founded the Accademia Platonica and installed Ficino as its head. Plethon and his students continued to teach there well after the council had ended.

Plethon's lectures were summarized in his book *On the Differences of Aristotle from Plato*. He was affectionately called the "Prince Among the Philosophers". Concepts of reincarnation were taught and became inherent when attendees discussed Plethon. Marsilio Ficino called him 'the second Plato' and Cardinal Bessarion openly asked, "Is Plato's soul in this body?" Plato's concept of the

---

⁹⁰ Epistole fol. xv iv: «Vidistis pictam in gymnasio meo mundi spheram et hinc atque illinc Democritum et Heraclitum, alterum quidem ridentem, alterum vero fentem»

transmigration of souls had itself been reborn. After Plato, the last major western philosopher to have dealt with reincarnation was Philo (20 BCE – 50 CE).

Concepts of reincarnation persisted into the first century and into the works of neoplatonist Philo of Alexandria. Sami Yli-Karjanmaa, in his book *Reincarnation in Philo of Alexandria*,[91] wrote, "This chapter deals with the four Philonic texts that most clearly seem to refer to reincarnation. In the overview of previous research, it was noted that *Somn*. 1.137-139 is actually the *locus classicus* of reincarnation in Philo. It is a comparatively straightforward case for which no other interpretation than reincarnation has been seriously suggested." Plethon gave the concept new life. Besides Plato and Philo, he also lectured on Plotinus, Zoroaster, (aka Zarathustra), astrology, the ancient mysteries, magic and the Egyptian Hermes Trismegistus. The excitement he caused lasted for generations.

---

[91] Sami Yli-Karjanmaa, *Reincarnation in Philo of Alexandria*, chptr 3, SBL Press, 2015

Figure 28 Plethon, Benozzo Gozzoli, Palazzo Medici Riccardi, Florence, Italy

After the council ended, unsuccessfully for John VIII, Plethon departed. Plethon's role was continued by his students at the Academy. In 1440, Plethon journeyed to his beloved Greece to found a mystery center in Mystra. In order to offer a mystery center, he obviously must have known how to administer initiation practices as a hierophant. Plethon died there in 1452, the same year in which Leonardo was born. Plethon obviously was much more than just a great teacher as we can deduct from the dramatic and dangerous decision fourteen years after his death of some of his Florentine students to sail to Mystra and steal his remains. These were reinterred in the Tempio Malatestiano of nearby Rimini "so that the great Teacher may be among free men." Surely Plethon was an initiate already during his time in Florence. Only an initiate could found a Mystery Center. Plethon brought with him a trunk full of ancient texts which have since disappeared. But Ficino was put to work to translate these to Latin. Likely, Ficino's *Orphic*

System of natural magic arose from his translation work on Hermes Trismegistus.

In his lectures, Plethon argued that the West had been influenced by an Arabic (materialistic) interpretation of Plato and especially of Aristotle. The teachers of Aristotle had come with envoys to Baghdad during Charlemagne's reign. Aristotelianism in Byzantium had been less penetrated by materialism. The companion book to this, the *Uncomfortable History of Christianity*, will cover more of Charlemagne's envoys to Baghdad who had returned with gifts from Harun al-Rashid: teachers for the fledgling Frankish kingdom. Naturally, these teachers brought such an interpretation of Aristotle.

Plethon practiced what would have been considered by the Inquisition to be a heretical ancient Greek paganism. But his academic presentation to an audience of dignitaries protected him. Plethon saw the Hellenistic beliefs as a prelude to Christianity. Moreover, like Augustine, he considered those who practiced the ancient mysteries as the Christians before Christianity, i.e. before the name "Christian" came into use. His lectures here inspired the Renaissance paintings that tied Greek mythological themes to Christian ones. After two years in Florence, in 1440, Plethon finally returned to Greece to fulfill his dream of founding a new mystery center which he did in Mystra, near Sparta. There he died in 1452, the same year that Leonardo was born! Imagine the stir in Florence when in 1466, Sigismondo Pandolfo Malatesta and other students, successfully stole his remains from Mystra that had become part of the Ottoman Empire. Plethon's remains were then interred in the port city of Rimini "so that the great Teacher may be among free men". Plethon was no ordinary teacher. Nor was the Platonic Academy an ordinary academy of its time (or whatever it was secretly known as).

Leonardo's Milanese Academy

In 2008, Jill Pederson provided the evidence of Leonardo's Milanese Academy. She wrote, "The recent rediscovery of the early sixteenth-century vernacular text of the *Isola Beata* (private collection, c. 1513) written by Henrico Boscano throws light on the Milanese intellectual circle of Leonardo da Vinci, and through the examination of this unpublished manuscript this article will put forth a new account in support of the existence of the Academia Leonardi Vinci."[92] The contents of the *Isola beata* [Blessed Island] places those of Leonardo's Renaissance community as characters upon a mystical island. Its author, Henrico Boscano (doc. 1513–1528), described members of Leonardo's group as representing diverse artistic, philosophic, and literary skills. Pederson concludes, "We can characterize the academy by comparing their varied interests. In the past, the Quattrocento Milanese academy, when its existence has been accepted at all, has been interpreted as an artistic school of the type headed by Vasari in the sixteenth century. Such a conclusion derives mainly from the historical ambiguity of the word 'academy'. In order to understand more fully Leonardo's circle, it is helpful first to examine the contents of the *Isola beata*, which provides a list of the members of Leonardo's group, as well as evidence for the existence of the academy."[93] Pederson's conclusions align with the central thesis of this essay that Leonardo's Milanese academy was based on the "Florentine counterpart, Ficino's Platonic academy." She reveals that Leonardo's "Milanese academy followed the same basic principle of dynamic exchange and entertained similar philosophical interests and pursuits."[94]

---

[92] Jill Pederson, "Henrico Boscano's *Isola beata*: new evidence for the Academia Leonardi Vinci in Renaissance Milan", *Renaissance Studies,* Vol. 22 No. 4, 2008
[93] IBID
[94] IBID

Why Were the Paintings Not Identical?

Figure 29 Comparing VoR Nat'l Gallery, London to VoR Louvre, Paris

These two paintings are indeed quite similar but as you study them, you will notice a number of significant differences. Take a moment to immerse yourself in this comparison. Look at the colors, the backgrounds, the foregrounds, and then at the characters. How are the hand gestures the same or different? Who touches which child? Are the plants different?

In the painting on the right, the one at the Louvre, you will notice that the staff with a cross at its end is held by the child on the left in one painting, but the staff is missing in the painting on the right. Also missing are the haloes around the two children as well as the central figure. Note that feminine figure on the right has wings but still no halo in either painting.

In the National Gallery's painting, the archangel's pointing hand is missing. This is the most dramatic difference.

With both paintings, if one divides the painting in half, then each child has a protective presence next to it with a unique background above it. The two halves are complete in themselves. Only the central figure's left hand crosses the boundary between the two halves. What does this left hand signify? She is also higher than the other three thereby giving her a higher iconological position, higher even than the archangel.

These differences will be clues to understanding what Leonardo intended to be portrayed in his original painting.

Many art historians denote the archangel as merely an angel. Modern simplification sometimes uses the term "angel" to mean any heavenly being. But in the time of Leonardo, the nine heavenly delineations of Dionysius the Areopagite were well known. The National Gallery, with this knowledge has deemed this feminine figure on the right to be the archangel Uriel because this is the archangel of the summer months when St. John was supposedly born (June 25). But this archangel's pointing hand was left out by the artist in the National Gallery's painting.

Note also, how its lighting seems to be from a full moon while the Louvre painting seems to be basked in sunlight. Is this also another clue from Leonardo for understanding what was intended to be portrayed in his original painting?

As discussed earlier, one theory by Angela Ottino della Chiesa is often cited to explain the existence of the two paintings. She claims that Leonardo painted the Louvre *Virgin of the Rocks* to fulfil the commission, thereby giving it a date of 1483, but then, he sold that painting to another client and replaced it with the London version. Although there is no data to support it, this theory further hypothesizes that the Louvre painting was sold in the late 1480s. The London painting was commenced about 1486 as a substitution for the "original" that eventually came to be in the Louvre. This second painting was not ready for installation until 1508, after prolonged disagreement and negotiation.

Unfortunately, this explanation by della Chiesa[95] has gained very wide acceptance becoming the version of events described on both the National Gallery[96] and the Louvre[97] websites. It puts into a mere financial transaction the complex issues associated with Leonardo's depictions. What is much more likely, is that the Confraternity accepted the original with the understanding it would be replaced by another Leonardo painting that would be aligned with the theology of the immaculate conception. The original, as beautiful as it was, left theological ambiguities aplenty. Possession of the original gave the Confraternity bargaining strength to receive a masterpiece that portrayed what they intended (and to get their money's worth). Leonardo failed to wear them down and eventually would be legally required to add finishing touches to a painting that Ambrogio de Predi had already varnished. Completing the copy for theological acceptance would come to painting haloes and a staff on top of the varnish!

---

[95] Angela Ottino della Chiesa, *The Complete Paintings of Leonardo da Vinci*. Penguin Classics of World Art, 1967

[96] https://www.nationalgallery.org.uk/paintings/learn-about-art/paintings-in-depth/mysterious-virgin?viewPage=3

[97] https://www.louvre.fr/en/oeuvre-notices/virgin-rocks

Double Identities?

Figure 30 Burlington House Cartoon, LdV, National Gallery

Art Historian James Kettlewell explains that Renaissance painters would, on occasion, depict a theme done by other artists but then give the characters additional possible identities. The following quote is from his analysis of The Burlington House Cartoon that is now in the National Gallery London.

"We do know from documents that Leonardo returned to this [immaculate conception] theme in drawings shortly after his return to Florence in 1499. The famous drawing in the National Gallery in London which represents the Virgin, her mother St. Anne, the infant Jesus and now, one more time, the infant St. John is another inventive variant on the theme of the Immaculate Conception, again with no precedents in Christian art. The infant St. John normally does not appear in Immaculate Conception subjects where Mary is seated on her mother's lap. Once again Leonardo was experimenting with Christian iconography. It is quite possible that, in the drawing, in the close relationship of St. Anne to the child St. John, we are to understand that St. Anne could also be St Elizabeth, the mother of John. There are many precedents in the art of the time, to give figures *double identities to convey certain meanings* [italics for my emphasis]. The artist is reminding us of the parallels that exist between the [immaculate] births of the two children of Anne [Mary] and Elizabeth [John]. And here the pointing hand appears again, now directing our attention overhead to heaven where both their children miraculously originated. The figures in the drawing are roughly the same size as those in the *Virgin of the Rocks*."[98] If Leonardo were to have "double identities" in The Burlington House Cartoon, then might the original *Virgin of the Rocks* also have such double identities? Might character ambiguity have motivated the Confraternity to have demanded modification to the painting intended to be installed in their chapel? And might Leonardo's knowledge-curiosity have led him to explore this new theme of the Immaculate Conception whereupon he arrived at a deeper mystery?

Heretical Identities?
According to Benvenuto Cellini, the French king, Francois I, believed that no other man "knew as much as Leonardo ... that he was a very great philosopher."[99] Leonardo absorbed the stupendous lectures at Florence's Platonic Academy and actively participated in the discussions within the Library and Garden of San Marcos in Florence with some of the greatest minds of his time.

---

[98] James Kettlewell, http://www.jameskettlewell.com/virgin.html, accessed 2Mar2018

[99] Benvenuto Cellini, "Della architettura," in Opere, ed. Bruno Maier (Milan: Rizzoli, 1968), p. 859, cited in Clark, *Leonardo da Vinci* (No. 389), p. 156.

Even within the Medici household, where young Leonardo lived, he was surrounded by renowned scholars exploring the depths of knowledge. New knowledge for Europe from an assortment of ancient texts had arrived during the reign of Cosimo de Medici (1434-1464).

Leonardo bristled at not only the Church's control of and restrictions upon science and anatomy, but also its control and restrictions on "Church" fields such as philosophy, theology, and artistic iconography. In his paintings, Leonardo, like the mischievous imp, could, safely behind his Muse's veil, quietly reveal what he felt was the Truth. The Veil of Art protected him from the enforcers of Church dogma who would have, had they known, labelled Leonardo a heretic and burned him at the stake.

Even towards the end of his life, our Renaissance Man silently fought against Church dogma. One of those who had loved Leonardo from childhood was Giovanni de Medici who had become Pope Leo X on March 9, 1513. As the second son of Lorenzo de Medici, Leo X had known Leonardo as he grew up. Leonardo had been part of the Medici household and likely inspired the young Giovanni regarding art. "Leo X's love for all forms of art stemmed from the humanistic education he received in Florence."[100] This education would have been similar to the education Leonardo received there a generation earlier. As a patron, Leo X provided Leonardo with an apartment near the Vatican in 1513. Leonardo writes in his notebook, "I left Milan to go to Rome on the 24th day of September 1513 with Giovan Francesco Melzi, Salai, Lorenzo, and Il Fanfoia." By December, they were settled into their apartment in Villa del Belvedere where both

---

[100] H. W. Crocker III, *Triumph: the Power and the Glory of the Catholic Church*, Crown Forum, 2003, cited in https://en.wikipedia.org/wiki/Pope_Leo_X, accessed 20Jan2020

Raphael and Michelangelo now resided. In October 1515, King Francis I of France would recapture Milan. In a gesture for peace, King Francis I of France then nominated Giulio de Medici, cousin of Pope Leo X, to become Archbishop of Narbonne. In December, a peace meeting with Francis I and Leo X took place in Bologna. Leonardo was present as an envoy. A few months later, in 1516, Leonardo agreed to enter into Francis' service. About this same time in 1516, the king named the Pope's cousin Giulio as the Cardinal Protector of France. In 1523, Giulio would be elected as Pope and he would subsequently take on the name Clement VII.

Further fighting with France subsided perhaps in small part because of Leonardo's influence but more likely because of the political marriages that followed. Giovanni's younger brother, Giuliano, was married to Filiberta of Savoy, a niece of the French king. An unfortunate fate awaited Giuliano who was murdered in 1516 by political opponents attempting to discontinue Medici rule of Florence. Lorenzo the Magnificent's eldest son, Piero the Unfortunate (1472-1503), had a son, also named Lorenzo (1492–1519) and like Giuliano, met an unfortunate early death. This Lorenzo had a daughter, Catherine (1519–89) who was married to Henry II of France (1519-1559) when both were fourteen. As queen of France, three of her four sons later became kings of France. The Treaty of Cateau-Cambrésis (1559) put an end to the Italian Wars. Henry II was the son of Francis I who had invited Leonardo to live near his summer residence in 1516. In commemoration of the youthful deaths of Giuliano and Lorenzo, the Medici family commissioned Michelangelo for the famous sculpture work at the Medici Tombs in Florence.

By this time in his life now in Rome, Leonardo's attention had turned strongly to philosophy, anatomy, alchemy, and esoteric subjects. Giorgio Vasari writes, "He [Leonardo] went to Rome with

Duke Giuliano de' Medici at the election of Pope Leo, where he applied himself very much to philosophical things and especially to alchemy."[101] What began when he abandoned his *Adoration of the Magi* had become a passion for Leonardo, a passion for Truth.

Despite friendly requests to stop by his patron, Pope Leo X, Leonardo continued his anatomical studies on cadavers at the famous Roman hospital in Santo Spirito (Holy Spirit). Imagine this gray-haired man in his sixties, snooping around in the hospital for opportunities to study anatomy. Naturally someone would object. That would be a German artisan named Giovanni degli Specchi who was so appalled that he alerted the pope's men. A bitter Leonardo, betrayed by an artist, bemoaned, he has 'hindered me in anatomy,' and now has 'denounced it before the Pope and also at the Hospital'.

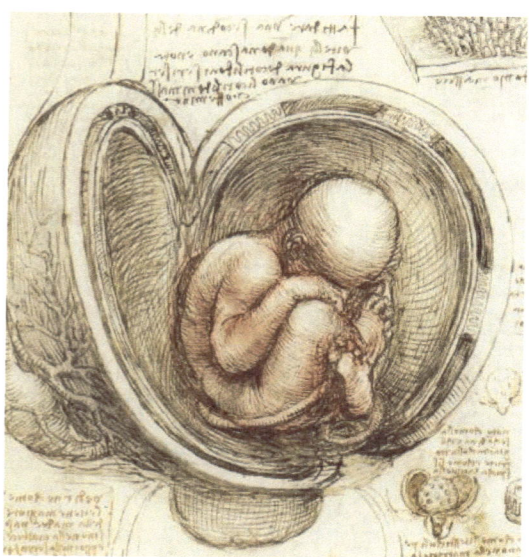

Figure 31 Sketch of fetus, Leonardo's notebooks

---

[101] Giorgio Visari (1511-1574), *The Lives of the Most Excellent Painters, Sculptors, and Architects*, Torrentino (1550), Giunti (1568)

Even worse, from the perspective of the Church, was Leonardo's studies upon a pregnant woman who had died. Leonardo describes the dead mother as having shared all of her animality including her desires and fears and sorrows with the fetus in her womb. Until birth, the baby is fully dependent on both its mother's soul and on her body. 'The same soul governs these two bodies.'[102] This would have been a blatant heretical statement for the hierarchy of the Church of Rome in 1515.

It is remarkable that Leonardo was never condemned as a heretic. The fact that Pope Leo X was a Medici and his patron probably helped to save Leonardo. Contrast this to Pietro Pomponazzi whose books on Aristotle were condemned as heretical and burned in 1516 and Giordano Bruno, a Dominican monk, who was burned at the stake in 1600 when he stated that the sun was the center of the universe and not the earth.[103] The astute biographer Vasari wrote about this trait of Leonardo in his first edition of 1550, 'He had a very heretical state of mind. He could not be content with any kind of religion at all, considering himself in all things much more a philosopher than a Christian'. Such was the Renaissance Man, a heretic hidden behind the veil of Renaissance Art. Likely, when invited by the French King Francis I to live in France, he saw it as an opportunity to continue his work without the threat of heresy hanging over his head beyond the reach of Rome. Likely his friends and perhaps even Pope Leo X gave their blessings to this move.

---

[102] Domenico Laurenza, *Leonardo On Flight,* Giunti Gruppo, 2004
[103] Oddly, in 1533, Clement VII had personally approved the work of Nicolaus Copernicus including his conclusion that the Earth revolves around the Sun. Galileo Galilei's heresy trial for similar ideas would happen 99 years later!

Depiction of a Heretical Mystery

Biographers of Leonardo commonly extol his virtues as both an artist and as a scientist. Some of the Renaissance's educated elite looked down upon Leonardo because of his lack of skills in Latin and Greek which meant he was not well-versed in contemporary authors who wrote in those languages. Of this, Leonardo wrote, "Though I may not, like them, be able to quote other authors, I shall rely on that which is much greater and more worthy — on experience, the mistress of their Masters." But none disparaged Leonardo for his art or for his accomplishments in science. Missing in these assessments was (and still is) Leonardo's religious and theological achievements. When his theology is examined, Leonardo the heretic becomes evident — heretic, that is, according to the Christian theology of his day. Of what he would have been accused in his day, is today just reemerging. Long has Leonardo's theology lain quiet within mysteries unspoken in public.

Although the Confraternity accepted a painting for their commission, it did not meet what they had desired. An existing legal document described what was desired, i.e., something akin to Fra Filippo Lippi's religious style that also depicted the immaculate conception. But they were under a time constraint to find an accomplished artist to fulfill the need for a suitable painting that would also fit within Giacomo's del Maino's altarpiece. They wanted a completed altarpiece for display by the first celebration of the newly blessed-by-the-Pope Feast of the Immaculate Conception. To have this ready by December 8th, they settled for a half-finished painting by the newly arrived "maestro" Leonardo.

Likely they saw sufficient value in having a masterpiece even though it did not fully fit their intentions. They could use their possession of the original *Virgin of the Rocks* as leverage to obtain their desired painting. But, in the ensuing negotiations, the

Confraternity imposed iconographic demands that Leonardo could not accept. They reached a compromise: Leonardo would complete as best as possible the original which the Confraternity would hold onto while they waited for its replacement. To speed up the work on the replacement, Leonardo could work with his new partners, the de Predi brothers. The new painting would be another masterpiece from the hand of Leonardo and one that they expected would be fully acceptable to the Confraternity. The Confraternity took the original, displayed it, and waited for the second version that promised to be more fitting for their chapel devoted to the Immaculate Conception.

Over the ensuing years, Leonardo and his two partners were frequently drawn away from this work for other duties or because of war. But this cannot account for length of time it took to complete the painting. Disagreements between expectations and artistic intentions persisted. Likely most of the painting was completed fairly quickly, but full completion awaited a settlement. Before the French captured Milan, the artists had appealed to Milan's Duke to resolve their differences. But this did not arrive at a solution. In 1503, more than twenty years after winning the commission, Leonardo's partner, Ambrogio de Predi, alone now in French-captured Milan, with Leonardo now back in Florence, and with his brother Evangelista now dead, became frustrated with thirteen years of unsuccessful legal wrangling and no payment for his work. He declared the painting to be complete by applying varnish over its surface! He then tried to deliver it to the Confraternity.

But the Confraternity would not accept the painting as it was. Thus, he appealed to the new king of the land, Louis XII who set a court date. To settle the dispute, the court called for an evaluation of the paintings. This was arranged for a day in April of 1506. The compromise judgment required that some small alterations would be required of the master, Leonardo (no record of the specifics of the requirements has been found). The Maestro was therefore required to travel to Milan and to complete the painting so that the Confraternity could accept it. Leonardo was to apply touchups to the varnished surface that would render the painting into one theologically acceptable by the Confraternity of the Immaculate Conception. What did Leonardo do to render it acceptable and what had been unacceptable?

Because the painting had already been covered in varnish, these touchups had to be applied on its surface. Simple paint and another layer of varnish would have been obvious and degraded the artistic quality and the value of the masterpiece. The genius of Leonardo shines through in his solution that would satisfy all parties. He gave to this painting a unique three-dimensional quality whose three-dimensional depth would be enhanced by the chapel's candlelight. He applied a "thick layer of metallic tin on top of which gold leaf was applied."[104] With this alteration, the Confraternity accepted the painting and paid for it. Leonardo, magnanimously, gave all of his share of this final payment to his partner Ambrogio. This indicates that Ambrogio's financial fortunes during the years of French occupation, without the Sforza patronage, had greatly suffered.

What was this modification that caused the Confraternity to gladly accept their new masterpiece? It was the iconic staff that identified the child on the left as John the Baptist. The three haloes that thereby identified three of the characters as Mary, Jesus, and John also were important. The fourth was obviously an angel or

---

[104] Larry Keith et al, National Gallery Technical Bulletin Volume 32, *Leonardo da Vinci: Pupil, Painter and Master,* Yale University Press, 2011

archangel and fully acceptable without a halo. Now the Confraternity finally had, not what was originally intended, but a venerable icon with high value for the small sum paid.

Presumably, at this time, in 1508, the original was returned to Leonardo. It now disappears until it is catalogued in the French royal collection in 1625. Presumably, it, like the *Mona Lisa*, traveled with the Maestro first back to Florence, then to Rome, and finally to Leonardo's last residence in Clos Luce, France.

As a final historical tidbit on this painting, in 1524, Milan experienced a renewed outbreak of the plague. The brethren of the Confraternity invited citizens of Milan to come and pray beneath their *Virgin of the Rocks.* It was believed that through the painting's iconic power, the Virgin Mary could help one to be personally spared or could provide help for one seeking a miraculous healing for a loved one. The Confraternity certainly got high value for their investment.

What Was the Painting's Heresy?
To explain the basis of the heresy, this section will explain the basis of this heresy through three events related to the portrayal in the *Virgin of the Rocks*. The three events are:

1. the two different birth stories of Jesus described in the gospels of Matthew and Luke,
2. the baptism of Jesus, and
3. the dramatically changed twelve-year old Jesus following Passover in Jerusalem as told in Luke's Gospel.

The Birth of Jesus
The painting shows remarkable left-right balance. Each half has a male child and a female figure present. Each side has a "window" to see the landscape beyond the so-called cave in the distance.

One "window" shows a river with many rock pillars while through the right window just one rock pillar is seen.

Figure 32 Foreground and background of VoR LdV, Louvre

Using customary Orthodox Christian concepts, these characters are the Madonna, the Christ Child, and John the Baptist. But, as we'll see, this is not what Leonardo has portrayed in the original! Under legal pressure, the master painted another that conformed to contemporary Catholic theology.

In the original painting, one sees a rocky scene indicating these four characters are upon the earth. The rocks tower over them. Whereas the religious characters of earlier painters, such as Lippi and Giotto, had their religious characters seem to hover above the ground, these have definitely landed.

In the foreground, appears still water[105] perhaps as a spring or as a reflecting pool. In the open and not within a cave they have assembled by this pool. Each of the two openings in the rocks invites one's eyes to perceive far into the distance.

A young woman towers over the other three characters. She is dressed in dark cosmic blue with a sun-gold waist sash. To her left kneels an archangel with wings. She looks upon the surface of the reflecting pool. The National Gallery has believed she is the archangel of the summer, Uriel, because the date of John's birth has traditionally been set as June 25th. Each of the two female beings is accompanied by a toddler. Note these are not newborns; rather, they are about 24 to 36 months old.

The toddler on the left has above him a window in the rocks through which one is given a glimpse into his past. In deference to the Greek philosopher Heraclitus, see the river of life flowing past a vast array of rock pillars, each representing a past life. This child on the left comes as one with immense knowledge about life on earth. He is the child described in Matthew's Gospel. He represents the kingly within the human.

---

[105] "he leadeth me beside the still waters" from Psalm 23:2 refers what a shepherd does for his flock for their drinkable water.

The toddler on right needs to be supported. This takes the hand of an archangel in order for this boy to be upright on the earth. His rock window reveals only one pillar, meaning only one prior life. This child can be identified as the one that the Kabbala calls Adam Kadmon.[106] When the Fall of Mankind happened, the archetype, the Godly intention for Mankind was held back in the heavens. Adam Kadmon represents what humanity was before the Fall in a sinless state. He had one life – in Eden. As such, he would be the Platonic Idea of the Human Being, the Cosmic Man. An example of this can be found in the Samothracian Mysteries where Adam was seen as the Archetype of Man.[107] Being from before the Fall and without sin, he would be karmically pure. He is the progenitor of the lineage that begins as the First Adam and continues to the Jesus described in Luke's Gospel. He represents the priestly within the human.

Obviously, reincarnation was not part of fifteenth century orthodox Christianity; but it was present as a heretical concept. It was certainly a part of the concepts the members of the Platonic Academy discussed when they studied Plato's Phaedrus and metempsychosis.

These two infants represent two "lineages" of mankind; one from Abraham[108] and one from Adam.[109] Both flowed together through David but diverge into a kingly line from David to Solomon (Matthew's gospel) and to a priestly line from David to Nathan (Luke's gospel).

---

[106] https://en.wikipedia.org/wiki/Adam_Kadmon
[107] Hippolytus, *The Refutation of All Heresies*, Book 5, chapter 3.
[108] Matthew 1:2-17 traces the lineage of the fathers starting with Abraham who "begat" continuing to Joseph who begat Jesus
[109] Luke 3:23-38 traces the lineage of the "Son of" from Jesus back to Adam who was the son of God.

Matthew traces the fatherly descent starting from Abraham down to Jesus while Luke ascends through the sons starting with Jesus and tracing back to Adam who was "the son of God." But the genealogies of Matthew and Luke are different! This contradiction did not seem to be an issue for Early Christianity, but it certainly had become so by Augustine's time (354 – 430 CE). Augustine offered this solution: "Joseph had a biological father who died allowing Eli [or Heli as stated in Luke] to become his adoptive father." John of Damascus (676 – 749 CE) argues this further claiming Joseph is *by nature* the son of Jacob [in the line of Solomon] but *by law* he is the son of Eli [or Heli who, in Luke was of the lineage of Nathan].[110] Unfortunately, no records exist to substantiate such claims. Such concern shows that the mystery of two messiahs was lost by the fourth century. The effort was underway to place the birth of Christ with the birth of Jesus. Note that Matthew 1:16 claims "Mary was the mother of Jesus who is called the Messiah." Christ was not called "the Messiah" by Early Christians. They would have applied the term "messiah" to both boys from Luke and Matthew.

Luke's words offer further clues, "And himself was Jesus beginning at about thirty years of age, being *as was supposed* the son of Joseph, the son of Eli, …" Was Luke saying "as was supposed" to indicate that Joseph was merely the foster father for Jesus and that Mary conceived Jesus without sexual procreation? In the other gospel with a birth story, namely Matthew, the virgin birth is not mentioned and Jesus has multiple siblings, including James who is mentioned in the biblical book Acts. This leads to the question, could there have been two different families each with the parents called Joseph and Mary and each family had a special child born

---

[110] John of Damascus, *An Exact Exposition of the Orthodox Faith*, Book 4, Chapter 14, reprint CreateSpace, 2012

with the name Jesus? Although it may sound far-fetched, hold your judgment until this can be explored in chapter 5.

It must be recalled that the ancient mysteries with their initiations[111] into super-sensible sight were fading away in Alexander's time and were essentially non-existent as a training for intercourse with spiritual beings by the start of the fourth Century. Gnosticism maintained a path of knowledge, some Greek mystery centers still offered initiations, and a form of Mithraism with its seven levels of initiation still existed throughout the Roman empire. No longer could any of these practices lead one to experience and to converse with beings of the heavenly host. With this door closed, knowledge of the hierarchies was left to books.

The Baptism of Jesus
This heresy concluded that neither child, that is neither the Matthew-Jesus nor the Luke-Jesus, was Christ from birth. Many Early Christians believed Christ's "birth" happened at the baptism in the Jordan River. Both the gospels of John and Mark begin with the baptism thereby proclaiming it as the moment when Christ descends and remains with the body of Jesus, as the birth of Christ into the body of Jesus of Nazareth. John's gospel begins with a being called the Logos. It tells the story of this Logos whose birth into a body happened at the baptism. Logos philosophy was basic to John's contemporary, the Jewish philosopher Philo of Alexandria. It was important in the works of many Greek philosophers such as Plato, Zeno of Citium, and Heraclitus, as well as to Christian Gnosticism.

Luke gives his genealogy immediately after describing the baptism thereby linking birth with baptism. The significance of this baptism, however, was lost during the early centuries of Christianity when it

---

[111] https://en.wikipedia.org/wiki/Greco-Roman_mysteries

was Romanized. The baptism became so watered down that to later theologians it represented merely a symbolic act of soul purification from original sin. Lost was the meaning from the three synoptic gospel passages that each say "As soon as Jesus was baptized, he went up out of the water. At that moment heaven was opened, and he [John the Baptist] saw the Spirit of God descending like a dove and alighting on him. And a voice from heaven said, 'This is my Son, whom I love; *today* [my italics] I have begotten thee'."[112] [113] [114]Almost identically, in John's gospel, the Baptist's own report says, "I saw the Spirit come down from heaven as a dove and remain on him. And I myself did not know him, but the one who sent me to baptize with water told me, 'The man on whom you see the Spirit come down and remain is the one who will baptize with the Holy Spirit'."[115] This Spirit that came down like a dove to the body of Jesus was the Spirit of Christ. Thus, although John knew well his cousin Jesus, he could correctly say, "I myself did not know him" for he spoke about the Spirit of Christ. It

---

[112] Matthew 3:16 NIV uses the words, "with you I am well pleased" but it is likely these are not the original words.

[113] From Luke, "the Holy Spirit descended on him in bodily form like a dove. And a voice came from heaven: "You are my Son, whom I love; with you I am well pleased." Luke 3:22, NIV, again changed words likely done in the 6th C.

[114] Bart Ehrman, in his book *The Orthodox Corruption of Scripture: The Effect of Early Christological Controversies on the Text of the New Testament*, offers multiple arguments that in Luke 3:22 the words originally were "today I have begotten you." On page 63 he states, "witnesses as far-flung as Asia Minor, Palestine, Alexandria, North Africa, Rome, Gaul, and Spain" where the texts of Luke 3:22 had these words. The Church Fathers such as Clement of Alexandria, Origen, and others, used "today I have begotten you." Justin Martyr in *Dialogue with Trypho* 88, "but then the Holy Ghost, and for man's sake, as I formerly stated, lighted on Him in the form of a dove, and there came at the same instant from the heavens a voice, which was uttered also by David when he spoke [Psalm 2:7], personating Christ, what the Father would say to Him: 'You are My Son: this day have I begotten You;' [the Father] saying that His generation would take place for men, at the time when they would become acquainted with Him: 'You are My Son; this day have I begotten you.'"

[115] John 1:32-33

appears clearly that the body of Jesus becomes, at the baptism, the earthly vehicle for Christ.

Although *Virgin of the Rocks* is not about this baptism, the heresy the painting depicts is fleshed out with an understanding of the change that took place when the Holy Spirit descended and remained upon Jesus of Nazareth. Materialistic concepts of the human being made it very difficult by the fourth century to grasp what happened at the baptism, and this problem of understanding this baptism is only worse today. Yet what happened at the baptism was fathomed by those Early Christians who still carried the Hellenistic concept of the human being, as evident in St. Paul's writings, as comprised of body (soma), soul (psyche), and spirit (pneuma). While what happened at the baptism was still comprehensible for some Early Christians, what happened on Golgotha and at Whitsun was, for them, even more difficult to grasp.

By the third Century, materialism had come to obscure such concepts that only initiates could still grasp what had happened to Jesus at baptism. Even in the time of Christ, materialism was usurping the throne upon which Greek concepts had ruled. The result was that the words "today I have begotten thee" were changed to "in whom I am well pleased."[116]

John the Baptist had a role to prepare people to grasp the coming of Christ. He would dunk the one being baptized into the river and hold them there long enough for a loosening of the individual's body-soul-spirit composition – essentially what would be called a near-death experience today. In this loosened state, experiences

---

[116] Bart Ehrman, *The Orthodox Corruption of Scripture: The Effect of Early Christological Controversies on the Text of the New Testament*, Oxford University Press, 2011

beyond the physical senses became possible. This was also similar to the initiation process conducted hundreds of years earlier by a hierophant within the Holy of the Holies, inside the Temple of an ancient mystery center. The neophyte was put into a death-like state for three and a half days during which they experienced some of the spiritual world before being called back by the hierophant to a new life. Similar spiritual experiences are reported today by people who undergo near-death experiences. Today's embedded materialistic concepts limit the experiences of those near-death occurrences. In the loosened state of Jesus of Nazareth when he was baptized, the Spirit of Christ was able to descend and take on the body of Jesus as his earthly vehicle.

Right after the baptism, Luke adds, "And himself was Jesus beginning at about thirty years of age." The words equally could be "And his self was in Jesus beginning at about thirty years of age." This translation has ties to the burning bush when Christ said who he was to Moses on Mount Sanai, "I am *the* I am."[117] Here, Luke was saying Christ was now the self, that is, the I-AM of Jesus when Jesus was at about thirty years of age. Christ had entered his earthly vehicle, Jesus of Nazareth. The spirit of Jesus had willingly allowed this by sacrificing his body to the Spirit of the Son, the Logos, the meaning of Mankind.

The Missing Twelve-Year Old Jesus
The middle event of importance, the disappearance of the boy Jesus, was reported only in Luke's gospel. Each year, Jesus' family took a pilgrimage to Jerusalem for Passover. While they were returning to Nazareth, they realized, after traveling much of a day, that they had left their twelve-year old son, Jesus, back in the city. They hurried back to the city to look for him. After being missing

---

[117] Exodus 3:14

for three days, they found him conversing with an astonished audience consisting of the doctors of the temple. The surprised parents questioned Jesus why he had remained behind. His answer, in addition to his surprising new-found wisdom caused his mother, Mary, to ponder over this event in her heart. Thus, the website BibleGateway wisely states, "Mary pondered all these things in her heart," an appropriate response to Jesus' somewhat enigmatic reply "did you not know that I needed to be in my Father's house?"[118] An esoteric interpretation explains that "Father's house" means the physical body as initially created by the Father. This could be a statement that the Matthew-Jesus knew that he had to now be in this prepared body that Luke traces back to Adam before the Fall. The mother of the Luke-Jesus, Mary, does what Luke suggests to his readers to do as well, namely, to pause and contemplate who this Jesus now is."[119]

By accepting that "my Father's house" means the physical body that is given by the Father, then one can grasp what was expressed in the Rosicrucian words "Ex Deo Nascimur."[120] When this gospel was written, not the slightest inkling of Darwinian evolution was present. The physical body was just a vehicle, just a sheath for the soul which, in turn, housed the individual's spirit. The soul until the time of Christ, had been the battleground. The body was a "throw away" until the Resurrection. Christian Gnostics saw the body as the creation of an evil God. Christianity had brought a new mystery. Christ had opened a new way in which the body played an important role.

---

[118] Luke 2:49
[119] https://www.biblegateway.com/resources/commentaries/IVP-NT/Luke/Twelve-Year-Old-Jesus-Goes
[120] Ex Deo Nascimur means Out of God [the Father] we are born and is attributed to Christian Rosenkreuz (b. 1378)

Merging of the Two Jesus Children

By now, this question has likely arisen, "if there were two children named Jesus, not one, then which one went on through the baptism?' The answer is, "it's complicated."

Only one Jesus would be baptized. Earlier in life, the Jesus described in Matthew and the Jesus discussed in Luke met and, essentially, merged. The secret of what happened requires us to look a bit deeper into chapter 2 of Luke's gospel. Again, this passage says, "Every year Jesus' parents went to Jerusalem for the Festival of the Passover. When he was twelve years old, they went up to the festival, according to the custom. After the festival was over, while his parents were returning home, the boy Jesus stayed behind in Jerusalem, but they were unaware of it. Thinking he was in their company, they traveled on for a day. Then they began looking for him among their relatives and friends. When they did not find him, they went back to Jerusalem to look for him. *After three days* they found him in the temple, sitting among the teachers, listening to them and asking them questions. Everyone who heard him was amazed at his understanding and his answers. When his parents saw him, *they were astonished*. His mother said to him, 'Son, why have you treated us like this? Your father and I have been anxiously searching for you.' 'Why were you searching for me?' he asked. 'Didn't you know I had to be in my Father's house?' But they did not understand what he was saying to them. Then he went down to Nazareth with them and *was obedient to them*. But his mother pondered all these things in her heart. And Jesus *grew in wisdom* and stature [maturity], and in favor with God and man"[121] [italics mine for emphasis].

---

[121] Luke 2:41-52, NIV

Note the duration that Jesus was missing, i.e., a little over three days. This compares to the length of time for a compositional change to manifest as the result of the hierophant-led ceremony of the mystery centers. Not only did the Luke family travel to Jerusalem for Passover, but the Matthew family also did. Here, somewhere in the city, perhaps in the Holy of the Holies, the boys exchanged "members" [soma, psyche, pneuma] of their composition. It was Rudolf Steiner who first grasped what happened at this Passover.[122] The Matthew Jesus brought to the Luke Jesus his kingly wisdom of many lifetimes. The two boys were preparing an appropriate vehicle for the Christ who would come at the baptism. It was a supreme act of sacrifice by each to allow for this exchange. Now the body of the original Matthew-Jesus, without its spiritual components, would not live for more than a few months afterward. [This merging is explained more deeply in Chapter 5].

Theological Basis for the Painting's Mystery

By the time Leonardo first settled into Milan in 1483, he was already known as a "maestro" or Master in painting. In addition, his genius in multiple fields was already legendary. Leonardo was beloved as a musician, an entertainer, a civil engineer, an inventor of war machines, and on and on went his immense capabilities. He had assimilated the wisdom that had been shared within walls of Florence's Platonic Academy and its Gardens of San Marcos. Leonardo describes his thirst for knowledge as being quenched by drinking from the fountain of wisdom itself. He wrote in his notebook, "the ['Adversary's' artistic and scientific] method will be good, if it is based on works of good composition and by skilled masters. But since such masters are so rare that there are but few

---

[122] Rudolf Steiner, *From Jesus to Christ*, Lecture 8: The Two Jesus Children, 12Oct1911, Karlsruhe, GA 131

of them to be found, it is a surer way to go to natural objects, than to those which are imitated from nature with great deterioration, and so form bad methods; for he who can go to the fountain does not go to the water-jar."[123]

A self-driven, self-taught genius, Leonardo's impressive inventory of inventions and ideas demonstrate his far-reaching creativity based on direct knowledge. Leonardo, in this sense, was a forerunner to the Goethean scientific method.[124]

In the age prior to the Renaissance, Faith in the Spirit had come to rule over Knowledge of the Spirit especially within Europe. While the Renaissance would eventually usurp Faith's throne and restore Knowledge, the emerging knowledge would be one wherein materialism ruled. During Leonardo's era, knowledge was still acceptable only so long as it supported The Faith. Leonardo knew well that the persistent Inquisition meant danger to one who wrote or spoke in a way that could be deemed heretical. Art provided the safe medium for this genius to express his garnered knowledge in art, science, and religion.

It appears that during Leonardo's last year or two before moving to Milan, something transpired within his inner life to awaken him to Christian mysteries once known during the first century of Christianity. He ceases work on his *Adoration of the Magi* and begins work on the *Virgin of the Rocks*. Likely Leonardo was exposed to or initiated into some of mysteries of Early Christianity.

---

[123] Emma Dickens, *The da Vinci Notebooks*, Arcade, 2006, pg. 63
[124] For more, see (1) David Seamon and Arthur Zajonc, *Goethe's Way of Science*, SUNY Press, 1998, (2) Rudolf Steiner, *Nature's Open Secret: Introduction to Goethe's Scientific Writings*, Rudolf Steiner Press, 2000, and (3) Henri Bartoft, *The Wholeness of Nature: Goethe's Way Toward a Science of Conscious Participation in Nature*, Lindisfarne Press, 1996

Once recognizing a truth, Leonardo could no longer add support to an untruth.

The Heretics

History is written by the victors. In the Christian theological battles up to the Renaissance, simple majority vote at an ecumenical council could cause anyone, despite the size of their following, to be labelled a heretic. Such a result led to the individual's excommunication plus exile or death. The theological battles of Early Christianity were intense, sometimes manipulative, possibly disrespectful to the truth, and often were settled by the intervention of the state (often the Roman emperor himself).

We've seen that the *Virgin of the Rocks* was begun in Florence, likely without a commission but as a work inspired by something Leonardo had learned. It revealed depths of Christianity that had been, since the third century, vile to the Roman Church. To understand what Leonardo portrayed that was heretical to his age, one needs to review theological history and its evolution from the fading of the ancient mysteries to start of the Renaissance, i.e. from about 800 BCE to about 1400 CE. This has been done in the companion text, *The Uncomfortable History of Christianity*.

From Multiple Mystery Centers to Multiple Christianities

Human culture began to change dramatically after the seventh century BCE. Arriving in the coming century would be waves of religious leaders including Moses, Gautama Buddha, Confucius, and Zoroaster. Leavening came from a steady stream of Greek philosophers that continued down to Plato and Aristotle. Deeply engrained into Greek as well as other cultures were their respective ancient mysteries with their gods, their temples, and their associated mystery centers.

Archeology suggests that all cultures, worldwide, had, during a period in their history, built temples that housed the local mystery center where in selected individuals received training that led to initiation into their mysteries.

Figure 33 Greek Mystery Centers by Marsyas

During these centuries the impressive temples of Isthmia (Corinth), Artemis (Corfu), Hera (Corinth), Apollo (Delphi), Aphaia (Aegina), Zeus (Olympia), and many more were built. History has recorded numerous Greek Mystery Centers such as at Eleusis,[125] Delphi,[126] and Samothrace.[127] (See map[128] above for locations). During this age, religion, science, and art were one. One of the Church Fathers, Hippolytus of Rome, wrote in the early third century, "the Athenians, while initiating people into the Eleusinian rites, likewise

---

[125] https://en.m.wikipedia.org/wiki/Eleusinian_Mysteries
[126] https://en.m.wikipedia.org/wiki/Delphi
[127] https://en.m.wikipedia.org/wiki/Samothrace_temple_complex
[128] https://www.ancient.eu/image/325/map-of-classical-greek-sanctuaries/

display to those who are being admitted to the highest grade at these mysteries, the mighty, and marvelous, and most perfect secret suitable for one initiated into the highest mystic truths: an ear of grain in silence reaped."[129]

Augustine

One Church father, Augustine, said of the leaders of these temples, "that which is called the Christian religion existed among the ancients, and never did not exist from the beginning of the human race until Christ came in the flesh, at which time the true religion, which already existed, began to be called Christianity."[130]

Augustine, in his book *Confessions* describes his own Manichaean [so-called heretical] initiation as a young man "Thus, step by step, was I led upwards from *bodies* to the *soul* which perceives by means of bodily senses, and thence to the soul's inward faculty, to which bodily sense reports external facts ... And when this power also within me found itself also changeable, it lifted itself up to its own intelligence, and withdrew its thoughts from experience, abstracting itself form the contradictory throng of sensuous images, that it might find out what that light was wherein it was bathed, ..."[131]

Augustine's initiation was, like those of the Gnostics, intended to awaken true knowledge. But by Augustine's time (354 - 430 CE), this could no longer reach the depths it once had. As was the case for nearly all by the fourth century, the initiation had failed to fully open Augustine's organs of spiritual perception. Thus, later in life, coincidentally in Milan, he is awakened by St. Ambrose to see the

---

[129] Hippolytus, *Refutation of all Heresies*, in ANF, vol. 5; 5, 3
[130] Augustine, *Retractions* Book I, chapter 12, section 3, from *The Fathers of the Church* trans. Mary Inez Bogan, Catholic University of America Press, 1968.
[131] Augustine, *Confessions*, Book IX, Chapter 8

need for Faith during the darkening age in which he lived. Only through Faith could Christianity survive through the Dark Ages. Christian leaders of the fourth century could foresee this direction.

Aristotle and Alexander

In the fourth century before Christ, Aristotle had commissioned Alexander to establish Hellenism in the known world as a healthy transition to a future consciousness. The ancient mysteries were everywhere failing and fading. Rising along with intellectual capabilities of the individual was human egoism. Prior to Aristotle, one had more of a group identity than an awareness of oneself as an individual. One was foremost an Athenian (or one of the other city-states). With this change came the inability to find and train those who would constitute the next generation of teachers and hierophants for the various mystery centers.

Consistent with the rise of individual intellectual capacity was the fall of memory capacity. Aristotle knew that the oral traditions were in danger of being corrupted by the loss of memory and the rise of egoism coming through the new intellectual capacities. Alexander was tasked by his teacher, Aristotle, to set up libraries, i.e., Alexandrias, across the cultured world. This goal was superbly accomplished. Many libraries are known to have been established within the conquered lands[132] and many more may have been hoped for but never were developed. Here, some of the content of the ancient mysteries would become recorded into texts before its oral tradition was lost or corrupted. This is similar to the role the Grimm brothers do centuries later to collect and record the so-called Fairy Tales. Much would have been lost had Alexander not succeeded.

---

[132] Plutarch, *Greek Lives*, Robin Waterfield (Translator), Oxford University Press, 2009

According to Greek historian Plutarch, Alexander's mother, Olympias, had told him that his father was Zeus himself. "When Alexander was setting out on his eastern campaign, she [Olympias] accompanied him during the procession, and told him in private the secret of his conception, that a lightning bolt had shot into her room and touched her womb, [note the similarity to the Holy Spirit overshadowing Mary for her conception of Jesus] and urged him to entertain ambitions worthy of his parentage."[133]

The connection of Alexander's birth with the demise of the ancient mysteries is told in the legend of the Greek goddess Artemis. She had come to attend Alexander's birth in 356 BCE. While she was distracted and away from her temple at Ephesus, Herastratus, egotistically seeking fame, was able to set it aflame so that, unprotected by Artemis, the temple burned to the ground thereby destroying one of the seven wonders of the ancient world.

Constantine and Helena
Jumping ahead in time, there is an historical reflection of Alexander in Constantine. In October of 312 CE, Constantine became the undisputed Augustus of the Western Roman Empire and later, from September 324 to May 337 CE, he was the Emperor of the entire Roman Empire. In 330 CE, he established his New Rome, naming it after himself Constantinople. It was from his mother, Helena, who, as a Christian, he had learned as a boy much of what he knew about the religion. Caught between his father's pagan religion and his mother's Christianity, he declared religious tolerance throughout the Roman empire. Constantine appointed his mother to the fully funded position of Augusta Imperatrix.

---

[133] Plutarch, *Greek Lives*, Robin Waterfield (Translator), Oxford University Press, 2009

With this office, she then took a delegation to Jerusalem to seek for the burial place of Jesus. She claims to have found it. Thus, Constantine funded in 326 CE the building of the first Church of the Holy Sepulcher on the site. (Other historical accounts claim Constantine had already ordered the church to replace the temple that emperor Hadrian had once built to cover the burial site). Helena discovered the actual grave while this new church was under construction. The church was completed after ten years of construction in 335.

Figure 34 Constantine and his mother Helena, Mosaic in Hosios Loukas, 11th C

Feeling divine intervention into his rise to emperor, Constantine wanted the capital of his empire to be closer to the Holy Lands. It remained the capital for over a thousand years. Legend has it that the Palladium that once protected Troy and later Rome, was moved to Constantinople. In each of these cases, the protection was said to be able to last for 1000 years.[134]

Halfway between Alexander and Constantine and their immense empires comes, in stark contrast, the Christ who said, "My Kingdom is not of this world."[135]

By accepting Christianity as one of the empire's accepted religions, Constantine inherited its century-old internal bickering. Because he was troubled by all of the different Christianities and their bitter rivalries, he used his authority as emperor to request that the leading theologians meet to resolve their differences. As new emperor of the reunited lands around the Mediterranean that had been divided by Diocletian in 293 CE, seeking peace was politically astute for him. He sought for all parties to peacefully agree to one doctrine. Thus, he called for the First Council of Nicaea to be convened in 325 CE. How would decisions be made? Being part of the Roman empire, the Council used Roman law and majority vote to determine what was truly Christian and what was heresy.

A majority of those present agreed to what is known as the Nicene Creed. Those in the minority did not expect what came next: strong state pressure to conform to and confess the new creed. Henceforth, the Western Christian church used the Roman style of governance. Future ecumenical councils would sometimes be called by the sitting emperor or be mediated by his representative.

---

[134] Some legends claim that the Palladium was found well after Constantinople fell and now resides in Moscow
[135] John 18:36-40, KJV

Simple majority vote by those present would determine truth and accepted belief.

Arius

At the time of the Council of Nicaea, the most important theological battle was between the proto-orthodox and the followers of Arius. The Nicene Creed was expressly anti-Arian. Arians were one of multiple branches of Christianity that had existed since the second century.[136] Each Christianity pointed back to one of the apostles or to one of the great converts to Christianity, such as St. Paul or Mani, as its divine source.

Of the written sources for Christian faith, Mark seems to have been the first Gospel to be written, appearing sometime around the year 70. This was followed by the Gospels of Matthew and of Luke, independent of one another, in the 80s and in the 90s respectively. Likely these gospels had been delivered orally to followers and then at the above dates, were finally recorded by a scribe. John wrote his gospel when he was in his 90s, just before the close of the first century. Then, in the second century, many new texts appear of questionable origin. Bart Erhman points out that this second wave of texts were largely meant affirm a particular perspective to the nascent Christian theology and were not spiritually inspired.[137] This second century and its sacred-sounding texts used to bolster non-Christian traditions within Christianity demonstrated how egoism and materialism continued to creep into human souls and theology.

As examples of the various Christianities, we will look at two more of its many leaders in addition to Arius. These revered three would

---

[136] Bart Ehrman, *Lost Christianities: The Battles for Scripture and the Faiths We Never Knew*, Oxford Univ. Press, 2005
[137] Bart Ehrman, Forged: Writing in the Name of God, Harper One, 2012

all become labeled as heretics. Their theologies illustrate the philosophical issues Christianity had to deal with as it emerged from paganism and the preeminent role that had previously been held by the oracles and its ancient mysteries.

As mentioned, the Council of Nicaea dealt with the theology of Arius (256 – 336 CE) who, in wrestling with the concepts of a one God or of a Trinity, opposed the new philosophy that would be accepted in the fourth century by Athanasius of Alexandria who proclaimed that the Son is of one nature, of the same substance (homoousios) as the Father God. In this debate over the *substance* of spiritual beings, we see the penetration of materialism into theology.

Figure 35 *Baptism, mosaic, Arian Hagia Anastasis, Ravenna*

Arians felt the Son was indeed from the Father but not the same as the Father and especially not of the same substance as that of the Father. They cite Christ's prayers to the Father and to the Gospel's implication that it was the Father who raised the Christ on Easter morning as proof that the Son God was subordinate to the Father God. Arians, in their theology, allowed for multiple gods in a hierarchy whose members were subordinate to the one God, the Father. Depicted was a lesser god in their fifth century baptistry in Ravenna. At the baptism of Jesus, the god of the River Jordan is portrayed in the mosaic of figure 35. Such iconography never existed in the sanctioned art of the Roman Church. But these mosaics in Ravenna, Italy were likely experienced by Leonardo. With his inquisitive mind, he would have become aware of the theological differences held by the Arians.

Where Arius questioned the *substance* of each member of the Trinity, a century later Nestorius (386–450 CE) questioned the *composition* of Christianity's most important individual, Christ-Jesus. Nestorians felt that Mary gave birth to a *human* Jesus naturally, even if as a virgin. As such, he opposed the fifth century concept of *Theotokos*, the Bearer or the Mother of God. There is no evidence that Nestorius opposed the Theotokos because he was aware of the two Messiahs, but his steadfast opposition to Jesus being God at birth remains notable in this context.

Nestorius
Nestorians would elaborate by saying that Jesus grew up as a man, not as a divine being; that is until his baptism when, at age 30, he united with the divine spirit of the Christ. After the baptism, the composition of this individual then became body (*soma*) from Jesus and spirit (*pneuma*) from Christ who replaced the spirit of the man Jesus. The middle entity, the soul (*psyche*), would have needed to be highly developed and purified prior to the baptism so that the

Christ spirit could inhabit this composition. During the coming three years, Christ would quickly penetrate and transform this soul and body. This is represented by the Temptation in the Desert that is described in both Luke and Matthew.[138]

Figure 36 Transfiguration, Raphael, Vatican, 1520

---

[138] Luke 4:1-13 and Matthew 4:1-11

Thus, what prepared the soul for the Christ, was the kingly Jesus of Matthew's gospel for its knowledge of the earth and its history while the priestly Jesus of Luke's gospel was needed for a karma-free and pure body. The Christ-transformed soul was revealed at the Transfiguration (see figure 36).[139] Later, the transformed body was ready just before the crucifixion when Christ-Jesus proclaims, "The hour has come that Son of Man should be glorified."[140] The transformed body was revealed at Easter to those who could behold it.

For Nestorians, Christ was a divine and cosmic being, i.e., the Son, the Logos. His home was the sun from where he descended in order to alter the course of earthly evolution, to become the Savior of the World.

By the end of the fourth century when Nestorius became active, the ways of the mysteries and their concepts were mere shadows among their ruins. Nestorianism could receive no support from the dead mysteries. Opponents to Nestorius felt that Jesus was Christ from birth, that there was only one entity and this entity remained himself from before and after the baptism.

Orthodox Christianity could not answer the theological question about what happened at the baptism when John experienced the spirit descending and remaining upon Jesus.[141] Did the composition of Jesus change when he emerged from the Jordan, or did he merely come to realize his divine commission through baptism?

The Nestorian opponents, led by Cyril of Alexandria, organized an ecumenical council in Ephesus in 431 CE and arrived early. Finding

---

[139] Luke 9:28-36 and Matthew 17:1-8
[140] John 12:23
[141] John 1:32-34

that John I of Antioch had not yet arrived with the eastern bishops who supported Nestorius, they quickly convened the council. They knew they had the votes to declare Nestorius a heretic. A few days later John and his bishops arrived. Naturally, they were furious to hear that Nestorius had already been condemned. Thus, they convened their own council, at which Cyril was deposed for acting against fairness and Christian principles.

Both sides then appealed to the emperor Theodosius II (remember, at this time the throne was in nearby Constantinople). To not appear to be taking sides, he ordered both Nestorius and Cyril to be deposed of their positions and exiled. But after bribing officials, Cyril was allowed to return to a position of church power while Nestorius abided by the terms. Then, with Cyril restored, emperor Theodosius II chose in 435 CE a politically expedient path. He decreed to have Nestorius exiled to an Egyptian desert oasis that was within Cyril's diocese surrounding Alexandria.

Figure 37 Wall painting of Palm Sunday from a Nestorian church in Qocho, China, Ethnological Museum, Berlin, 7th Century

The intolerance of Cyril caused the devoted followers of Nestorius to split off and associate with the Christian Church of the Orient. In the subsequent decades, Nestorianism permeated much of the Church of the East. Many relocated to live in the Sasanian Empire of Iran, home to a vibrant but persecuted Christian minority. In 489, the Nestorian School of Edessa moved to the Persian city of Nisibis (modern-day Nusaybin in Turkey). Here it became known as the School of Nisibis.

By the end of the first Millennium, the Church of the East with Nestorian zeal had become the largest Christian church in the world. With Nestorianism, it had spread rapidly through Persia, India, Kazakhstan, China, and had outposts as far away as Japan.

After Nestorius was defeated at the Council of Ephesus in 431 CE, the concept of Christ-Jesus as one entity from birth becomes cemented, lasting into modern times. Even the words of Luke and Matthew's account of the baptism were then altered to better fit the new theology as discussed earlier (see footnote 141).

Prester John

In Leonardo's time, this history was still known. The theology of the Eastern Christian Church, although it was fading, was still known. Among the texts brought to Italy, some must have described this heretical theology. Interestingly, in twelfth century a popular legend of a Prester John[142] arose. The legend drew from accounts of travelers to the East where they encountered Nestorian Christian communities. A letter in 1165 to the Byzantine Emperor Manuel I Comnenus claimed Prester John was a descendent from a recent King of India who was from one of the Three Magi.[143] The tie to India is not surprising because Christian legends also had the Apostle Thomas traveling to India to found one of the Christianities there. This branch later merged with Nestorian Christianity. However, the Prester John legend most likely was drawn from the life of Genghis Khan.

---

[142] Prester John (Latin: Presbyter Johannes) was a legendary Christian patriarch, presbyter (elder), and king. He was popular in European chronicles and tradition from the 12th through the 17th centuries. He was said to rule over a Nestorian (Church of the East) Christians amid the Islamic caliphates and pagan lands of the Orient.

[143] https://en.wikipedia.org/wiki/Prester_John

Hulagu Khan and Doquz Khatun

Figure 38 Hulagu Khan and his Christian wife Doquz Khatun depicted as the new "Constantine and Helen" in a Syrian Bible.

Genghis Khan, a pagan, was tolerant of other religious faiths so long as those subjects did not resist the expansion of his empire. He was the first East Asian ruler to invite clerics from the three major religions (Christianity, Islam, and Buddhism) to a symposium so that he might learn about their beliefs. Genghis Khan's grandson of was Hulagu Khan. His army greatly expanded the southwestern portion of the Mongol Empire, founding the Ilkhanate of Persia, a precursor to the modern state of Iran.

Both Hulagu's mother, Sorghaghtani Beki, and his wife, Doquz Khatun, were Nestorian Christians. Compare figure 38 to figure 34. His army was seen as Mongol Christian crusaders. They were known to royalty and state in Europe. Letters spanning a hundred years between these Mongols and various kings of Europe including French King Philip IV are extant. Under Hulagu's leadership, the siege of Baghdad (1258) destroyed Baghdad's standing in the Islamic world and weakened Damascus, causing a shift of Islamic influence to the Mamluk Sultanate in Cairo and ended the Abbasid Dynasty.

When Islam first spread to the same territories where Nestorian Christianity was established, the two co-existed. But following the Crusades and the Mongol invasion by Hulagu Khan, this peaceful co-existence was ruined. Hulagu's mother was a very influential Nestorian Christian who favored Nestorians over all others. Hulagu's brutal conquest of Islamic caliphates brought extreme enmity upon the Nestorians. Once tolerated within Islamic lands, after the fall of Baghdad, Nestorian Christians became enemies of the state. Little remains of the Eastern Christian Church today. Remnants became the Assyrian Church of the East whose center is in Erbil in northern Iraq.[144]

It is not that Arius or Nestorius came up with the theology that is attributed to them. Rather, it is that they became the one to champion a particular theological perspective that had already existed. In the theological battles that followed, the winner sought to not only ban those who became labelled as heretics but also to prevent any retention or return of the so-called heresy. Thus, all of

---

[144] Erbil is the capital of Iraqi Kurdistan and the most populous city in northern Iraq. The remnants of Nestorian Christianity, some 100,000, fled when Mosul fell to ISIS in June, 2014. Some 40,000 Nestorians live there now.

their texts were confiscated and destroyed. All the followers were required to convert or seek exile.

Often today, and certainly in Leonardo's time, almost all that was known of these heretics was what was written one-sidedly by the victors. Honest descriptions of the so-called heretics did not get recorded for history as the victors sought to justify their cause, their verdict, and their often-cruel actions. Truth fell to expediency. Tribunals caused the heretical faithful to convert just to save their lives.

Origen
The last significant early heretic that will be examined was Origen (184 – 253 CE). Destroying his works was far more difficult because he was one of the Church Fathers and a prolific writer. From Origen came the concepts for the Trinity that eventually were accepted. Analogously, Origen explained that there are three possible interpretations for sacred writings, (1) spiritual, (2) soul-wise, and (3) flesh-wise or historical. Each inspired passage can be interpreted from one or all of these perspectives. Because Origen was so talented at snuffing out forgeries in the growing collection of texts used by some of the Christian churches, he was thought to be a Christian initiate by his contemporaries. His review of the available literature led to the later selection of the Christian canon.

After being celebrated during his lifetime, nearly two hundred years later Pope Theophilus of Alexandria assembled a council in Alexandria for the expressed purpose of having Origen condemned as a heretic. Christian theology had changed that quickly! Because Origen had agreed with Plato concerning the transmigration of souls (reincarnation), Theophilus called Origen the "hydra of all heresies."[145]

The call for a Holy War on the Mysteries was sounded. By the sixth century, currents of Origen's "heresy" persisted causing, in 543 CE, the Emperor Justinian I to essentially declare a state-sponsored holy war on everything and everyone associated, directly or indirectly, with Origen. Throughout the empire, church leaders, fearing for their lives, sided with the state to condemn Origen and his writings. Justinian sanctioned soldiers and mobs to destroy the temples of the pagans including the schools of the once venerable Mystery Centers. Even the Christian Mystery School of Athens, initiated by St. Paul, was closed by decree from Justinian I. Materialism had ascended to the throne.

Justinian's decrees defamed one of the most important Christian theologians of all time and sealed materialism's victory by sweeping away all proponents of Hellenism along with any who maintained lingering spiritual concepts that had persisted from even earlier ages. These teachers fled eastward, out of the Christian Roman Empire to safety. With them went culture. Without this leavening, Europe would slide backwards for centuries to come. To the recipients of these teachers came the blossoming of new culture. The great school of Gundi-Shapur, for example, received many such emigrating teachers. From its center near Baghdad, world culture advanced and spread throughout the Islamic world and in particular to Cordoba in Spain. When Charlemagne was crowned King of the Franks in 768, he would compare the primitiveness of his own realm to the city wonders and the intellectual marvels of Cordoba.

---

[145] Geddes MacGegor, *Reincarnation as a Christian Hope*, Springer, 1982

This chapter has begun an exploration into the theological views that Leonardo as a young man had pondered. Theological differences at that time were resolved not with the search for truth but with Roman senatorial procedures and majority voting. Yet, Leonardo claimed to have drunk from the Fountain of Wisdom. Chapter 5 will explore whether any heretical views found their way into Leonardo's knowledgebase. Could Leonardo have brought any of this theological drama to expression in his original version of the *Virgin of the Rocks*?

Florence and the Early Renaissance Infusion of Eastern Knowledge

Because of the expected fall of Constantinople to the Ottomans, teachers and texts had come to Italy and in particular to Florence where Leonardo as a member of the Medici household had heard these eastern scholars speak. He listened to stories of the ancient mysteries and the meaning of mythologies that sounded in the Platonic Academy of Florence. These stories were tied in an Augustinian way[146] to Christianity itself. Teachers inspired by George Gemistus Plethon[147] offered insights into the relationship of Christ and Jesus that had been known to Eastern Christianity. Leonardo realized he had drunk from the fountain of wisdom. His

---

[146] Augustine felt that what had been practiced in the mystery centers was a form of Christianity before Christianity. "What is now called the Christian religion already existed among the ancients and was not lacking at the very beginnings of the human race. When Christ appeared in the flesh, the true religion already in existence received the name of Christian." *Retractions* Book I, chapter 12, section 3, from *The Fathers of the Church* trans. Mary Inez Bogan, Catholic University of America Press, 1968.

[147] Encyclopedia Britannica: "George Gemistus Plethon, also spelled Pletho, (1355 - 1450/52), Byzantine philosopher and humanist scholar whose clarification of the distinction between Platonic and Aristotelian thought proved to be a seminal influence in determining the philosophic orientation of the Italian Renaissance. Plethon studied in Constantinople and at the Ottoman Muslim court in nearby Adrianople."

Renaissance spirit forbade him to squash his enthusiasm for this wisdom despite its risks. With the "hounds of God", the Inquisition, still active, public non-adherence to the Church's dogmas typically meant death. Thus, Leonardo expressed his voice in art.[148]

With the supremacy of materialism engrained today in our sciences and religion, it is difficult for the modern mind to grasp the importance of the spiritual debates of the Early Christians. Today, those debates seem to be arguments over mere nuances.

We must keep in mind that the multiple Christianities arose at a time when a transition from tribal identity to self-identity was giving rise to egoism. As scribes copied sacred texts, leaders of the new religion were rightfully wary of possible modifications. Even the great leaders of Christianity were not immune to alterations to the faith as evidenced by the confrontation of Peter by Paul.[149] Paul battled against those who had retreated from the Proclamation of Pentecost to settle upon a Christianity that was merely an extension of Judaism. It was a time when sacred texts were adulterated, and full fake sacred texts were written in order

---

[148] The recent discovery by researcher Roberto Biggi of a dog portrayed but blended into the background could be Leonardo adding commentary on the hounds of God as the Inquisitors were known. Silvano Vinceti, president of an Italian national heritage committee commented on Biggi's find, "That dog is an act of indictment by Leonardo Da Vinci against the corruption of the papacy of the age." See http://www.ansa.it/english/news/2017/03/02/dog-found-behind-leonardos-virgin-of-the-rocks-expert_393a4af5-6950-43cf-a559-1546a1ef8f4b.html

[149] Galatians 2:11-14, "When Cephas [Peter] came to Antioch, I opposed him to his face, because he stood condemned. For before certain men came from James, he used to eat with the Gentiles. But when they arrived, he began to draw back and separate himself from the Gentiles because he was afraid of those who belonged to the circumcision group. The other Jews joined him in his hypocrisy, so that by their hypocrisy even Barnabas was led astray."

to hold onto certain traditions or beliefs that were threatened by Christianity.

Figure 39 Saint Peter and Saint Paul, El Greco, Catalunya National Museum, Barcelona, 1590

The new tenets through Paul were upsetting to many traditionalists. The temptation, therefore, to alter these disruptive tenets was present. By the third century, who knew what Christ had intended? Many fake texts were spreading through the Christian communities. Leaders realized that a canon had to be established. And this then led to the attempt to unify Christianity under Constantine. But later, under Justinian I, it was used to rid the empire of everything that was not Orthodox Christianity.

The spirit of knowledge that arose with the Renaissance rebelled against the control of knowledge that the Church had held for centuries. But by then materialism was well established; the yoke of the Church was unknowingly being exchanged for another.

4. Fusing the Fragments of a Mystery

In her 1967 book (published in English in 1985), author and art historian Angela Ottino della Chiesa cites four paintings that apparently were derived from Leonardo's *The Virgin of the Rocks*.[150] These are:

- The *Thuelin Madonna* by Marco d'Oggiono now part of the Thuelin collection in Paris
- The *Holy Infants Embracing* also by Joos van Cleve in Naples' Capodimonte Museum
- Joos van Cleve's smaller copy of *The Virgin of the Rocks* that resides in a Berlin private collection
- The *Holy Family and St. John* by Bernardino Luini now in the Museo del Prado in Madrid.

Remarkably similar themes run through the paintings by four artists all of whom were associated with Leonardo's Academy in Milan. Chiesa's book implies that the artists participating in Leonardo's Milan Academy had access to the original *Virgin of the Rocks* at the Confraternity or to its copy or to both. The class of artists enrolled at the Milan Academy used, in addition to the *Virgin of the Rocks*, the theme from Leonardo's *Holy Infants* for their training.

Flemish painter Quentin Matsys (1466–1530) may have been the first from Antwerp to study at the Academy followed by Joos van Cleve (1485 – 1541), a fellow Flemish artist. Like Quentin Matsys, "Joos van Cleve appropriated themes and techniques of Leonardo da Vinci. This is apparent in the use of sfumato [a painting style] in the Virgin and Child. Multiple versions of a soft, sentimental

---

[150] Angela Ottino della Chiesa, *The Complete Paintings of Leonardo Da Vinci*, 1986

Madonna and Child and the Holy Family were discovered, produced in his [Joos'] workshop."[151] Joos was nicknamed, the "Leonardo of the North" for his accurate adoption of Leonardo's style. This leads to the conclusion that he studied directly with Leonardo in Milan.

Holy Infants Embracing

Figure 40 Holy Infants Embracing, copy of lost work by LdV

---

[151] Campbell, Lorne (2000). The fifteenth century Netherlandish paintings, National Gallery catalogues (Repr. ed.). New Haven: Yale Univ. Press

Figure 41 Holy Infants Embracing, Luini? private collection, London

Of particular interest to our study are the many paintings done by Leonardo's students that depict two holy infants embracing and kissing. Many of Leonardo's students would copy this *Holy Infants* theme. Why? What was so remarkable about it? Because of Joos, the theme was carried to Antwerp where Flemish artists continued to work with this theme.

None of Leonardo's own kissing babies' paintings are known to still exist but the two above are from his Milan Academy and show his artistic touches. Both paintings are thought to be a student's faithful copy of a Leonardo original on this subject. Both are also a variation on the *Virgin of the Rocks*, having very similar backgrounds of rocks and exquisitely and accurately painted plants suggesting the presence or even the hand of Leonardo.

In all of these *Holy Infants Embracing* paintings, the position of the two boys remains identical. The background, the hair color or length, all may change, but the two boys remain in the same position and embrace. Some have wondered if this was some homosexual statement by Leonardo and all of these students. Such theories detract from the beauty and seriousness of what these paintings depicted.

Figure 42 Thuelin Madonna, Marco d'Oggiono, Paris

The identities of the two infants has typically been assumed as "Christ embracing his cousin John the Baptist" and the subject matter relates to "the two paintings of the *Virgin of the Rocks* by

Leonardo and numerous other Renaissance works by Raphael and others of the meeting of the two children on the road to Egypt while escaping the Massacre of the Innocents."[152]

As we have seen, this explanation does not hold water. By using the word "Christ" rather than "Jesus" here, the theological position that Jesus was also the Christ from birth is assumed although nothing from the gospels states this. But Leonardo's students will give us convincing evidence that they had a different theological understanding, one that has Christ entering the body of Jesus of Nazareth when he was thirty at the baptism.

Remarkably, we now find that some of Leonardo's students merged the *Virgin of the Rocks* and the *Holy Infants Embracing* themes. Two of the students who did this were Maro d'Oggiono and Bernardino Luini.

Compare the two *Holy Infants Embracing* (figures 40 and 41 above) to the *Thuelin Madonna* by Marco d'Oggiono[153] (figure 42) and the *Holy Family* by Bernardo Luini (figure 43). A third painting by Bernardino de Conti that was very similar to d'Oggiono's would be shown here but it was lost during World War II. Bernardino de Conti played an important role in these paintings.

In these paintings by students in Leonardo's Academy, each Madonna appears very much like she does in the *Virgin of the Rocks*. Her position is similar. Her hand gestures are nearly identical although in d'Oggiono's her left hand holds open a book on her knee while her right hand is farther away from the infants. When we look more closely, we see that her hand gestures are reversed from those of *Virgin of the Rocks*! With her left hand she

---

[152] https://en.wikipedia.org/wiki/The_Holy_Infants_Embracing
[153] Marco d'Oggiono painted two similar Madonnas. One was lost.

is drawing wisdom from the book and with her right hand she is bestowing this wisdom upon the child near to her right hand. In the actual Virgin of the Rocks, it is with the right hand of the central figure that wisdom was drawn and with the left bestowed. Thus, we may assume that the infants are also reversed intentionally in this painting.

Figure 43 Comparing the hands of VoR Louvre and Holy Family by B. Luini

Shown here is the Virgin of the Rocks side-by-side with Luini's Holy Family to reveal similar gestures and geometry. As a pupil of Ambrogio Bergognone, Luini was likely present with Leonardo's students when this theological subject of the children was studied. His painting of the *Holy Family* includes the two infants embracing. Here the Madonna's hand gestures are identical to the *Virgin of the Rocks*. Yet, her hands do not pertain to the embracing infants. Her raised left hand has no relationship to the infants. Its position in front of Joseph is artistically awkward and can only be seen as a conspicuous attempt to copy the hand gestures of Leonardo's original. Luini has merged the study of *Holy Infants Embracing* with the *Virgin of the Rocks.* Luini replaced the archangel with Joseph. Why did Marco d'Oggiono and Bernardo Luini merge two of

Leonardo's paintings? Was this just some painting exercise done for some class?

Antwerp's Holy Infants Embracing

Below are some of the thirty known copies of this theme begun by Leonardo. The paintings here are all attributed to Joos van Cleve or his studio in Antwerp, Belgium. Note the inclusion of the descent of the holy spirit in the form of a dove! Why would Joos include this icon? Is Joos saying that coming is an event when the Christ spirit will descend upon the merging of these two?

Figure 44 Joos van Cleve, Private

Figure 45 Joos van Cleve, Art Institute Chicago

Figure 46 Joos van Cleve, Museo di Capodimonte

Figure 47 Joos van Cleve, Minerva Auction

Van Cleve has placed these two kissing boys on a stage with curtains. What is point of the stage? Perhaps, a reenactment of another scene? Van Cleve must have struggled on how to depict the descending white dove in an artistic and meaningful way.

We continue with more *Holy Infants Embracing* now with a landscape replacing the curtains.

Figure 48 Joos van Cleve, Private

Figure 49 Joos van Cleve, Private

Figure 50 Marco d'Oggiono, Royal Collection

Notice that the dove has been replaced by a bird that has hopped to a new perch in the top two van Cleve paintings.

Marco d'Oggiono's landscape is nearly identical to van Cleve's! Obviously, they knew each other and each other's work. Is there more to this?

And lastly, one more of van Cleve's with a different setting.

Figure 51 Joos van Cleve, Museum Catharijneconvent

Were these multiple copies mere student lessons being repeated until perfect? Or is there a Leonardo-inspired theological drama being portrayed in them?

Pistis Sophia

As mentioned, art historians associated with the museums where the two *Virgin of the Rocks* are hung have assumed that there must be an apocryphal text to the Bible that tells this story. Wikiwand explains the accepted explanation for these paintings, "The subject matter relates to the two paintings of the *Virgin of the Rocks* by Leonardo and numerous other Renaissance works by Raphael and others of the meeting of the two children on the road to Egypt while escaping the Massacre of the Innocents."[154] As we've seen, none of the apocryphal books have this story. In the Luke's Gospel, the holy family have no need to flee to Egypt but in Matthew's Gospel they must flee. Since the fourth century, it has been assumed that these two gospels described the same birth of Jesus but with different details.

The Pistis Sophia is a Gnostic text that was discovered in 1773 although copies of it may have existed in the Middle Ages somewhere in Christendom. Of the many Greek and early Christian texts arriving in Florence and Venice and elsewhere in Italy, the Pistis Sophia or other Gnostic texts were likely to have been in one of the caches of sacred books such as the trunk brought by George Gemistus Plethon in 1438 to Florence.

This Gnostic-Christian text describes twin messiahs and their two families. Its chapter 59, states [with my italics], "And Jesus answered and said: 'Thou also, Mary, hast received form which is in Barbēlō, according to matter, and hast received likeness which is in the Virgin of Light, according to light, *thou and the other Mary, the blessed one*; and on thy account the darkness hath arisen, and moreover out of thee did come forth the *material body* in which I

---

[154] Jane Darnell et al, https://www.wikiwand.com/en/The_Holy_Infants_Embracing, accessed 1May2018

am, which I have *purified* and refined, --now, therefore, I bid thee proclaim the solution of the words which Pistis Sophia hath uttered.'"[155] [Pistis means Faith and Sophia means Wisdom]

Later, in chapter 62, a second Mary is mentioned. "The *other Mary* came forward and said: 'My Lord, bear with me and be not wroth with me. Yea, from the moment when thy mother spake with thee concerning the solution of these words, my power disquieted me to come forward and likewise to speak the solution of these words.'" The Pistis Sophia has described two mothers both with the name Mary.

In between these mentions of two women both named Mary is chapter 61 that refers to a second Jesus, "When thou wast small, before the Spirit came upon thee, while thou wast in a vineyard with Joseph, the Spirit [of the other Jesus] came forth from the height, he came to me into my house, *he resembled thee*. And I did not recognize him, and *I thought that he was thou* [she is saying that she had experiences of her Jesus out-of-body and this other spirit was alike to the spirit of her Jesus]. And the Spirit said to me: 'Where is Jesus, my brother, that I meet him?' And when he said these things to me, I was confused, and I thought that he was a phantom to tempt me. But I took him, I bound him to the leg of the bed in my house, until I came out to you in the field, thou and Joseph, and I found you in the vineyard, as Joseph was hedging the vineyard with reeds.

Now it happened, when thou didst hear me speaking the word to Joseph, thou didst understand the word and thou didst rejoice. And thou didst say: 'Where is he that I may see him? Or else I await him in this place'. But it happened when Joseph heard thee saying these words, he was agitated and we came up at the same time,

---

[155] http://gnosis.org/library/pistis-sophia/ps063.htm

we went into the house. We found the Spirit bound to the bed. And we looked at thee with him, *we found thee like him*. And he that was bound to the bed was released, *he embraced thee, he kissed thee*. And thou also, thou didst kiss him and *you became one*."[156] This scene would be taking place in Nazareth when the boys would be about twelve (or more) years old. Was this story related to Luke's story of the missing Jesus after Passover when he was twelve? Does it shed some light on the merging of the two boys?

If the unknown apocryphal book that the museums cite existed and if it applied to background of *Virgin of the Rocks*, it would need to have the Matthew Jesus just days old and John the Baptist at six months when the meeting on the road to Egypt took place. In *Virgin of the Rocks,* neither of the two boys are newborn babies. Rather, they are toddlers, perhaps 18 months old. Not only is there no such apocryphal book, but the depiction by the scientist Leonardo clearly does not fit such a made-up tale of a meeting on the road to Egypt.

While not conclusive, the *Pistis Sophia* is likely an inspirational source for the *Holy Infants Embracing*. Because of Leonardo's arrest when he was seventeen, he knew that a depiction of twelve-year-old boys kissing and embracing would bring up calls of homosexual indecency. His accusers could point to his earlier arrest. By using the innocence of infants to depict the mystery of a spiritual transfer from one child to the other, Leonardo and his students together depicted this scene as part of the sequence leading up to the coming of Christ at the Baptism.

---

[156] http://www.pseudepigrapha.com/PistisSophia/pistisSophia_Book1.html

Haloes

Figure 52 below shows that in the original, Leonardo did not place a halo over either of the two children nor over the figure we are calling, for now, the Madonna.

Figure 52 Detail of both boys, VoR, Louvre

Did his students follow this practice? One of Leonardo's students was Bernardino de' Conti who was also a pupil at Bernardo Zenale's (c. 1460 – 1526) Milanese school. As a friend and associate of Ambrogio di Predis, de' Conti got to know Leonardo and joined his academy.

Figure 53 Thuelin Madonna, Marco d'Oggiono, private, Paris

De Conti's Madonna (figure 54) is remarkably similar to the *Thuelin Madonna* by Marco d'Oggiono (above) that was shown earlier. This is not just another *Holy Infants Embracing* copy!

Here we see haloes but one of these is not a typical halo for the Renaissance period. Look closely at the halo of each child. The one on the left has for his halo three crosses over its head pointing prophetically to the hill of Golgotha where two others would be crucified with Jesus Christ.[157] De' Conti is telling us: this is the one who will die on the cross! Note by using three crosses for the halo, de' Conti is also proclaiming that this child will first receive a three-fold transfer from the child on our right.

Figure 54: Madonna, Bernardino de Conti, private collection

---

[157] See Kabbalistic Roots: Zohar section where the following quote may be found, "he will be killed and will become alive again, when the little hill [the skull] receives life upon the great hill [Golgotha, the place of skulls]." This shows that de Conti, through Leonardo, was aware of this mystery. Some see three nails instead of crosses.

But what does that say about this other child? Is that child John the Baptist? If so, then his position has been switched from the left in the *Virgin of the Rocks* to the right here. One might look for further clues and inquire again about the symbol of the book. It is on the right side suggesting that the child on the right has to do with knowledge. This implies that the child on the left is the "sacrifice", the one whose body will die on the cross but before dying, the wisdom of the book or the child on the right will be bequeathed to the child on the left. Here the Madonna's left hand is drawing out the wisdom on her left and with her right hand she, through grace, transfers it to the other.

Figure 55 Madonna, B. de Conti, private in comparison to the Virgin of the Rocks, Louvre

When compared with the *Virgin of the Rocks*, we notice that the Madonna's hands have been reversed in Conti's painting. The bestowing hand was her left one but now in Conti's work is her right. This confirms that the two children are also reversed. It further implies that in all thirty copies of *Holy Infants Embracing* derived from Leonardo's Milan Academy, the two children are the same two children in *Virgin of the Rocks* but in reverse order. Why the reversal? Was it to disguise and yet to reveal?

Further, note that Conti's work has the same background as *Virgin of the Rocks*! But here both children are under the "window" through which many rock pillars are shown while the other window with one rock pillar has neither boy underneath. What is the meaning of these windows? This will be answered in chapter five.

Figure 56 Three Holy Children, B. de Conti, private collection

From the similarities of backgrounds, foregrounds, and hand gestures, we can conclude that de Conti was fully aware of the original Virgin of the Rocks. It should be obvious that de Conti is explaining the Virgin of the Rock using the disguising language of art. We can further conclude that he is saying that in the Virgin of the Rocks, neither child is John the Baptist.

In case the above painting was not convincing enough, Bernardino de' Conti set out to make certain one can grasp who is who in in his masters *Virgin of the Rocks*. This painting of his, known as the *Three Holy Children,* verifies our conclusion.

Here, in place of the Madonna is John the Baptist! We know this because of his iconic staff. Behind him and between his legs is the River Jordan. To each side of him, on separate sides of the river, are the two boys from *Virgin of the Rocks*. The boys are in exactly the same position as *Virgin of the Rocks*. Thus, de' Conti is not showing these two as twins but as the two who are in Leonardo's *Virgin of the Rocks*. Even the foreground rocks are suggestive of the original.

Although the boys are in the same position as in *Virgin of the Rocks*, only one of the holy children has a "halo" and that is the boy on the right. Again, it is not the circular halo but the three crosses that indicate this is the boy who will hang on the cross. The hand gestures of John the Baptist are very similar to those of the Madonna of *Virgin of the Rocks*. He indicates that something from the boy on the left will be drawn out and granted eventually to the boy on the right. Lastly, the boy on the left has fine, royal cloth draped around his body and, although it is difficult to make out, it appears that a regal cape lies on the ground behind him indicating this boy's kingly heritage and his connection with the three Magi. Three Magi, three crosses, and three hands, there is more mystery to be discovered in these paintings that is beyond the scope of this

book but notice that neither the boy to the right nor the boy to the left are touching the ground!

It as if they are floating above the earth. Only John the Baptist can stand on the rocky ground with his bare feet.

This next painting, again by Bernardino **de' Conti**, also has two children. One is in the same kneeling position as that of the child on the left in *Virgin of the Rocks*. Remarkably, adorning this child is the iconic staff of John the Baptist! The staff is identically angled as Leonardo had positioned the staff in the second of the *Virgin of the Rocks*.

Here are the same halos. Again, there are two "windows," one with an up-close castle and the other showing a distant landscape. In the left hand of the nursing child is a bird, suggesting his awareness of the bird in Joos van Cleve's *Holy Infants Embracing* paintings. Note further that this Madonna is holding this nursing baby and is not involved in a "transfer."

Bernardino **de' Conti**, we've seen, knew of the secret of *Virgin of the Rocks*. Why would he insert the iconic staff of John? Perhaps because his prior painting could well have been met with threats of heresy causing this painting to be his "escape path."

Figure 57 Nursing Madonna, Bernardino de Conti, private collection

But more probable is the conclusion that he painted this after 1506, after Leonardo touched up the second version of Virgin of the Rocks.

Thus, **de' Conti** is telling us, "I know what Leonardo did – see this staff? It is in the same position as in the second *Virgin of the Rocks*. In my prior painting, *The Three Children*, I painted John the Baptist with two other boys in the same positions as in Virgin of the Rocks. Thus, John the Baptist was not this second boy. But here, in

Nursing Madonna, I've put in the staff to avoid being called a heretic, as did Leonardo." De' Conti's clues are clear.

How the Two Children Were Merged

Probably to protect each painter from the Inquisition, Leonardo decided that the full story of the *Virgin of the Rocks* could safely be told as a composition where each chapter was painted separately by each of his willing students. Bernardino de' Conti revealed that neither of the two boys in *Virgin of the Rocks* nor in *Holy Infants Embracing* were John the Baptist. It fell to other students to explain the story of the merging of the two boys.

Bergognone

The first student we will examine was Ambrogio da Fossano Bergognone (1452? – 1524). Like de Conti, Ambrogio was a student of Leonardo and a pupil of Zenale in Milan. Figure 58 shows the scene at the Temple in Jerusalem as told in Luke's gospel. His parents had traveled to the city to partake in Passover festivities. When they left with many others in their group for their return to Nazareth, they assumed that Jesus was with the group. But he was not. Later that day they realized their mistake and returned to Jerusalem. They searched but it was not until the *third day* that they would find him in the temple having discourse with the doctors of the temple who were amazed at his knowledge.[158] Even Jesus' parents were amazed at his newfound wisdom. After this, "Jesus grew in wisdom, maturity, and grace before God and men."[159] Note the mention of a threefold change in Jesus. This suggests that before this event, Jesus may not have been so obviously filled with wisdom or with maturity. Likely, the meaning of grace is not readily available to people today. In any case, it was

---

[158] Luke 2:41-52
[159] Luke 2:52

likely that this Jesus was, before this event, considered a slow-learner in regards to earthly things and knowledge.

Figure 58 Jesus Among the Doctors, Bergognone, Saint Ambrogio Basilica, Milan

Simon Cade Williams brilliantly describes Bergognone's painting *Jesus among the Doctors* as a depiction of the merging of the two Jesus children in the autumn 2009 issue of the cultural magazine New View.[160] Given that Bergognone appears to have known about two Jesus children, one can ask how did he come upon this knowledge? Was it within Leonardo's Academy?

One of the great insights of Rudolf Steiner had to do with this event. This was developed further by biblical scholar Edward R.

---

[160] Simon Cade Williams, *Christ Among the Doctors*, New View, Issue 53, 2009

Smith.[161] The two boys, the Jesus from Luke and the Jesus from Matthew, underwent a merger during these three days following Passover. Steiner described the transfer from one to the other as that which in the Matthew-Jesus had become spiritualized was then incorporated into the spiritual entities of the Luke-Jesus. Only what had been spiritualized by the Matthew-Jesus (from previous lives) was transferred to the other.[162]

This may have happened behind the curtain concealing the Holy of the Holies where, in its past, initiations had taken place. Or perhaps only the Luke-Jesus went into the Holy of the Holies while the Matthew-Jesus was working with his father when this event occurred as suggested by the *Pistis Sophia*. The important outcome is that something spiritual from the Jesus with the kingly lineage (in Matthew) merged with the constitution of the Jesus with the priestly lineage (in Luke). According to Rudolf Steiner, the earthly-wise Matthew Jesus, now without its spiritual component, would die within months of this event while the Luke Jesus would now display the worldly wisdom of a king.[163] This would continue until age thirty when the baptism would take place.

In this Bergognone painting above, it is the Luke Jesus that is sitting on the chair as on a throne. The other child, Mary, and Joseph have customary haloes. The halo of the seated Jesus could also be an object inside the Holy of the Holies whose curtain is behind him. This halo is magnified by the succession of arches overhead. Around this Jesus are the Temple doctors who were asking him questions with the aid of their books.

---

[161] Edward R. Smith, *The Incredible Births of Jesus*, Anthroposophic Press, 1998
[162] Rudolf Steiner, *The Gospel of St. Luke*, lecture 7, 21Sep1909, Basel, GA 114
[163] IBID

From the left entered Mary and Joseph. Both have been weeping for their lost son. These are the parents of the Matthew-Jesus. This scene shows the moment when they have finally found their son who is the Jesus that is standing and departing. The hand gestures, hair, and robes of both boys are almost identical. This gives Bergognone the option of declaring to an Inquisitor that he has depicted one Jesus shown twice to reveal a sequence in time.

Jesus the King was now merged with Jesus the Priest. Notice the gaze of the enthroned Jesus. He looks intently upon the other boy with a loving expression.

Pinturicchio

Besides Bergognone, several of Leonardo's students painted this scene.

Figure 59 Jesus Among the Doctors, Pinturicchio, Bagloioni Chapel, Spello, Italy

Figure 59 shows a fresco by Bernardino di Betto, who was better known as Pinturicchio (c. 1452-1513). He studied under Bergognone and joined the work at Leonardo's Academy. This was painted in 1501 for the Bagloioni Chapel, Santa Maria Maggiore, in Spello, Italy. It is a depiction of the two Jesus children right after their merger.

Here again are two boys, actually three, who are central to the story depicted. Joseph with a weeping Mary holding onto his belt are entering from the right. Joseph points to their son who is the boy in blue on the left without a halo. He is no longer filled with what he had once had. Without his spiritual member part of his constitution, he will not live long afterward. The other Jesus has a bright halo around his head. Within the halo is a cross designating his fate.

As with other paintings from Leonardo's school, the hands help to explain the story. Here, the spiritually enhanced human Jesus is telling what just happened. His left hand shows two fingers for the two children with his right hand indicating that they have become one.

Figure 60 Close-up of the feet, Jesus Among the Doctors, Pinturicchio

Note that the boy on the right is barefoot, he stands now on the earth, while the boys on the left are lifted progressively from the earth by wearing socks and then by wearing shoes. The one with red socks wears clothing of a poor boy and carries a white sack in his left hand, presumably his schoolbooks, while the other boy wears a rich outfit of a purple vest, red pants, and shoes. The colors of his stockings and shoes are the reverse of the red socks with black tops of the poor boy. The noble boy carries his book of wisdom close to his body and secured with his right arm. He is touched at his left elbow by the right hand of the poor boy.

This poor boy's face has an expression of acceptance of his fate as his contented face looks down upon the earth as if saying "I've successfully done my part." The rich boy appears to be slightly older and somehow connected to the poor boy as he too shares in a countenance that looks down upon the earth. They appear resigned of a fate together. Their demeanor indicates a sense of imminent departure in contrast to the boy at the center of attention on the right who stands barefoot and vibrant upon the earth.

Pinturicchio has depicted in scene on the left the joining of the Matthew-Jesus (the rich boy) and the Luke-Jesus (the poor boy). We are witnessing the combining of their two streams, two lineages. Norwegian scholar and philosopher Trond Skaftnesmo, in his book *Verdensordet*,[164] comes to the same conclusion. He states, "The two Jesus children have been given their own image in the lower left corner. And the 12-year-old Jesus who teaches the scribes is almost the sum of both of them. [By his blue cape, one

---

[164] Trond Skaftnesmo, *Verdensordet*, Paradigmeskifte forlag (Paradigm-change), 2018, pp 86-88. Also, Trond's book *Prince Immanuel of Bethlehem and Yeshua of Nazareth*, draws from several sources to show the expectation of a royal as well as a priestly messiah.

can see] physically he is still the Luke-child." Indeed, the central figure is the twelve-year-old Jesus. His outer sheaths are a color combination of the other two boys with his purple robe matching the purple vest of the noble boy while his blue fancy cloak matches the heaven-blue of the poor boy's outer wrap. He reveals himself in radiance as a merger of the other two boys. This is Jesus of Nazareth who will, eighteen years later, sacrifice this bodily vehicle for the incoming spirit of Christ at the Baptism.

Behind the boys stand three well-dressed men although two of these are remarkably feminine. Both the one in gold with blue standing directly behind the poor boy as well as the one directly to his or her left (our right) are beardless and fair. Both carry books that have not been thrown to the ground. Neither are perplexed nor amazed by the coming of the wise child on the right.

Figure 61 Comparison of feminine faces, Pinturicchio and Raphael's School of Athens

In fact, the one wearing a green and rose robe looks serenely upon the scene. Her/his robe matches the color of the top worn by the richly dressed boy.[165] She/he wears a richly-embroidered hat and,

---

[165] Interestingly, this magenta color is that color found by Goethe when he examined the colors that arise through the use of a prism. Goethe realized that it is not that the light is split up by the prism, but that a picture, simply an image

like the noble boy, holds a book close to her/his body secured by her/his right arm. She/he carries what appears to be a royal purse of gold and red colors. She lifts up her left hand to face the two boys. Meanwhile, the feminine figure to her right gazes above the two children in front of her (or him). Her appearance is reminiscent of Raphael's self-portrayal in his *School of Athens* painting.

Figure 62 The Hierophant with his Four Assistants, Pinturicchio

There is a third richly adorned individual who stands between the scene of the two boys on the left and the one radiant boy on the right. His adorned sky-blue hat is rimmed with white fur and his gold sleeved right hand reaches through his light blue robe. Combining this right hand with the left hand of the green and

---

of the circular aperture of the light source was being projected. The aperture has edges, and where the colors occurred it was not that they were drawn out of white light but because in passing through the prism the light of the image was mixed with darkness. Because this image has edges, the image of the edges became the mixing area where colors arose. Here too the fact is that where light adjoins dark, colors appear at the edges, when a dark center surrounded by light is rayed through a prism. The Newtonian spectrum arises when a thin light source is shown through a prism. In this "dark" spectrum, the magenta is found in the middle where green is found in the Newtonian spectrum

magenta feminine figure, makes for a gesture that draws from the two boys on the left and is given to the one boy on the right. While not the same hand gestures of the *Virgin of the Rocks*, there is a similar drawing and bestowing quality here in Pinturicchio's painting.

These three represent something significant for this event. When one sees that Pinturicchio has displayed here the esoteric Christian theme of the merger of the two Jesus boys in the temple, then one can see these three as representing the hierophants of the Temple who would have conducted the merger within the Holy of the Holies.[166] The gold one looks out at the viewer, the world, the present, while the magenta hierophant looks at Joseph and Mary who approach from the right, the past, and the third hierophant in violet looks toward at the future, that is, the twelve-year-old Jesus.

Digging deeper, we find that the gold sleeves of the noble boy match the color of the first hierophant whose large book is held close to her heart. The covers of this book have an earthy color in contrast to her solar gold. She represents psyche or the astral body in Christian esotericism. Her large book is the Book of Life containing the many prior lives of the noble boy. His green and rose (or magenta) top resembles the color of the second hierophant who would thus represent soma, the transformed life (or prana or chi) body. Lastly, the third hierophant, pneuma, stands with his back to these two boys showing they are the past while he faces the future in the new Jesus of Nazareth. This twelve-year-old Jesus makes a distinctive gesture with his hands that sums up what this painting portrays. The left hand shows two fingers and the

---

[166] They may further represent the life body in magenta, the soul body in gold, and the ego in violet.

right-hand points with one finger, saying "the two have become one."

Interestingly, the Luke-Jesus is backdropped by a gold robe that acts as a halo or aura around him. Behind the Matthew-Jesus is a man whose black robe surrounds the Matthew-Jesus. This indicates that this child will soon die. The white cloth in his left hand forms a shape similar to a handle over this child's head as if he could pull out the spirit of this child. There is also a man in rich blue holding a white bag. The black and blue men appear behind the Matthew-Jesus while the gold and rose feminine figures stand behind the Luke-Jesus. Thus, there are four individuals who stand behind the two boys and behind a fifth who appears to be the head hierophant. The colors of the four range from black to blue then to gold and finally magenta whose shadows appear green. Together they represent the four-fold nature of the human being, physical and I (or ego) in black and blue, the astral, and life bodies in gold and rose. The hierophant in purple worked with these four to bring about the merger.

The floor is littered with books tossed by the doctors because they cannot match the boy's wisdom. The floor tiles are squares and triangles. In the geometry taught at Leonardo's Academy, the wisdom of geometry was an essential part of the training. These geometrical shapes have to do with the soul (triangle) and with the physical earth (square).

Luini

Our next student we've seen before, namely Bernardino Luini. He was a student of both Leonardo and Bergognone.

Figure 63 Jesus Among the Doctors, B. Luini, National Gallery, London

His *Jesus Among the Doctors* was painted around 1515. Leonardo's signature appears 3 times on the back. Like the second *Virgin of the Rocks,* this painting can be found in The National Gallery, London. Here, clearly displayed in figure 63 is the hand gesture of the "two becoming one".

Ferrari

Our last student, Defendente Ferrari (1490 – 1540), painted this *Jesus Among the Doctors* in 1526. It hangs in Staatsgalerie in Stuttgart. Defendente was an apprentice to Giovanni Martino Spanzotti who had participated in Leonardo's Milan Academy.

Circled are the second Jesus and the two-becoming-one hand gesture offered by one of the doctors. Instead of the round golden halo that is above the heads of the other Jesus, Joseph,

Figure 64 Jesus Among the Doctors, D. Ferrari, Staatsgalerie, Stuttgart

and Mary, the enthroned Jesus has a radiating halo that shines out from within. This indicates something more than heavenly holiness; it indicates a glowing wisdom garnered from lives on earth while it anticipates the coming of the God from the Sun.

This chapter explored the role that the students of Leonardo's Academy played in telling the rest of the story that the *Virgin of the Rocks* could only partially tell. Similar backgrounds and hand gestures invited us to relate the paintings. The known thirty copies of *Holy Infants Embracing* showed the same two children in exactly the same embrace in every copy. These students have told us that these two were the same two children that appear in the original *Virgin of the Rocks*.

These paintings revealed that of these two children of *Virgin of the Rocks*, neither could be John the Baptist. This led to the initial conclusion that the two children could be depicting a heretical theology that the Jesus of Luke and the Jesus of Matthew are actually separate boys and neither is the Christ. Leonardo, again using his students, then tells us how these two came together and out of this union one of the children would grow up to be Jesus of Nazareth.

The companion book, *The Uncomfortable History of Christianity*, explains that this was the theology of some of the early Christians. For them, Christ was a spiritual being who, at the baptism. entered the prepared body of Jesus of Nazareth. For those early Christians, the baptism was also the birth of Christ. This relief shows a large John the Baptist representing the heights that one could attain in pre-Christian times. It is an artistic depiction of the Baptist's words "He must increase, but I must decrease" from John 3:30.

Figure 65 Sarcophagus, c.270, Baptism of Jesus by John (right), Santa Maria Antigua, Rome

Next, the theological basis for two Messiahs in the Kabbala, the Dead Sea Scrolls, and other ancient texts will be explored.

Summary of the Role of Leonardo's Students

The mythology of Osiris was certainly available to Leonardo from teachers and books and lectures during his early adulthood in Florence. It took the Goddess of Wisdom, Isis, to be able to put together again Osiris' dismembered body. The body of this mystery of the two Jesus boys was dismembered to protect each student from accusations by the Inquisition. Leonardo's *Virgin of the Rocks* begins the composition that completes with his *John the Baptist*. In between the students tell the story of the merging of the two boys as preparation for the baptism, the birth of Christ into and for humanity.

5. Lifting the Veil of Isis

Recall the depictions claimed by the National Gallery. If true, then the infant John the Baptist is with Mary while Mary's son Jesus is seated with and supported by the archangel. These depictions leave out the mother of John the Baptist. Further, they have placed neither infant with its own mother. If the younger child on the right is Jesus, then why is he not with his mother? It is doubtful any renowned painter would swap the children so that its own mother is not situated near it or embracing it. Leonardo used standard artistic techniques of his time to give further clues on how to interpret his enigmatic *Virgin of the Rocks*. These clues will help to fully realize the heretical views of the artist and genius Leonardo.

Secrets of the Background

Figure 66 Close-up of the background, VoR Louvre

Employing symbolism was a common practice in the Florentine school and throughout the Renaissance. Leonardo left us numerous symbols to lead the inquiring mind into the mystery he intended to reveal. By dividing the original painting in half, a set of symbols corresponds with each child. Especially the backgrounds communicate symbolically.

There are two openings in the rocky wall which we will call 'windows.' Each window corresponds to one of the toddlers. The window on our left is lower and displays countless rock pillars plus a stream or river flowing through them. The window on the right side is higher, narrower, and reveals only one central rock pillar. Here Leonardo is revealing something of the infant that sits below its respective window.

When one senses this rocky background as symbolic of past earth lives, it then whispers deep wisdom regarding reincarnation. This wisdom begins to glow when one associates each pillar with a past life. In this way, these windows tell something about the past lives of these two boys. By its window, the child on our left has had multiple past lives. And, by the size of its pillars, these were significant past lives. Further, the river running through these pillars represents the River of Life.

The Fall of Mankind and Reincarnation
In this exegesis, the window on the right side is telling us that its corresponding child has had but one incarnation. Why should this child miss out on incarnations while the other one seems to have had a generous apportionment? A close examination of the Kabbala and the gospels of Luke and Matthew reveal what this painting's background is declaring to us. In order to fully appreciate what this Jesus of Luke's gospel represents, that is the toddler on the right in *Virgin of the Rocks*, we will explore esoteric

traditions related to Luke 3:38. Luke traces a lineage that completes with the words "the son of Enos, the son of Seth, the son of Adam, the son of God."

Assuming that what was portrayed through these two 'windows' in *Virgin of the Rocks* represented each child's past lives, one can conclude that because it is higher, a higher spiritual relationship to reincarnation existed. This leads to the question, who was the individual who had a higher incarnation than any other human and yet only had one? The Kabbala reveals who this was, namely the Pre-Fall Adam who is called Adam Kadmon.[167] Adam simply means "mankind" (and can mean more than just one individual) while Kadmon expresses our pre-Fall state, i.e. the heavenly man in the Garden of Eden.

Prior to the Fall, humanity lived in a very different environment than we do today. Genesis 3 describes the Fall of Man who had been living in a paradise. One interpretation of the Fall is that mankind was evicted from a higher state, spiritually, to a lower state, one in which humanity had to descend into a physical body, into flesh, and then to live upon the mineral kingdom. For this lower bodily state humanity felt ashamed. Adam was now in a gross body that absorbed and retained mineral substance rather than of a higher body similar to angels.

Born of Eve into this fleshy state are Cain and Abel who represent the two types of humanity during the transition from Eden until sexual procreation could truly begin in the physical realm. Genesis explicitly tells us that it was Seth who was the first to be born via a mix of both parents.

Abel represented in humanity that which accepted what God gave as sufficient. Abel desired no more. He sacrificed to God from the

---

[167] Isidore Singer, *Adam Kadmon*, Jewish Encyclopedia, Funk & Wagnalls, 1906

abundance of what came from God. Cain, however, represented that which sought to work upon and transform this new environment, to spiritualize matter. Thus, to Cain and his descendants are attributed, by Freemasonry, the origin of the Arts, Sciences, and Technology.[168] But because the sacrifice from Cain was a product of the earthly, Yahweh rejected it. Why was it rejected? The last chapter explains how a number of Early Christian and Gnostic texts claimed that, because of the Fall, a different human evolution than originally intended had to be. The Fall required a descent into matter, into the earthly where each life was to experience death. The earthly realm was purposefully not pure and thus, these theologians concluded, must have been created by another god, perhaps an imperfect if not evil one, rather than by the Father God. The name often attributed to this god was the Demiurge.

Humanity, however, had gained something through this Luciferic temptation at the Tree of Knowledge, namely the ability to garner knowledge for itself. This became a step, through knowledge, toward freedom. Eventually, this path of knowledge would lead the ego within each human to feel a freedom even from God. Eating this fruit began a process that required humanity's evolution to take place differently than what had been divinely intended so that what Lucifer enabled at the Fall could be redeemed and made holy.

After the Fall, humanity would no longer be able to eat from the fruits of Eden but must, afterward, eat from the fruits of a lower realm, that which grew upon the mineral kingdom. With that step out of Eden, humanity was placed onto its journey to fully realize its freedom. In order that humanity could develop true freedom, our 'residence' with the beings of the heavens had to gradually

---

[168] Manly P. Hall, *The Lost Keys of Freemasonry: The Legend of Hiram Abiff*, Martino Fine Books, 2013

come to an end. Then our awareness of a spiritual world also had to come to an end. The path of knowledge from Eden had to lead away from God so that the human ego could stand alone in freedom. According to this theology, a time will come when this freedom will be attained. Then, like the prodigal son,[169] humanity can work its way back to God. For these Early Christians, Christ was the enabler of this return path.

In this heretical history, humanity after the Fall eventually found itself in a body of flesh that needed nourishment from the plants of the earth. By consuming plants of the earth and their minerals, humans became like other living things on the earth; that is, their physical life needed to end in physical death. During Eden, death was merely a change in state, similar to a snake shedding its skin. One's offspring came through an androgynous, painless birth. Such offspring looked like a clone of the male-female parent whose blood and memories lived on in the offspring. Hence, the long lives in hundreds of years attributed to these early humans.

This theology reads Genesis to conclude that there was a transition from the androgynous Adam and Eve to the sexually produced Seth who would have been the first to be a mix of both parents. The transition species were Cain and Abel. They were still androgynous but during this transition, Cain evolved toward the masculine physical body while Abel evolved toward the feminine.

---

[169] See Luke 15:11-32. Prodigal means wasteful. A father has two sons. The younger son takes his inheritance and explores the world but squanders his fortune. He becomes destitute and is forced to return home empty-handed. Rather than being chastised, this son is welcomed back with celebration and fanfare. The faithful older son refuses to participate in the festivities. The father reminds him that "everything I have is yours." Thus, celebrating the younger son's return is right because once he was lost, but now he is found.

Life, death, and life again became a necessary evolutionary process in this theology. Reincarnation was a breathing between life on the unholy earth and life in the holy heavens. Karma would be the teacher, the guide toward perfection. Gradually each individual would achieve freedom. Only a truly free individual could choose each individual's goal. Through the lessons of death and multiple lives, mankind could, one day, develop to become like a god. Mankind could return to be like the archetype, Adam Kadmon, once more. But, with the fruits of freedom, the new Adam, a perfected human, would be more than originally intended.

Because of this long journey of the soul, longer than originally intended, mankind would return with more than what was given at creation. This was embedded in the parable of the talents.[170] Such a future individual will be one who will act in moral freedom out of wisdom. According to such esoteric teachings[171], the temptation by the serpent Lucifer caused the divine guiding spirit(s) to adjust their plan for mankind to incorporate freedom as a result of Lucifer's successful temptation of mankind.[172]

But lacking was love. Towards this end, humanity also had to be given 'fire' in order to develop love on this long journey of the soul. The beginning of love was implanted by God into post-Fall humanity in the mother-child relationship. Because the child came from her body, this love was natural, instinctual. Love grew to exist

---

[170] The story is found in both Matthew 25:14-30 and in Luke 19:12-27. A master was to take a trip. He gave his three servants a portion of his goods to administer while he was away. Upon his return, the three are assessed. One hid the goods so that he could safely return all of the goods in the same state as they were given. The other two used the goods as investments. The master was pleased with these two but not with the safe one.

[171] Bill Ellis, *Lucifer Ascending*, The University Press of Kentucky, 2015 plus Annie Besant and Richard Smoley, *Esoteric Christianity*, Quest Books, 2006.

[172] Rudolf Steiner, *The Michael Mystery*, Steiner Books, 2015

within a family. Family love became tribal love. But, love within the bloodline would need to expand to all of humanity. The founders of religion came to implant a wider love within humanity.

This is why Luke traces the ancestry of his Jesus back to Adam whom he says was the son of God. Adam represents this archetype of mankind from creation that existed through the whole period when humanity was within a non-physical existence in the Garden of Eden. When humanity partook of the Tree of Knowledge, a change in human destiny was necessitated. Mankind would need to fall into matter where death could be experienced. Adam Kadmon is the name for that archetype that was retained in the spiritual world when mankind fell into matter. Adam's lineage continues into the post-Eden phase of humanity that was required to live upon the mineral kingdom.

To summarize, the symbolic nature of the background tells us that the child on the left has had many past-lives but none as high as that of the child on the right who had but one incarnation. This symbolism tells us that the Jesus on the left has had many significant incarnations as represented by the many majestic pillars through which the river of life flows, while the Jesus on the right has had just one incarnation but one of highest significance. Above his 'window' are rocks suggesting the form of a bridge, a bridge, that is, from a former existence on the right that was crossed with the Fall to a different existence on the left.

Sacred geometry

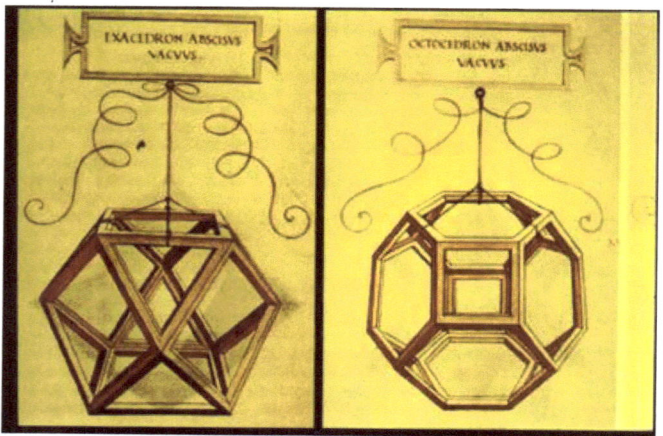

Figure 67 Illustration by LdVinci in Pacioli's On Divine Proportions

The inscription over the entrance to Plato's Academy said, "Let no man enter here who is not a geometrician." According to Vasari's biography of Leonardo, he was, as a boy, accepted to be an apprentice to Andrea del Verrocchio where he "soon proved himself a first-class geometrician." After his studies in Verrocchio's school, Leonardo, as a member of the Medici household, likely was able to attend lectures and other educational events at the Platonic Academy in Florence. [173, 174] Historians have long suspected that Piero de Medici, as a 20-year-old in fear of Savonarola and his mob who found the Platonic Academy to be

---

[173] James Hankins argues in 1994 that the Platonic Academy in Florence may never have existed as an accredited school. His paper *The Myth of the Platonic Academy of Florence* appeared in *Renaissance Quarterly*, Vol. 44, No. 3 (Autumn, 1991), pp. 429-475. Hankins points out that there are few references to the academy. This author claims it was hidden because of the content was deemed to be heretical and thus secrecy had to be maintained.

[174] In *Ficino's Little Academy of Careggi* Christophe Poncet makes a strong case that this academy existed at the farm Cosimo de Medici gave in 1463 to Marsilio Ficino after completing translations of Plato's works. Poncet shows that this farm was established in the same style as the first Platonic Academy of Athens which was also a small farm just outside of Athens similar to how this farm in Careggi was just outside of Florence.

teaching heresy, poisoned two of its prominent professors.[175] By this time, Leonardo had established a similar academy in Milan safe from the foreseen troubles in Florence. Little is known about his Milan academy which probably existed as part of his studio.

Leonardo would later borrow from Plato to write in his notebook, "Let no one read me who is not a mathematician."[176] These notebooks contain numerous drawings of the five Platonic solids, namely the cube, tetrahedron, octahedron, icosahedron, and dodecahedron.

As it was for Pythagoras, geometry was sacred in Leonardo's school. Plato's inscription was said to be over the entrance to Leonardo's Milan Academy. Leonardo, in his earnestness to study the sacredness of mathematics, collaborated with one of the leading mathematicians, Luca Pacioli, in the 1498 publication of *On Divine Proportion*.

The book was subsequently republished in 1509 in Venice and thereby established Leonardo as a skilled illustrator of geometric shapes. Pacioli devoted the entire second part of *On Divine Proportion (Divina Proportione)* to the Platonic solids. relating the Platonic solids to the golden ratio like this: "As God brought into being the celestial virtue, the fifth essence, and through it created the four solids ... earth, air, water, and fire ... so our sacred proportion gave shape to heaven itself, in assigning to it the dodecahedron ... the solid of twelve pentagons, which cannot be constructed without our sacred proportion, as the aged Plato has

---

[175] Malcolm Moore, "Medici philosopher's mysterious death is solved". The Daily Telegraph. London: Telegraph Media Group Limited. Retrieved 7 February 2008. https://www.telegraph.co.uk/news/worldnews/1577958/Medici-philosophers-mystery-death-is-solved.html

[176] Translated by Edward MacCurdy, *The Notebooks of Leonardo da Vinci* (Volume 1), Braziller, 1958.

described in his *Timaeus*."[177] This quote reveals how religion and mathematics and philosophy (in this case Plato) were still woven together in the great minds of the Renaissance.

Figure 68 Tetrahedron, Cube, Octahedron, Dodecahedron, Icosahedron

All of the illustrations were magnificently done by Leonardo. Pacioli wrote of his work with Leonardo, "Shortly afterwards, as hopes nourished my courage, I dedicated to Ludovic Sforza, Duke of Milan, the treatise entitled *On Divine Proportion*, with such ardor that I included shapes and volumes by the hand of Leonardo da Vinci, so that the reader could picture them more easily."[178]

Interestingly, in 1596, Johannes Kepler published his book *Mysterium Cosmographicum*. The book brought sacred geometry to the cosmos where Kepler expected to find it employed. Kepler discovered that by representing the orbits of the six known planets as spheres, each platonic solid, namely the cube, tetrahedron, dodecahedron, icosahedron, and lastly the octahedron fit between those six spheres almost perfectly. Kepler arranged each platonic solid so that the center of each face was tangent to the inner planetary sphere. He found that the sphere of the next planet contained all the vertices of the platonic solid! The sequence he found was octahedron between sun and mercury, then

---

[177] Luca Pacioli and Leonardo da Vinci, *De Divina Proportione*, CreateSpace Independent Publishing, 2014
[178] George Tombs, *Man the Machine, A History of a Metaphor from Leonardo da Vinci to H.G. Wells*, PhD thesis, McGill University, Montreal, November 2002

icosahedron, then dodecahedron, next tetrahedron, and lastly the cube between Jupiter and Saturn.

It was already a common Florentine practice during the Renaissance to arrange a religious scene according to sacred geometry. The characters and the action often were often placed within a central isosceles triangle or within a tetrahedron (pyramid).

Triangle
The woman in blue and gold, thought to be the Madonna, occupies the central position of the composition. If any character is to be considered a spiritual being it would be this central character who is cloaked in the colors of the heavens, the rich deep blues with inner gold shining through. She towers over all the others

Figure 69 Original Virgin of the Rocks with isosceles triangle

including the archangel. She could represent Mary or a divine being or both at the same time (recall our discussion of double identities). In other paintings of the Madonna done by students of Leonardo, she is holding a book suggesting that she could be related to the Greek goddess of wisdom, Sophia. Keep in mind, that this book is making the point that these students were participating in a larger 'body' of work intended to reveal Christian mysteries. And recall that these Renaissance artists often painted scenes from Greek mythology that were felt to have a relationship to Christianity.

In the original *Virgin of the Rocks,* she receives with her right hand through the shoulder of the child on our left. She transfers this through her heavenly means to the child on the right. Even the archangel is participating in carrying for what is to be transferred to a lower level of the constitution of the child on the right.

Note that the child who is to be the recipient is not fully within with the triangle. His left hand and his body's trunk are outside the triangle meaning that nothing of the physical body will take part in the action of this future transfer. It is this child's earthly body that will be the vehicle for the merged two. This one will be the earthly basis for Jesus of Nazareth who will later sacrifice this body for the use of the Christ to become the first Son of Man.

Only the child's head and right hand are within the triangle suggesting that only what is above the physical will be received from the other child. That is, the child on the right will receive three spiritual entities, namely the I (Ego or spirit) plus two of its purified members that have been spiritualized already by the child on the left.

The lineage of the child on the right is traced back by Luke to Adam, to that Adam who was the son of God, namely Adam Kadmon. Because Adam Kadmon retained the purity of Man before the eviction from Eden and never again incarnated until the Luke-Jesus was born, it therefore lacks any wisdom of earth as well as culture.[179] Thus, those who met this child, would conclude this loving child was intellectually challenged. This is why, at the event in Jerusalem when he was twelve, his parents were so shocked by the wisdom that he was suddenly able to express. The other child, the Matthew-Jesus, would have been deemed exceptionally wise from birth, full of royal wisdom.

---

[179] Christian D. Ginsburg, *Kabbalah: Its Doctrines, Development and Literature*, Kessinger, 2003.

Tetrahedron (pyramid)

Figure 70 Original Virgin of the Rocks with tetrahedron

Outlining a pyramid, as in figure 70, reveals much in each visible facet. The left facet fully contains the left child, all of the central figure except for her bestowing left hand, plus the blessing gesture and legs of the sitting infant on the right. The left facet shows from whence these three gifts come.

The right facet contains the trunk and head of the infant on the right including his left hand that touches the mineral kingdom. Nearly all of the archangel is also contained. And her pointing right hand along with the bestowing left hand of the central figure all appear in this, the receiving facet.

Let us look at the expression of will of both of the children. The one kneeling shows himself to be a doer, active, while the one sitting is a receiver who can bless. These two exemplify Cain and Abel. In this mystery, Cain was the earthly doer and Abel was one who received what came from above (via the hands of the heavenly hierarchies) down to the earth. Further, in Masonic traditions, the Cain lineage eventually becomes the kingly that rules over the earthly. According to Freemasonry legends, Hiram Abiff was foretold that he would be the father of such a lineage after the passing of King Solomon.[180]

The Abel lineage represents the priestly in the human. While they lived upon earth, they believed they had divine roots. They sought guidance for their earthly lives from the divine. For this, they established initiations and the mysteries.

The Cain lineage felt endowed to work upon the earth, to spiritualize it. They grew in earthly wisdom that became the wisdom of Magi, of Kings. Thus, the child on our left represents this Cain lineage while the other child represents the Abel lineage.

Color Analysis
The above interpretation is supported by an analysis of the colors. The left tetrahedron facet has to do with wisdom as it displays blues and golds while the right facet has to do with life and love based on its green and red colors. Again, the wisdom revealed in the left facet will be transferred to the love and life forces of the right facet. Note that in the copy of *Virgin of the Rocks*, the archangel has different colors.

Vitruvian Man

---

[180] See Rudolf Steiner, The Temple Legend, Rudolf Steiner Press, 1997

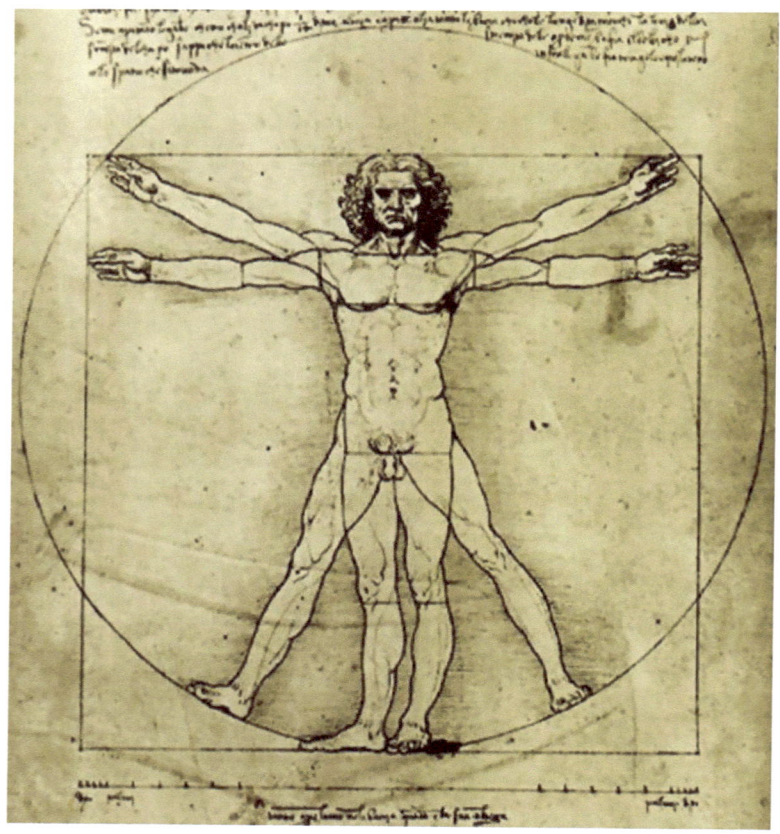

Figure 71 Vitruvian Man from LdV notebook

Sacred geometry was inspired in Leonardo by his studies of Marco Vitruvius Pollio (author and architect in Rome during the first century BCE) who wrote: "... in the human body the central point is naturally the navel. For if a man be placed flat on his back, with his hands and feet extended, and a pair of compasses centered at his navel, the fingers and toes of his two hands and feet will touch the *circumference of a circle* described therefrom. And just as the human body yields a circular outline, so too *a square figure* may be found from it. For if we measure the distance from the soles of the feet to the top of the head, and then apply that measure to the outstretched arms, the breadth will be found to be the same as the height ..." Leonardo sketched the Vitruvian Man in his notebooks around 1490, about a decade after he abandoned his *Adoration of the Magi* and began work on the *Virgin of the Rocks*. He was interested in the relationship of geometry with the form of the human created by God the Geometrician. Clearly, Leonardo sought to reveal geometry's sacred qualities and did so in his *Virgin of the Rocks*.

Hand Gestures

Throughout history, how the human hand was used has had special meaning. Ancient India called this *mudra*. "The term mudra applies to the use of hand gestures during meditation that carry specific goals of channeling your body's energy flow."[181] Native Americans made hand gestures as they spoke. Caricatures of Italians claim their speech coincides with hand gestures.

"In Hinduism and Buddhism, there exists a large body of gestures known as mudras which appear in ritual and especially in religious dance. Mudra are also described in mythology and depicted in

---

[181] The Chopra Center, https://chopra.com/articles/10-powerful-mudras-and-how-to-use-them

iconography. There are many dozens of mudras each having a very specific form and meaning."[182]

Figure 72 Original Virgin of the Rocks, LdV, Louvre, Paris

In the West, reverence for hand gestures has gradually vanished along with most spiritually based expressions and symbols. But the need for hand gestures has remained and evolved into gestures with a non-obvious spiritual basis such as the military salute, the victory sign, the OK sign, the thumbs up sign, and the middle finger "I'm angry at you" sign. For those who knew back then, Leonardo's hand gestures were as meaningful as these hand gestures are to those in the know today.

---

[182] David Calabro, "Understanding Ritual Hand Gestures of the Ancient World," Ancient Temple Worship, The Expound Symposium Proceedings, 14May2011, Eborn Books, 2014

What Do the Hands Tell Us?

There are four hands on the right and two on the left. Two hands are partially hidden, one on each side. The child on the left has his two hands together in a prayerful gesture leaving only one hand visible. On the right, a fifth hand, namely the left hand of the kneeling character, is mostly hidden behind the left arm of child on the right. Why are these hands depicted with such strong gestures? Each hand is doing something meaningful.

It is unlikely that an archangel would be depicted by Leonardo as providing a gentle yet firm physical brace for the child on the right whose left-hand rests upon the earth just above the reflecting pool. Leonardo knew that archangels have no physicality to offer such support. So, what does this archangel's hand mean or do? Could it mean, "I've got your back"? Her gaze appears to be directed at the group's unseen reflection in the pool. This is indicative of an archangel's inability to see into the physical world. Rather, archangels see not the physical but our soul's 'reflection' of our experiences within the physical world recorded into memory.

The Four Hands

Just to the right of the middle of the painting are four hands, three of which are stacked. Beginning with the left hand of the child on the right we see that since it rests on the earth suggesting that once the two children are combined this will be the remaining physical body. In the Greek model, the physical body relates us to the Mineral Kingdom or the Earth element.

His right hand is raised in a blessing gesture which we also see in this closeup of Leonardo's cartoon, The Virgin with St. Anne, above. To help us identify the children of the Virgin of the Rocks, Leonardo has here brought John the Baptist into the cartoon as a character farther to our right. When compared to the Virgin of the Rocks, the position of the Luke-Jesus child who was offering his blessings has been turned around here to bless John. This further verifies that Leonardo did intend this younger Jesus to represent the Jesus from Luke's gospel in which John the Baptist appears. In

Matthew's gospel, John does not appear until Jesus is thirty when he come to be baptized.

Continuing vertically, the next hand belongs to the archangel who kneels beside this Jesus child on the right. She is pointing with her right hand at the other child. This is meant to be part of the action of this painting and is why it is central in the triangle. It is noteworthy that this pointing hand is absent in the theologically-acceptable copy of the Virgin of the Rocks.

Note further that in the copy, the iconic staff was added to identify one child as John the Baptist and haloes were also added to the presumed humans but not to this archangel. As mentioned, these were the required theological 'touch-ups' Leonardo applied after his partner had varnished the surface of the painting in order to declare it finished.

Lastly, the fourth hand, the left hand of the woman who is central in the composition expresses bestowing. As we've discussed here, her right-hand will transfer from the Matthew-Jesus and bestow it to the Luke-Jesus. Her bestowing hand represents a fourth element.

Leonardo is revealing that he had knowledge of the Greek fourfold concept of the human being.

In figure 73, two of the hand gestures are repeated. The Jesus child has the same two finger gesture that is commonly claimed to be the gesture of blessing. Note the left hand of the Madonna is strikingly similar to the right hand of the archangel in figure 74, only here the point is vertical towards the heavens while the archangel is pointing horizontally to the Jesus child. Now notice how this hand gestures matches that of John the Baptist seen in figure 11.

Figure 73 The Virgin with St. Anne, LdV, National Gallery

Using the Greek Model of the Human to Understand the Painting

St. Paul named the members that constituted the human being. He used the terms soma, psyche, and pneuma meaning body, soul, and spirit.[183] As materialism took hold of the human intellect, first spirit and later soul too were lost to our understanding. For the Hellenistic Greek, the human was known as a microcosm of the macrocosm. Within us, therefore, existed something that corresponds to each level of a heavenly hierarchy.

---

[183] 1 Thessalonians 5:23, "May your wholeness of spirit, soul, and body be kept blameless," NIV

Figure 74 VoR depiction of the Greek model of the human
Figure 75 VoR depiction of the heavenly hierarchies

The first esoteric Christian school was initiated by St. Paul in Athens with Dionysius the Areopagite as its head. Dionysius and his school explored the heavenly hosts, their hierarchy, and their relationship to the human being.

Here in this Christianity-based school, the details of this microcosm were elaborated.[184] As a reflection of the Holy Trinity, the heavenly hierarchy also had three levels and each of these, in turn, had three levels for a total of nine. Now the human had to share in such a division. Soma related to the lowest hierarchy, psyche to the middle hierarchy, and pneuma to the highest. Then each of these were further divided in three yielding a total of nine levels. The Godhead was the source and thus the tenth level in both the

---

[184] Being the first 'hierophant' of this school, the name Dionysius became the title given to each successor

macro and the microcosm. Likewise, soma, psyche, and pneuma were each further divided by three. There were Greek terms (as well as Sanskrit) for each of these nine human members.

The School of Athens tied the three aspects of soma, the body, to the elements, to, namely, earth, water, and air (solid, liquid, and gaseous). The fourth element, fire, was given to humanity, according to Greek mythology, by Prometheus who was the god of foresight and one of the Titan gods from the earlier Kronos generation of gods that had preceded Zeus. One can, in this case, compare Prometheus to Lucifer for the gift of inner fire.

Where in our body (soma) did the Greeks, with these concepts, place this fourth element? They associated fire in the bodily home with the human I, or spirit. According to the Greek model, spiritual Fire must be within the human. It is thus connected with our blood which is the carrier of our warmth. In our soma, it was considered our blood that supported our divine spark, our I.

Just as the element fire or warmth is able to be in each of the other elements, so is our I, our *Fotia*, able to permeate each of our other three bodies. This sets it apart from the other elements. Other than this level of fire, each of the nine hierarchical levels is reflected in a human member as shown in the following table.

Term	Greek	Meaning	Hierarchy
Spirit (top level)	Atma (Sanskrit)	Spiritual Body	Seraphim
Spirit (2nd level)	Buddhi (Sanskrit)	Spiritual Life	Cherubim
Spirit (3rd level)	Manas (Sanskrit)	Spiritual Human	Thrones

Soul (top)	Dianoetikon	Consciousness Soul	Kyriotetes
Soul (2nd level)	Kinetikon	Intellectual Soul	Dynamis
Soul (3rd level)	Orektikon	Sentient Soul	Exusiai
Body (Fire)	Fotia	I	Divine spark
Body (Air)	Aisthetikon	Astral, Wisdom	Archai
Body (Water)	Threptikon	Etheric, Chi, Prana, Beauty	Archangeloi
Body (Earth)	Gaia	Physical, Strength	Angeloi

Notice how each tripartite (soma, psyche, and pneuma) is also divided into three (red, green, blue).

This **tripartite** reflects the three activities of the human soul, namely, thinking, feeling, and willing and in the physical body in head, trunk, and limbs. The physically immobilized head is the home for our soul's thinking. Through our limbs we express our soul's willing. In the breathing and blood circulation centered in our trunk we find the home for our soul's feeling that mediates between the thinking with breathing and the willing with the circulation of the blood. The ratio of our heart beats to lung breaths is maintained at 4:1.

Within the Platonic Academy of Florence, Leonardo certainly learned these Greek concepts. His notebooks have multiple entries mentioning the human soul. In one he wrote, "Though human ingenuity may make various inventions which, by the help of various machines answering the same end, it will never devise any inventions more beautiful, nor more simple, nor more to the purpose than Nature does; because in her inventions nothing is wanting, and nothing is superfluous, and she needs no counterpoise when she makes limbs proper for motion in the bodies of animals. But she puts into them the soul of the body, which forms them that is the soul of the mother which first constructs in the womb the form of the man and in due time awakens the soul that is to inhabit it."[185]

Applying this Greek model to the *Virgin of the Rocks*, clues are found as to how these two children, although from separate births and parents, will become united. That which has been spiritualized, that is, any of the three spiritual members from the child on the left will be merged into the child on the right. This could include, along with the I, whatever exists of what is called in Vedic traditions Manas, Buddhi, and Atma. Wisdom (not mere knowledge) is found in Manas, creative and spiritual love in Buddhi, and Father in Atma. In esoteric traditions, a redeemed Lucifer (who is a separate being from Satan) leads to Manas, Christ to Buddhi, and after that Atma, experience of the Father God, can be attained in the far future.

At the time in evolution when the birth of Jesus occurred, evolution had led to where only the I, Manas, and some existing Buddhi structure would have possible as spiritual entities available in the most advanced child, whom we've called the Matthew-Jesus, to be transferable to another, in this case, to the so-called Luke-Jesus.[186]

This is only possible, of course, under the concept of reincarnation. Certainly, the concept of reincarnation existed before Christianity, but did this concept exist at any time within Christianity? While this

---

[185] Leonardo da Vinci, Notebook XIV Anatomy, Zoology and Physiology, Transl Jean Paul Richter, 1888

[186] For more on these future spiritual entities, see Rudolf Steiner, *According to Luke*, lectures 4-7, 1909

discussion will take us too far afield, it may be noted that this concept, although fading, had existed in nearly all cultures up to the time of Plato. Christian theologian Edward Reaugh Smith, arrived at such a conclusion, in his tome, *The Burning Bush*. He argued that Early Christians did know of this concept but allowed it to be suppressed so that the importance of each life would become paramount.[187] The concept is present, for example, in the questions posed to Christ-Jesus concerning the man born blind.[188]

We can now review the four hand gestures on the right side in vertical order in the light of reincarnation.

- The lowest hand is outside the triangle, is not fully vertically aligned, and is touching the earth. We can say it tells the viewer that the physical body of this child will, at merger, remain the same. This body was pure, without karma.

- Next, is the child's right hand that is offering a blessing. This right hand represents, in Greek philosophy, the Life Body, prana, which is related to the life-giving element Water. This is what relates us to the plant kingdom in which life is found. Into this life-body of the Luke-Jesus on the right will be merged what of the Matthew-Jesus' life body had spiritualized. Buddhi is the Sanskrit name for the spiritualized life body. This could only have been a partially developed Buddhi body at this point in evolution. In the three years when Christ inhabited this body, the Buddhi body was completed.

- Applying the Greek model of the Human, the third hand, the pointing hand of the archangel, would represent the Astral Body which is related to the element Air and is the seat of consciousness. The central female represents the cosmic spirit. Likewise, the archangel represents the cosmic soul. She points

---

[187] Edward R. Smith, *The Burning Bush*, Anthroposophic Press, 1997. See also, *The Incredible Births of Jesus*, 1998
[188] John, 9:1–12

to the other child from whom will be transferred its Manas, its spiritualized astral body.

- Lastly, is the bestowing hand of the central feminine figure. Through her cosmic capabilities, the I of the Matthew-Jesus, its divine spark, will transfer to the sitting child, the Luke-Jesus.

The transfer of these three bodily members will not occur until the Luke-Jesus has become twelve years old. To keep these members pure, the merging needed to occur just before the onset of puberty.

Gnostic Esotericism: Androgyne, Cain, and Abel

The earthly humanity that arose when humanity descended to the physical earth following the Fall, is represented by Cain and Abel. In esoteric traditions of Freemasonry, the duality of Abel and Cain represented humanity during the great transition time from Eden to earthly life. The Adam and Eve asexual lineages both continued and existed alongside the asexual lineages of Cain and Abel. When one from the Abel lineage was killed by one from the Cain lineage, the Abel lineage did not come to an end. But it lost the source of its lineage. The asexuality of these four lineages eventually comes to an end. The Abel lineage tended towards expressing the female while the Cain lineage more readily expressed the male. But the first sexual union of beings came from the Adam and Eve lineages that also had been dividing into male and female. Seth is the first to inherit from both parents. With this transition from Eden to earthly life now at an end, Seth took the place of Abel in both lineage and role.[189] Thus, Luke traces his lineage through Seth to Adam.

The fratricide of Cain remained as a karmic debt within humanity. From it arose the distrust and the hatred of those who refuse to

---

[189] Rudolf Steiner, *The Temple Legend*, 20 lectures, 1905, GA 93

work upon the earth by those who do. This emotion became directed at the priests and priestesses. Hidden within these traditions lies the esoteric reason why women were barred from Masonic lodges until in the late nineteenth century when women were finally admitted to Adoptive Lodges.[190]

A careful examination of the Hebrew text of Genesis 1:27 and 5:2 helps to grasp humanity's body pre-Fall and during the transitional period and then the change to the human body once sexual procreation began. With materialism ruling modern concepts, translators have rendered these passages to say "He created them male *and* female" but a translation that says "He created them male-female" is more accurate. But if fourth century Christians could no longer understand 'the two became one' for the two children named Jesus, then an androgynous procreation would have been just as difficult to grasp, if not more so.[191]

Conception during the time in Eden was through a spiritual knowing, a penetrating light. Hence the expression "he knew her and thus she conceived." There was no sexual procreation until after the Fall. After all, according to Genesis, the Elohim [often translated as God] had created mankind in their image and they did not sexually procreate. What was this godly image used by the Elohim? Androgynous beings! Reliefs and statues of an early Zeus had multiple breasts such as this Zeus Labraunda shown below.[192]

Such concepts would have been part of Plethon's lectures about Plato. In *Symposium*, Plato says, "First you must learn what human nature was in the beginning and what has happened to it since,

---

[190] IBID

[191] For more, see Rudolf Steiner, *Genesis, Secrets of Creation*, Rudolf Steiner Press, lectures August, 1910, GA122

[192] Robert Fleischer, *Artemis von Ephesos und verwandte Kultstatuen aus Anatolien und Syrien,* Leiden, Brill, 1973

because long ago our nature was not what it is now, but very different. There were three kinds of human beings, that's my first point—not two as there are now, male and female. In addition to these, there was a third, a combination of those two; its name survives, though the kind itself has vanished. At that time, you see, the word 'androgynous' really meant something: a form made up of male and female elements, though now there's nothing but the word, and that's used as an insult. ... Those who are interested in members of the opposite sex are halves of formerly androgynous people."[193]

In some esoteric traditions such as Anthroposophy, an individual would commonly, but not always, alternate gender with each incarnation.

Greek mythology, in picture form, reaches back to the Fall. With the post-Fall change for humanity, Zeus becomes the new ruler of the Gods. The myths speak of the dramatic changes that took place for humanity following the Fall. Even the Greek gods would have to change. Zeus and Hera, although brother and sister, would marry and have children. Marrying within the bloodline and within the family would be normal and healthy for thousands of years (but even this would evolve). As it was below, in humanity, so it must have been above, with the gods.[194] Thus we see here images of the gods that depict a feeling-knowledge by the artist for this Eden period and the transition time of Cain and Abel when humanity was male-female.

---

[193] https://www.laphamsquarterly.org/eros/platos-other-half
[194] Hermes Trismegistus' *The Emerald Tablet* is a short work that contains the phrase "as above, so below" meaning that as things are in the macrocosm, so they are in the microcosm or the spiritual makes the physical in its image.

Figure 76 Artemis of Ephesus, engraving Fleischer

Figure 77 Zeus Labraunda, Robert

Figure 78 Roman copy of Artemis of Ephesus

In the second century, Lucian of Samosata wrote *Dialogues of the Gods* wherein he describes the birth of Dionysus from Zeus, "[Hermes and Poseidon are conversing] 'I see,' says Poseidon, 'Another birth from the head, as with Athena? What a fertile head.' 'On the contrary,' says Hermes, 'it was his thigh this time. He had

218

Semele's baby there.' 'Incredible!' says Poseidon. 'He conceives throughout his body, wherever he wants.'"[195] Although intended to be satirical for the contemporary Roman, it illustrates this fading knowledge of the male-female ability of these ancient times.

The background to this Greek mythological scene satirized by Lucian should be noted here. Zeus would have multiple children including some with mortals. One was a Theban princess, Semele, who was the daughter of the hero Cadmus and Harmonia of Thebes. Despite being a mortal, Zeus fell for her beautiful qualities. When she became pregnant from Zeus, his wife Hera became jealous. She set out to punish Semele but, instead they became friends. Hera decided her gift would be to instill doubt in her about her affair with Zeus. Thus, the pregnant Semele came to Zeus asking him about their affair. When confirmed she asked him to grant her a wish. She wanted to see him in his full glory. But being only a mortal, when she saw the glory of Zeus she burst into flames. Zeus managed to save her unborn baby by sewing it inside his thigh.

Some months later, Dionysus was born. He would be her immortal son, a god, who would later rescue Semele from the Underworld. She now became an immortal named Thyone. One conclusion from this story is that the depictions of the gods and goddesses had, like the humans, separated by sex but were still in transition from their former androgynous times.

Ernest J. Ament, in his paper *Aspects of Androgyny in Classical Greece*,[196] describes how the Greek gods were depicted as androgynous, as both male and female during the early periods of Greek art prior to 500 BCE. He cites Nikolai A. Berdyaev with the

---

[195] Lucian, Dialogi Deorum 9
[196] Joy K. King, *Woman's Power, Man's Game: Essays on Classical Antiquity*, Bolchazy-Carducci, 1993

words, "The Fall of Man is the Fall of the androgyne." Berdyaev, in one of his essays adds, "Man, as the image and likeness of God, is an androgyne."[197] The androgyne of mankind from Adam to Seth is consistent with multiple lecture cycles from Rudolf Steiner's body of work.[198]

We've traced the ancestry of the Luke-Jesus back to Adam, or more appropriately, to Adam Kadmon. Now let's examine the other toddler. In the Gospel of Matthew, Jesus' genealogy is listed by the father-of rather than the son-of as it is recorded in Luke. Matthew listed the father-of back to Father Abraham (or Ibrahim).

Whereas Luke listed seven times eleven generations back to Adam, Matthew lists fourteen times three generations from Abraham to Jesus to represent the periods before the Babylonian captivity, during this captivity, and the period after captivity. While Luke traces through David's son, the priest Nathan, Matthew traces through David's son, the king Solomon. The table below lists several of the key differences between these two gospels.

---

[197] Nikolai Berdyaev, *La Philosophie de Jacob Boehme*. Paris. Librarie Philosophique. translator Fr. S. Janos, 1929
[198] Rudolf Steiner, (1) *The Temple Legend* GA 93, (2) *The Apocalypse of St. John* GA 104, (3) *Egyptian Myths* GA 106, and (4) *Genesis*, GA 122. SteinerBooks, 1905-1910.

	Matthew's Gospel	**Luke's Gospel**
Gospel Passage	Matthew 1:1-25	Luke 3:23-38
Theme	Kings, Magi - Star	Shepherds, Heavenly hosts
Lineage	Through King Solomon	Through Priest Nathan
Generations	42 (14x3) from Abraham	77 (7x11) from Adam
Angel speaks to	Joseph	Mary
Original home	Bethlehem	Nazareth
Slaughter of the innocents	Yes	Not mentioned
Escape to Egypt	Yes	No
John the Baptist's birth	Not mentioned	Mary visits Elizabeth
Brothers and Sisters	Yes	No
History at birth	Many lives, wisdom	Purity, no karma
Founder Assumption	Abraham / Zarathustra	Adam Kadmon

The Jesus in Matthew's story is of kingly blood and heritage. When the concept of reincarnation is integrated, this infant is the one who is bringing supreme kingly wisdom that was garnered from many incarnations as a king.

Figure 79 Awakening the Three Kings, Master Gislebertus, Cathedral of St. Lazarus, Autun, France

Historically, one of the kings who figures prominently in ancient lore as one who brought significant cultural growth with increased wisdom of the earth was the Persian Zarathustra. Rudolf Steiner cautions researchers, "Not the Zarathustra of whom history tells; he lived later. The Zarathustra I am referring to is a much more ancient teacher of mankind. In those olden times it was, you know, quite a common custom for the pupils of a great and lofty teacher to continue for a long time to bear his name; and the Zarathustra found in history is in reality the last of a succession of pupils of the great Zarathustra."[199]

Zarathustra beheld the divine being of the sun. He called him Ahura Mazdao. When one speaks of a Christianity existing before the coming of Christ, one must include Zarathustra (and Zoroaster) in this category. The Christ who was in the beginning had a home in the sun before coming to earth at the baptism. The sun being

---

[199] Rudolf Steiner, *Planetary Spheres and Their Influence on Man's Life on Earth and in the Spiritual Worlds*, 24APR1922, GA 211.

perceived by Zarathustra was the Christ. The fact that the three magi were told of the birth of their spiritual master by the stars offers further evidence of Zarathustra connection. By their ancient astrology, they came to pay homage to his rebirth. In this sense, Zarathustra and Zoroaster are the same being but in different incarnations.

Because Luke's lineage runs through Seth, the successor for Abel of the priestly line, then it is logical to examine Matthew's kingly lineage for a relationship to Cain. But Matthew traces back only to Abraham. In the story of Abraham, his kingly abilities were blessed by the high priest of Salem, Melchizedek. They share bread and wine. This scene symbolically represented Abel forgiving Cain for fratricide. The connection to Cain was deepened in the building of Solomon's Temple. Masonic traditions claim that the builder of this Temple was Hiram Abiff. In the legend of the building of this temple, Hiram Abiff is called a descendant of Cain and Tubal Cain.[200] Finally, the karmic resolution of the fratricide can take place. It was the event in Luke that took place in the Temple of Jerusalem when Jesus was lost to his parents for three and a half days. Here, the Jesus who represented Cain, the Matthew Jesus, sacrificed his physical body to join the other Jesus. Luke's Jesus offers up the body to the spiritual members of the Matthew Jesus. These two were two expected Messiahs who were to be made one. With the merger complete, their karma is fully resolved. Now the Christ can enter one human body for all of humankind.

There are fascinating details in this Masonic legend that fill out our story of Solomon's Temple. When the Queen of Sheba, Balkis, heard about Solomon she traveled to meet him. His beauty and grandeur caused them to quickly become married. Later Balkis

---

[200] Rudolf Steiner, *The Temple Legend*, lecture 18, 23Oct1905, GA 93

wished to meet the master builder of this amazing temple. On first glance, she felt a powerful passion for this man, Hiram Abiff.

Eventually, she would slip off her wedding ring for a pre-arranged rendezvous with Hiram. They would spend one night together. The next day, three apprentices who had been rejected for promotion, killed Hiram.

But Hiram had been promised during a spiritual experience, that he would be the father of a lineage that would take on a leading role in the future evolution of humanity. How could this story end without the listener hearing how this lineage will come about? Was Balkis impregnated by Hiram that one night? Rehoboam becomes king after Solomon and is listed in Matthew's lineage. But the mother of Rehoboam was Naamah the Ammonite,[201] not Balkis. Thus, the lineage promised to Hiram must not be a bloodline. When Balkis is seen as representative of the human soul, then this event would be a spiritual fertilization of the human soul.[202]

So far, we have seen that the *Virgin of the Rocks* was revealing the two Messiahs, as two Jesus children. One represented what emanated from the highest kingly line belonging to Zarathustra and the other represented the karmic purity of Adam Kadmon.

---

[201] 1 Kings 14:21: "Now Rehoboam, Solomon's son, reigned in Judah. Rehoboam was forty-one years old when he became king; he reigned seventeen years in Jerusalem, the city where the Lord had chosen from all the tribes of Israel to put his name. Rehoboam's mother's name was Naamah the Ammonite." See also 1 Kings 14:31: "Rehoboam rested with his ancestors and was buried with his ancestors in the city of David. His mother's name was Naamah the Ammonite. His son Abijam[a] became king in his place."

[202] Rudolf Steiner, *The Temple Legend*, lecture 5, 4Nov1904, "Hiram is the representative of the initiates among the Sons of Cain belonging to the fourth and fifth epochs. The Queen of Sheba is the soul of humanity — every female character denotes the soul in esoteric terminology. She has to choose between the detached piety which does not concern itself with worldly conquest, and the masterful wisdom which is achieved through the overcoming of earthly passions and desires. She is the representative of the true human soul, taking her position between Hiram and Solomon and uniting herself with Hiram in the fourth and fifth epochs, because he is still engaged in building the Temple."

Leonardo reveals their past lives in the two rock 'windows.' Through the left window which is the lower one, is seen the representation of multiple lives. Through the right and higher window is seen the single rock pillar that points us to the godly purity of the human archetype, Adam Kadmon.

Ancient Expectations of Two Messiahs

Dead Sea Scrolls

The Jewish mystical group, the Essenes, stored scrolls in caves near to their Qumran community. When Rome defeated the Jewish Revolt in 70 CE, this community was closed, and its members forced into exile. These Dead Sea Scrolls remained untouched until they were discovered in 1946-47. In these scrolls, the term "messiah" appears in their prophecies of the coming of a savior. Messiah is the Hebrew word for the anointed one.

These Dead Sea Scrolls reveal that the Essenes were expecting two Messiahs.

The Dead Sea Scrolls were discovered in 1947. More scrolls were found up through 1979 in eleven caves in and around the ancient Essene settlement of Qumran. Dating techniques determined that these Dead Sea Scrolls were being written around 150 BCE and these writings continued until the Roman army dispersed the Essenes in 70 CE, a period of 220 years. During those years, the initiates of Qumran wrote 872 scrolls in Hebrew and Aramaic. Of these two messiahs that were expected, one was to be of a priestly lineage and one of a kingly. "Its members [the Essenes of Qumran] were looking forward to a 'Messiah of Israel' and a 'Messiah of David', who resembled the priestly and kingly descendants."[203]

---

[203] http://www.livius.org/men-mh/messiah/messiah_14.html

But these scrolls contain many references to two messiahs. Sometimes the word "messiah" is expressed in the plural, sometimes in the singular. The scholar Millar Burrows claims that a later scribe who was not familiar with the idea of two Messiahs changed the plural to the singular.[204] Often the two messiahs are referred to as the "Messiahs of [the priest] Aaron and of Israel."

Dutch historian, Jona Lendering, has studied these scrolls for decades. His article in Livius[205] offers multiple examples of how "the Qumranites expected the coming of not one, but two Messiahs." One would be of a priestly lineage [Aaron] and the other a kingly [Israel] lineage. "Its members [Essenes of Qumran] were looking forward to a 'Messiah of Israel' and a 'Messiah of David' who resemble the priestly and kingly descendants."[206]

Some of the documents found among the Dead Sea Scrolls were already known to scholars before the discovery of these scrolls. For example, a copy of the *Damascus Document* had been found in Cairo in the nineteenth century.[207] Another copy of it was known to have existed in medieval times.[208] As such, it was likely that, in Renaissance Florence, Leonardo had become aware of contents of ancient texts where two messiahs were mentioned. However, even without any knowledge of the contents of the documents that later were found in the Dead Sea Scrolls, the availability of the

---

[204] Millar Burrows, *More Light on the Dead Sea Scrolls: New Scrolls and New Interpretations*, Viking Press, 1958
[205] Jona Lendering, *Qumran's dual Messianism*, http://www.livius.org/articles/religion/messiah/messiah-9-two-messiahs/, accessed 25Sept2018.
[206] http://www.livius.org/men-mh/messiah/messiah_14.html
[207] Scholars refer to this Cairo document as "CD".
[208] John Allegro, *The Dead Sea Scrolls: A Reappraisal*, Penguin Books, 1956; see also http://www.blackelectorate.com/articles.asp?ID=857

Kabbalistic books and the Old Testament supplied sufficient support for Leonardo as we shall see.

In Manuscript A, Fragment 3 of 4Q286-287, entitled *The Chariots of Glory*, contains a passage of the two Messiahs after they have been made into one. It says, "the Holy Spirit will settle upon His Messiah."[209] Compare this passage to Isaiah 11:2 "The Spirit of the Lord would settle on Him" and to John 1:32-33 "I saw the Spirit come down from heaven as a dove and remain on him. I would not have known him [his cousin] except that the one who sent me to baptize with water told me, 'The man on whom you see the Spirit come down and remain is he who will baptize with the Holy Spirit.'" This change in Jesus' entelechy at the Baptism completed the preparation made by Jesus of Nazareth for the Logos to become flesh, to become Man.

Most of the references to two messiahs in the Dead Sea scrolls are found in the *Damascus Document*. Below is a partial list from the Dead Sea scrolls where two messiahs are mentioned.

- Damascus Document 7.18-21: "And the star is the seeker of the law, who came to Damascus; as it is written A star has journeyed out of Jacob and a scepter is risen out of Israel. The scepter is the Prince of the whole congregation, and at his coming he will break down all the sons of Seth."
- Damascus Document 12.23-13.1: "during the time of ungodliness until the appearance of the Messiahs of Aaron and Israel"
- Damascus Document 19.9-11: "But others will be delivered up to the sword at the coming of the Messiah of Aaron and Israel."

---

[209] http://www.scribd.com/doc/3649853/Dead-Sea-Scrolls-Uncovered, accessed 20Jul2009, no longer available

- **Damascus Document 19:11**: "when the Messiahs come from Aaron and Israel"
- **Damascus Document 20:1**: "until there arises the Messiahs from Aaron and from Israel"
- **Messianic Rule 1Q28a 2.11-21**: "And when they gather for the community table, or to drink wine, and arrange the community table and mix the wine to drink, let no man stretch out his hand over the first-fruits of bread and wine before *the Priest* [the Messianic Priest was mentioned earlier]. For it is he who shall bless the first-fruits of bread and wine, and shall first stretch out his hand over the bread. And afterwards, the *Messiah of Israel* shall stretch out his hands over the bread. And afterwards, all the congregation of the community shall bless, each according to his rank."
- **Q266 frag. 18 col.13 line 12**
- **Manual of discipline 9.9b-11**: "... but they shall be governed by the first ordinances in which the members of the community began their instruction, until the coming of the prophet and the anointed ones of Aaron and Israel."
- **Rules of Community 9:11-14 p.13**

Much more could be written here about the Dead Sea scrolls. The reader is encouraged to discover more in the book *The Meaning of the Dead Sea Scrolls* by James VanderKam and Peter Flint.[210]

Two Messiahs in Other Sacred Texts

The *Testaments of the Twelve Patriarchs* were written in either Hebrew or Greek. Evidence from currency terms proves that it could have been written only between 330 and 150 BC. The book reached its final form in the second century CE. It was translated

---

[210] James VanderKam and Peter Flint, *The Meaning of the Dead Sea Scrolls: Their Significance For Understanding the Bible, Judaism, Jesus, and Christianity*, HarperCollins, 2013

into Latin in the thirteenth century by Robert Grosseteste, Bishop of Lincoln, whose translation became very popular in Leonardo's time. Renaissance scholars believed the book to be a genuine sacred text.

The book contains this passage, "My children, be obedient to Levi and to Judah. Do not exalt yourselves about these two tribes because from them will arise the Savior from God. For the Lord will raise up from Levi someone as a high-priest and from Judah someone as king. He will save all the gentiles and the tribe of Israel."[211]

Commenting on this passage, Hippolytus of Rome (170 – 235 CE), in his book *On the Benedictions of Isaac, Jacob and Moses*, wrote, "For we have found it written that the Christ must also appear from the tribe of Levi, as a priest of the Father, from a commingling of the tribe of Judah with the tribe of Levi, so that the Son of God should be made known from both as King and as Priest."

Modern scholars continue to publish their analysis of "the parallels in the Testaments to the doctrine of the two Messiahs, a priestly and a royal one, which is found in the Qumran documents."[212]

Kabbalistic Roots: Zohar

Ample evidence of knowledge of this theme is found in the Zohar of the Jewish Kabalistic traditions. The Zohar is a group of books describing the mystical aspects of the Torah. It includes scriptural interpretations as well as material on mysticism and mythical cosmogony. They form the foundation for Jewish Kabbalistic traditions. The Zohar first appeared in Spain in the thirteenth century. Within fifty years it was being quoted by many kabbalists,

---

[211] *Testaments of the Twelve Patriarchs, Testament of Simeon, 7.1-2*
[212] Marinus de Jonge, *Jewish eschatology, early Christian Christology and the Testaments of the twelve Patriarchs*, Brill, 2014

including the early fourteenth century Italian writer Menahem Recanati whose mystical work includes Perush 'Al ha-Torah (published in Venice in 1523). Hand written copies of the Zohar may have been available to Leonardo.

Of particular interest to us in the Zohar is this passage, "Another Messiah, the son of Joseph, will unite himself with the Messiah, the son of David. But the son of Joseph will not remain in life, he will be killed and will become alive again, when the little hill receives life upon the great hill."[213] This passage indicates that the son of King David will unite with the son of Joseph and the son of Joseph will remain in life for a while. But this son of Joseph will be the one who is killed. After death, he will become alive again. This story sounds remarkably alike to the story of the merging of two Jesus boys into the Luke-Jesus's body which will later be crucified and then resurrected. In this interpretation, the Messiah is a human being into whom the spirit of Christ descends.

Old Testament Prophecies

The prophecies from the books included in the Old Testament are slightly more ambiguous but they too speak of the two who will become one. The following passages could be interpreted as an anticipation of two Messiahs. "NIV" stands for New International Version.

Zechariah 4:14: "So he said, 'These are the two [the priest Joshua and the 'king' Zerubbabel] who are anointed to serve the Lord of all the earth.'" [NIV]

---

[213] Arthur Edward Waite, *Holy Kabbala*, Kessinger Publishing, 2003

Zechariah 6.11: Two crowns are mentioned, one placed on the head of Zerubbabel as a kind of king, the other upon the priest Joshua.

Zechariah 6.12-13: Concerning how the high-priest Joshua was crowned and ruled jointly with the governor Zerubbabel, God ordered the prophet Zechariah to say, "Here is the man whose name is the Branch, and he will branch out from his place and *build the temple* of the Lord. It is he who will build the temple of the Lord, and he will be clothed with *majesty* and will sit and rule on his throne. And there will be a *priest* on his throne. And there will be *harmony between the two*." [my emphasis using italics] Note the reference to (re-)building Solomon's temple.

Numbers 24:17: ""I see him, but not now; I behold him, but not near. A star will come out of Jacob; a scepter will rise out of Israel." [NIV] This passage suggests that the Messiah would have sources from the pure beginnings of Man (the star out of Jacob) and from the heights of what Man had accomplished, that is, from the kingly side (the scepter out of Israel).

Ezekiel 37:15-17: "The word of the Lord came to me: "Son of man, take a stick of wood and write on it, 'Belonging to Judah and the Israelites associated with him.' Then take another stick of wood, and write on it, 'Belonging to Joseph (that is, to Ephraim) and all the Israelites associated with him.' Join them together into one stick so that *they will become one* in your hand." [NIV, my emphasis using italics.] This passage implies that two branches (sticks) will become one in the Messiah. Unlike Abraham from whom came many nations, Jesus reverses the process of creating new branches to begin the process of fusion, of uniting all of humanity.

Summary

Jewish prophets were expecting two messiahs to be born, one from a priestly lineage and one kingly. These writings spoke of a later merging, and a time when a holy spirit would settle upon the merged body. Princeton professor James Charlesworth concludes in an article, "Over forty years of labor on over three hundred scrolls and fragments and archaeologic work on Khirbet Qumran and the Qumran caves have produced ... They [the Qumran Community] held firmly to the belief that God would soon vindicate them by sending one or, most likely, two Messiahs."[214]

John's Book of Revelations also makes references to the kingly and priestly aspects in his first chapter, "and has made us to be a *king*dom and *priests* to his God and Father."[215]

Applying Our Insights

With this background, we can now return to the centerpiece of our study: the two paintings called the *Virgin of the Rocks*.

Stage Curtains

It was no accident that all three hands are framed by the sleeve of the supposed Madonna in the original *Virgin of the Rocks*. Leonardo uses this sleeve like theater curtains to point our eyes to the action of the painting.

In the copy, the archangel's pointing hand is no longer involved in the action; rather, it lays limp in front of her. The archangel's gaze is no longer beholding the reflection in the pool but now dreamily looks across the scene perhaps to the other infant.

---

[214] James Charlesworth, *Jesus and the Dead Sea Scrolls*, Yale University Press, 1992, p.144
[215] Revelations 1:6

Figure 80 Sleeve as Stage Curtains, VoR National Gallery and VoR, Louvre

In the original, the right hand of the central figure is drawing forth from the infant beside her while with her left-hand, she guides what she has drawn forth into place in the constitution of the infant whose hand touches the mineral kingdom, the rock. Of course, this scene is a foreshadowing of what will happen when the receiving child on our right becomes twelve years old.

John's Staff

In this closeup, we can clearly see that the iconic staff of John the Baptist and his halo were 'applied and artistically fitted' after the varnishing of the painting by Ambrogio de Predi.

This retrofit strongly indicates that the painting on the left is the copy and this retrofit was done to render the composition into one that was theologically acceptable to the client, the Confraternity.

Figure 81 Close-up: Child with Staff, Same child from Virgin of the Rocks Paris

The Details

Geologist and Renaissance art historian, Ann Pizzorusso, points out the botanical accuracy on the original (right) while the copy (left) has multiple botanical flaws. For example, the flower bundle on the lower left sometimes have five and sometimes six petals. Such a mistake Leonardo would never have made![216]

Ann Pizzorusso adds to scientific and artistic grandeur of the Louvre's version with the analysis, "The Louvre version is a geological tour-de-force, she says, a complex landscape in which each rock formation can be identified: 'To the right of the virgin's head is weathered sandstone, and above it is a contact surface with a strata of diabase and above that is spheroidal sandstone.' In the London version, she says, the rocks are unrealistic. The artist — whoever that was — lacked both technique and appreciation for

---

[216] https://www.theguardian.com/artanddesign/2014/dec/09/leonardo-da-vinci-virgin-rocks-louvre-national-gallery

geology. 'The rocks are all angular and blocky, with no distinctive texture.'

She notes that the Louvre version positions plants where they would grow naturally: 'At the top of the grotto, the sandstone would have decomposed sufficiently to allow roots to take hold.' No plants grow out of the diabase, because it's too hard and resistant to erosion to allow growth."[217]

Participation of Florentine Artists

Although a generation later than Leonardo, this painting probes us to ask whether or not Raphael had knowledge of the two Jesus children. His Madonna Terranuova, painted in 1505, shows two holy children with a Madonna and the infant John the Baptist.

---

[217] IBID

Figure 82 Madonna Terranuova, Raphael, c.1505

From whence came his knowledge? Perhaps the theological basis was still being discussed within academic circles of Florence even after Leonardo relocated to Milan in 1482. Or perhaps Raphael's training had connections to Leonardo during which such a topic may have arisen. In any case, Raphael's Madonna Terranuova certainly reveals both Jesus boys along with the infant John the Baptist. Here, the child in the Madonna's lap would be from Luke's gospel while the royal gold robe of the toddler on the right reveals this is the kingly Jesus from Matthew's gospel.

Lombard Artists' Participation

After Leonardo moved to Milan in 1483 and set up his Academy, we found plenty of evidence that his students there were aware of this mystery. But did other artists in the Lombard area also become acquainted with this birth mystery? With the reach of the Inquisition, it seems unlikely that Leonardo would allow for discussions to ensue outside of the Academy.

Figure 83 Madonna with Kissing Babes, Martino Piazza, Museum of Fine Arts (Budapest)

But perhaps Martino Piazza (1475/80 - 1523 aka Martino de' Toccagni) was somewhat aware. Very little is known about him save that he worked mostly in Lodi, Lombardy from where he probably became acquainted with Leonardo and his work. Likely he traveled to experience trainings that took place in Leonardo's Milan Academy. This Madonna shows that Piazza was aware of use of the *Holy Infants Embracing* theme by students who placed the theme within their Madonna painting. Even the hand gestures of Piazza's Madonna resemble those of the central figure of *Virgin of the Rocks* but here the children are reversed rendering the drawing and bestowing direction to be incorrect according to the conclusion reached in this book.

Clearly, we cannot conclude from this painting alone that these two boys represent the two Jesus children. However, when one adds to this another Piazza painting of *John the Baptist*, then its reference to the *Virgin of the Rocks* becomes obvious.

Note the similarity of this scene to that of the original *Virgin of the Rocks*. Two "windows" are depicted with the right one higher than the left. Even the plank-like rock at a 45-degree angle in the higher window appears here proving Martino was quite aware of the *Virgin of the Rocks*.

Saint John, as a young man, is about to take a drink from the waters of the same reflecting pool in front of which the infants had been placed by Leonardo. John is kneeling but his position has the right and left legs reversed from that of the Jesus child in *Virgin of the Rocks*.

Figure 84 Saint John the Baptist In the Desert, Martino Piazza, National Gallery, London

Here the rock types have also been reversed! In *Virgin of the Rocks*, the flat, horizontal rocks were in the foreground, while the upright rock pillars were in the background. This seems to be deliberate. Why would Martino have copied the *Virgin of the Rocks* scene for his painting other than to show he too was a part of this revelation? The deliberate reversals support our conclusion. It tells us that John was not part of the scene in the original; he comes later to these waters when he takes up his mission to be the

Baptist and the Witness.[218] The artist may be portraying the mystery of that which was last will later be first.[219]

Did Eastern Christianity Know of These Two Children?

This book has suggested that Leonardo's understanding of the mystery of the two Jesus boys came to Florence from the Byzantine empire just before the fall of Constantinople. It may also have arrived via the Cathars or even the Knights Templar. In any case, the question, did others of Christianity's East ever reveal this mystery? An answer to this question can be found in Kiev's Khanenko Museum of Art.

Figure 85 The Bohdan And Varvara Khanenko Museum of Art, Kiev

Here the two teen-age Jesus boys each have a halo. Between them, also in a halo that merges with the other two, is the Christ. Each boy carries a cross because both will be participating in this event. Note that each ornamentation around their necks has three jewels

---

[218] John 1:7 [NIV], "He came as a witness to testify concerning that light"
[219] Matthew 20:16, "So the last will be first, and the first will be last."

reminiscent of the three key hand gestures in the original *Virgin of the Rocks*.

The Archangel

The National Gallery has correctly identified the second feminine figure in *Virgin of the Rocks* as an archangel. She is sometimes identified merely as an angel. When that is done, the designation is to mean any heavenly spiritual being. This book has distinguished between heavenly beings according to the nine names and descriptions given to each of the levels of the heavenly hierarchy as defined by Dionysius the Areopagite.[220]

The National Gallery identified her as the archangel Uriel. By so naming her, they attempted to solidify their claim that the child on the left is John the Baptist because Uriel is the archangel of the summer season.[221] John's birthday had been established by the year 500 as being on the summer solstice which, by the sixth century, was set on June 24th.

This birthdate, according to Luke's gospel had to be six months before the birth of Luke's Jesus. To those in the fourth or fifth century who set these dates, placing these birthdays on the solstices made good cosmic sense. Perhaps, as surmised by historians, placing these on top of existing pagan festivals could more easily win over the masses.

The winter solstice of December 25th thus became the birthdate for the Jesus of Luke's gospel with the summer solstice of June 24th as

---

[220] *Dionysius the Areopagite, Works* (1899) vol. 2. p.1-66. The Celestial Hierarchy, translation by Roger Pearse, Ipswich, UK, 2004, see
http://www.tertullian.org/fathers/areopagite_13_heavenly_hierarchy.htm accessed 5June2018

[221] The other seasons are: autumn – Michael, winter – Gabriel, and spring - Raphael

the date to celebrate John the Baptist's birth. Calendar reform in 1582 moved both solstices to the 21st but these two nativities remained on the 24th and 25th respectively.[222]

According to Luke's gospel, the nativity of John the Baptist was three months after the celebration of Gabriel's Annunciation to Mary. Thus, the Annunciation festival was set for March 25th (before calendar reform, this was the day of the vernal equinox). Archangel Gabriel also told Mary that her cousin Elizabeth was already six months pregnant. Cycling backwards, we arrive at the conception of John on the autumn equinox which was September 25 before calendar reform (now the autumnal equinox is September 22).

Figure 86 Comparing Gabriel's Annunciation, Leonardo da Vinci, Uffizi to Archangel VoR, LdV, Louvre

While still a young lad in training in Verrocchio's studio, Leonardo painted an Annunciation. Figure 86 shows a kneeling archangel Gabriel holding her hand in the blessing gesture. Note the color of

---

[222] https://en.wikipedia.org/wiki/Nativity_of_Saint_John_the_Baptist

her robes, the white lily in her left hand, a sign of purity, and her fixed gaze. She has a radiating halo very similar to Defendente Ferrari's *Jesus Among the Doctors* (figure 64).

In *Virgin of the Rocks* (right), the archangel is quite similar but not identical. Her right hand no longer expresses the blessing gesture, as that now belongs to the right hand of the Luke-Jesus, but it is pointing one finger. Instead of the symbol of purity, the white lily, her left hand has the karmically pure Luke-Jesus who is the incarnation of Adam Kadmon.

What is it that the archangel will source from the far child and place into this child beside her? Her left hand touches the body of the infant beside her indicating that her action will bestow a member that is closer to the physical body. This indicates that she will transfer the spiritualized life body from the Matthew-Jesus' prana (or chi) that has been purified. The red and green colors of the robes of the archangels are similar. These garments are indicative of the life body.

Are these the same archangel? Would archangels be significantly different to Renaissance painters? Perhaps she is Gabriel,[223] the archangel used for announcements. If an archangel, perhaps she is depicted here as the one to announce what will happen for the infant beside her when he becomes twelve?

Conclusion
Depicted in the original version of *Virgin of the Rocks* were the two Messiahs expected in prophetic writings by the Essenes and others.

---

[223] I had gender difficulty here. Gabriel is a masculine name as is the name for the other well-know archangels: Raphael, Uriel, and Michael. But angels and archangels are commonly referred to with the feminine pronoun.

These Messiahs were the two Jesus boys separately described in the books of Luke and Matthew.

Leonardo depicted on the right side an infant whose karma was untarnished-by-the-Fall. This purity of Adam was described in Luke's gospel. On the left, kneeling in honor to the original Adam was depicted the kingly Jesus whose lineage began with Abraham, continued through David, and then through King Solomon as described in Matthew's gospel.

As foretold in the Kabbala and the Dead Sea Scrolls, this kingly Messiah was destined to unite with the priestly Messiah later in life to complete preparations for the descent of the Holy Spirit into this body. This theology that became labeled as heretical, placed the birth of Christ at the baptism. During the ensuing three years, the Christ would penetrate the members of this constitution. By the time of Golgotha, the Christ had permeated all of these members. God had become Man and now could die so that the Son of Man could arise from Death.

Leonardo, through his participation in the Platonic Academy of Florence, had likely become familiar with such heresies. Teachers such as Ficino and Argyropoulos, plus the successors to George Gemistus Plethon, knew of the concept of reincarnation through Plato and other Greek philosophers. Even the secretive schools left over from the Cathars or the Knights Templar, likely had similar mystical wisdom that had flowed into Leonardo's mind and hence into his art.

Likely Leonardo found it unacceptable that fifteenth and sixteenth century Christianity clung to dogmas while potentially greater understandings of the Christ were brutally suppressed. With the spirit of the Renaissance in his blood, Leonardo likely sought such wisdom. And, once found, he wove it into his art.

In the theology the Gnostics and other heretical sects, Christ did not enter Jesus until the baptism when the Holy Spirit descended to remain upon Jesus' bodily organization. Ancient writings of the Gnostics such as the *Pistis Sophia* indicate a knowledge the two Messiahs was known. Was this why Leonardo and his students used it as the theme for so many paintings?

What happened in the temple over those three days described in Luke's gospel when Jesus, at twelve years of age, was alone in Jerusalem? One explanation came from Rudolf Steiner (1861 – 1925) whose research showed that the "I" of Jesus, his human ego, transferred from the Jesus of the Matthew story to enter the Luke-Jesus when this boy was twelve. This was accomplished in the Holy of the Holies within the Temple in Jerusalem. Then, at the baptism at age thirty, the Holy Spirit united with the constitution of Jesus so that God could become Man. The name Christ-Jesus reflects this combined constitution.

After the Roman perspective of Christianity had been established by Constantine, the so-called heresies were purged with Roman military might. With Emperor Justinian, the heretics were purged and their books destroyed so that all their thoughts were rooted out of Christendom.

But not all books could be destroyed. And not all of the heretics could be rounded up and slaughtered. Some escaped. Some went into exile. And many traveled east. Some would carry on oral traditions. Some would write books while in eastern exile.

Inspired by Byzantine teachers such as Manuel Chrysolorus and Gemistus Plethon, Italian libraries sent buyers to the east seeking such books. These texts eventually found their way in the early days of the Renaissance to Florence and Venice.

Although the Human was described by St. Paul as being of body, soul, and spirit, over time the Human was reduced to only body and soul. At the Eighth Ecumenical Council in Constantinople, the bishops decreed that the eternal quality of spirit must not yet be present in the human. They reasoned that this was a reward that was to come only on Judgment Day and only to the righteous. Spirit is already eternal. Thus, if the human already had a spirit, then reincarnation must also be accepted.

In our time, a thousand years after Religion removed the spirit, it has become a form of scientific heresy for a learned person to speak about soul as a reality. Thus, today the concept of the Human has been reduced to physical body alone. We need today a new Renaissance, a Renaissance 2.0.

With the concepts of soul and spirit missing today, it should be no wonder that it has become so difficult to see what this painting depicts! Leonardo would rail against the tyrannies today as he did against the dogmas of his Renaissance.

What Did the Symbols Tell Us?
In the foreground of the original is a reflecting pool that is symbolic of the Hermes Trismegistus philosophy "as above, so below" where the macrocosm is to found in the microcosm (the human) and vice versa. If we see these four beings in the painting as beings depicted as both in the spirit and in the physical, then the placement of the pool just below the child's hand (which represents the physical) indicates that the Spirit can view the physical in its reflection in the water. Water represents the life forces, the prana or chi. It appears that the archangel is gazing over the child on the right into this reflecting pool.

Two Messiahs, Two Jesus Boys, A Priest and a King
Why were there two? Was it somehow necessary? Read carefully about the ascending lineage of Luke and the descending lineage of

Matthew. Luke traced from a Jesus child back through Nathan, the *priest*, all the way to Adam. Matthew began with Abraham and followed the fathers through Solomon, the *king*, until he got to "Jacob begot Joseph, the husband of Mary, of whom was born Jesus." Matthew's story is about kingship and the royal bloodline. Luke traced back through Seth to Adam or rather to Adam Kadmon who was born of God. These two stories, one about a king and one about a priest, aligned with the expectations of two messiahs, one kingly and one priestly. These were mentioned in numerous ancient texts.

Due to Leonardo's sense of privacy and to the continued power of the heresy hunters, it is unlikely that one can find self-incriminating "hard proof" that Leonardo da Vinci was attempting to display an understanding of a theme of two messiahs. Had Leonardo belonged to a secret society where such views were discussed, their membership and their knowledge would have been kept secret. But, through the works of his students, what was written in the Old Testament (e.g. *Ezekiel* chapter 37), and mentioned in the Zohar, and was to be found in the Dead Sea Scrolls, can be seen as revealed in the paintings by those of Leonardo's school.

In the original version of *Virgin of the Rocks*, it is this author's conclusion that Leonardo da Vinci was portraying not only the two messiahs but also his understanding of how these two would be resolved into one person. Because of this heretical portrayal in the original, it likely was rejected by the Confraternity necessitating a second painting more acceptable to contemporary theology. In order for Leonardo and his partner, Ambrogio de Predi to be paid and for the original to be returned, an acceptable copy had to be painted. Safe from the Inquisition and inspired by these Mysteries, several of Leonardo's pupils depicted supporting scenes, yet scenes that still could be explained according to contemporary theology.

Through the participation of his students, we can easily see now the depiction of a grand mystery worthy of the entry of a cosmic Christ into earthly evolution.

6. The Emergence of a Mystery

What We've Covered

We began our journey by tracing the history of at least two paintings known as the *Virgin of the Rocks*. This history led us to conclude that the painting at the Louvre was the original and why. We found the history of these paintings to be intimately connected with Leonardo's own life story. We then tied it all together with the history of Christianity (in the west) in order to understand not only Leonardo's disposition towards the Church of his day but also to his motivation for this painting.

We came to appreciate the struggles of a truly great pioneer who had abundant knowledge that he wanted to bring to mankind. But he was fenced in by the Inquisition. He used his privilege as a master who was revered by the powerful to reveal this so-called heretical wisdom from Early Christianity through his art.

We found that in the original painting of *Virgin of the Rocks*, he depicted two innocent infants. Each one represented one of the two original spiritual streams of humanity. These infants, we concluded, depicted the separate Jesus infants from the Gospels of Luke and Matthew.

Then, through his students, Leonardo explained how these two streams merged when these boys were about to enter puberty. The remarkable work by Pinturicchio fully illustrated those involved in the sacred act that merged the two boys within the Temple in Jerusalem.

We speculated that these two streams that were merged represented the Cain and Abel streams. A free-willed sacrifice by each boy but especially by the Matthew Jesus, solved the human karmic debt from the fratricide of the Cain stream. With this resolved, then the Christ, at the baptism, could enter into Jesus of Nazareth who now represented the one stream of humanity.

With the expectation of two Messiahs, one a priest and one a king, must have flowed into the knowledge of these two births. Gnosticism placed the birth of Christ at the baptism. This knowledge was present in Early Christianity. But the theological emphasis of Early Christianity was not on the birth but on the resurrection. Much of this knowledge was essentially lost by the fourth century as human consciousness changed. Christmas was first celebrated in Rome in 321 CE but not in the Roman empire until midcentury.[224] With Roman authority, other Christianties became heresies.

In this context, giving the name *Christ* Child for the infant portrayed in Renaissance Madonna paintings would be incorrect. To many Early Christians, Christ's 'birth' happened at the baptism when Jesus of Nazareth was thirty years old. The spiritual being called Christ would take on this body for his three years on the physical earth. During those three years, this God would become a man and go through death which had become part of human life since the Fall.

Leonardo, through what he learned at the Platonic Academy and other institutions in Florence, gave new life to this lost wisdom that had long been declared a heresy. Leonardo was, therefore, the hidden heretic of the Renaissance reviving Knowledge to its former prominence.

Bernardino de Conti's painting, *Three Holy Children*, was shown to provide convincing proof that neither boy in *Virgin of the Rocks* can

---

[224] William Abruzzi, *in The Date of Jesus' Birth*, lists 321 as the start of when Christmas was celebrated in Rome.

be John the Baptist! De Conti painted the same two boys as seen in *Virgin of the Rocks* and he placed John the Baptist between the boys to prove that neither of them could be considered to be John the Baptist.

Figure 87 Comparison of Virgin of the Rocks, LdV and Three Holy Children, B.de Conti

Understanding Why Leonardo Choose Two Infants

Leonardo was a very patient painter. He went to pains to portray faces and gestures in the right way. He struggled with Judas in his *Last Supper*. Apparently, when pressured by the head of the monastery why he wasn't finishing his work, he described the difficulty in finding a suitable model for Judas. When further pressured to finish, he retorted to the prior that perhaps he would select the prior as the model for Judas if he continued to push with such impatience.

Obviously, when Leonardo painted *Virgin of the Rocks,* he was aware of Matthew's gospel that advised, "Unless you change and become like little children, you will never enter the kingdom of heaven."[225] By virtue of being freshly arrived from the spirit realm,

---

[225] Matthew 18:3, NIV

children represent an uncorrupted, divine nature on earth. Out of a divine world they have come full of innocence.

This book showed that these two children represent, spiritually, the streams of Cain and Abel. To depict them, Leonardo used toddlers who could stand on the earth yet retained their heavenly nature. Toddlers symbolically represented the early stages of human development when Cain and Abel walked on the earth.

Cain's stream flows into Matthew's story about kings while Abel's stream appears in Luke's story of heavenly hosts and shepherds. Cain dug into the earth while Abel was a shepherd.

The following table shows the differences in the two gospel stories.

	Luke	Matthew
Home of Parents	Nazareth 1:26, 2:39	Bethlehem 2:1, 2:23
Genealogy from David	From Eli … from Nathan 3:23-31	To Solomon … to Jacob 1:6-16
Bloodline source	Adam (Kadmon) from God 3:38	Abraham 1:2
Annunciation	Archangel Gabriel to Mary 1:26-38	"Angel of the Lord" to Joseph 1:18-25
Angel speaks to	Mary 1:26-38	Joseph 1:18-23, 2:13, 2:19, 2:22
Visit to Elizabeth	Described 1:39-45	Not described
Birth of John the Baptist	Described 1:57-66	Not described
Parents of John the Baptist	Zacarias & Elizabeth 1:5-25	Not described
Song of Mary	Described 1:46-55	Not described
Song of Zacarias	Described 1:67-79	Not described
Census	Cause of travel 2:1-5	Not described
Birth location	Stable 2:7	Home 2:11
Who visits	Shepherds 2:8-20	Three Magi 2:1-12
Guide to visitors	Heavenly hosts 2:8-20	[Astrological] "Star" 2:9
Following the birth	Circumcision 2:22-24	Escape to Egypt 2:13-15
Temple prophecy by	Simon & Anna 2:25-38	Not described
Slaughter of the Innocents	None – family returns to Nazareth	All boys <2 years 2:16-17

It should be noted that the other two gospels begin with the 'birth' of Christ into the body of Jesus of Nazareth! It was believed by some of these Early Christians that a divine being, especially the Christ, could not enter a body that was corrupt with matter nor into one that had unresolved sin or karma built into its flesh. But the Logos had to become flesh.[226]

The Two Streams of Humanity
Because Cain's fratricide was a human act, another human act was needed to compensate for that sin. Only after that sin had been compensated, could the Christ enter a purified, sin-free body. This is what was meant in the prophetic words, "and the Two became One." The merger of the priest Abel and king Cain was the merger of the two that Leonardo's students depicted.

The Jesus boy on the left in *Virgin of the Rocks* would sacrifice his body and resume his life in the body of the other Jesus whose lineage Luke traced all the way back to the pure Adam from before the Fall. This had to happen before the baptism when the Christ spirit would be witnessed by John the Baptist as descending to and remaining upon this unified and purified body of Jesus of Nazareth.

Christ could then compensate for the original sin, that is the sin caused by the act of a divine being, namely Lucifer. If not for Lucifer's temptation, the Fall would not have happened. This act involved a being higher than humans; it was enacted by Lucifer. It thereby needed a higher being, a divine being, to compensate for it.

At the baptism, Christ entered a human body. It took three years for Christ to work upon this body before he could say "the hour has

---

[226] John 1:14, And the Logos became flesh and dwelt among us.

now come for the *Son of Man* to be glorified."[227] We can now understand this concept of the "Son of Man" as something new that comes as offspring of the purified soul. This was foretold in the Mythological stories such as that of Horace in the myths of Osiris and Isis.

Because Christ was born in one human, namely Jesus of Nazareth, then the Cathars as well as other heretical groups claimed that Christ can be born in anyone. Many Christian mystics spoke similarly. Angelus Silesius (1624 – 1677), a German mystic, wrote "If Christ were born in Bethlehem a thousand times and not in thee thyself; then art thou lost eternally."[228]

This gives an image of the fullness of what Leonardo was depicting in his original *Virgin of the Rocks* painting.

On the Mystery of the Two Children

We have explored Leonardo's depiction of the two children in *Virgin of the Rocks* as the Jesus from Matthew's gospel and the Jesus from Luke's gospel. With the concept of reincarnation, can this be explored any deeper? We saw in the rock formations through the two "windows" that the Jesus from Matthew had many pillars next to his river while the "window" corresponding to the Jesus from Luke had but one pillar. This pointed to many prior incarnations for the Matthew-Jesus while only one for the Luke-Jesus.

The discussion of the Mithraic Mysteries and their own stated connection to Zoroaster gives us a possible lead. The three magi that come to visit the baby boy also indicate the astrology of

---

[227] John 12:23
[228] Angelus Silesius (1624 – 1677), German mystic, https://www.goodreads.com/author/show/2045255.Angelus_Silesius, accessed 25July2018

Zoroaster as it flowed into Mithraism. The coming of the Cosmic Christ from the realm of the Sun was central to the Mithraic mysteries. With the concept of reincarnation, one might trace Zoroaster to the original Zarathustra.[229]

Luke's gospel traces its Jesus back to Adam before the Fall. We've shown that in Kabbalistic traditions, this before-the-Fall Adam is denoted by the name Adam Kadmon. Such a human would have been the archetype of what the Elohim had intended when they created Man. After the Fall, Adam had to change. The degradation of their post-Fall bodies caused shame as they took on such base elements as earth. Humanity had to change after eating from the Tree of Knowledge. It meant separation from the only world they had known, the spiritual world. The Adam of Luke goes back to the human archetype that was embodied in the Luke-Jesus.

In these two infants of *Virgin of the Rocks* are representatives of not only the two streams of Cain and Abel but also of the earthly (Matthew) and the heavenly (Luke). The Matthew-Jesus was full of earthly wisdom attained from multiple kingly incarnations. The Luke-Jesus might have been considered to be an odd child, a slow learner of earthly knowledge but one who showed great capacities for love.

This story of two Jesus children aligns with the two Messiahs expected by the Essenes. And this expectation was also described in other prophetic writings. The Quran mentions two different Annunciations. In both instances Mary (Maryam) is told that she was chosen by God to deliver a son. The first Annunciation is by the

---

[229] Rudolf Steiner, *From Jesus to Christ*, lecture 8, 12Oct1911, Karlsruhe, GA 131. The name, Zarathustra belonged to the original Zarathustra. The next head of his school would have used the same name. Zoroaster could be a later incarnation of Zarathustra.

archangel Gabriel (3:42-47). The second Annunciation is by an angel who takes the form of a man well-proportioned [in body, soul, and spirit] (19:16-22).[230] Most believe this also to have been the archangel Gabriel in both cases.[231]

Then, at age twelve, a dramatic change happened for the Luke-Jesus when the two boys went through an experience similar to an initiation. During an initiation, what is soul-spiritual in one, leaves the physical body. To an outsider, the neophyte appears to be dead. Yet, their consciousness is not dead; it is similar to dreamless sleep, only one remains fully conscious while outside one's body. One's perceptions are no longer from the physical senses but now from spiritual senses known as chakras in Indian lore. While the boys were outside their physical body, they could exchange their spiritual entities so that upon return, the spiritual entities belonging to the Matthew Jesus could enter the physical body that had belonged to the Luke Jesus. Thus, they fulfilled the prophecy of the "two becoming one." They were merged so that the height of human culture and wisdom that had resided in the Matthew-Jesus could now work on in the body of Jesus of Nazareth. What had been the physical Matthew-Jesus no longer had a purpose and so it faded, became ill, and died within a year.[232]

In the original version of *Virgin of the Rocks* as well as in *Holy Infants Embracing*, Leonardo da Vinci portrayed the babes from the priestly and from the kingly lineages. In *Virgin of the Rocks,* Leonardo depicted on the right-side, the priestly Messiah, the purity of Adam, untarnished by the Fall, as the Jesus of Luke's gospel. On the left, he portrayed the Jesus whose kingly lineage

---

[230] See https://quran.com/19/16-22
[231] For more depth, see Oddbjørn Leirvik, *Images of Jesus Christ in Islam*: 2nd Edition, Bloomsbury Publishing, 2010
[232] IBID

from David through Solomon is described in Matthew's gospel. As foretold in the Kabbala, these two united later in life.

Through his students, Leonardo spoke of how these two would be resolved into one person. It is likely that the Confraternity of the Immaculate Conception rejected the original for theological reasons. If Leonardo and his poor partner Ambrogio were to be paid, a second painting was needed, one that would be more acceptable to contemporary theology.

Knowledge of various heretical traditions arrived in Florence with the Byzantine envoys and texts. Many of these theologies had lent themselves to the concept of reincarnation. Such heresies saw the human as comprised of body, soul, and spirit. The human spirit, the ego, that was in the Jesus of the Matthew story, entered the Luke Jesus at age twelve. Later, at the Baptism at age thirty, the Logos descended and remained upon Jesus of Nazareth whose ego sacrificed his body to the Christ spirit so that God could become Man.

Before God could enter the body of a Man, a special body had to be prepared; that is, a body with human and earthly wisdom and, at the same time, no unresolved karma.[233] The merging of the two Jesus boys, a human act, was a true sacrifice, that brought great wisdom attainable from many incarnations together with a human body free of karma. Thus, could the Christ enter the stream of humanity. This is embedded in the mystery behind the *Virgin of the Rocks*.

---

[233] Resolution of the karma of Cain's fratricide can be seen as having taken place via the merging of the two Jesus boys in the Temple of Jerusalem. As Abel was a shepherd, so shepherds came to witness the birth of Jesus in Luke while Cain's story comes in the three magi of Matthew, making this case would take another book.

Leonardo had likely become familiar with these concepts through the schools of Florence. But out of concerns about the Inquisition, Leonardo had to keep such thoughts secret. He spoke therefore through his remarkable skill as a painter.

Resolving the Archangel and Central Figure
Leonardo abhorred the chains of dogma. He felt his soul had experienced divine wisdom, the divine goddess Sophia herself. He had drunk from this fountain and such wisdom should not be held within like a dragon hoarding over its treasures. Thus, comes the conclusion that in the central figure of *Virgin of the Rocks*, Leonard was likely depicting Sophia.

The Goddess of Wisdom in Greek mythology is Sophia and Isis in Egyptian mythology. In the Egyptian myth, Osiris is the representative of the spiritual sun. He is killed by Set (aka Typhon who is Satan in Christianity and Ahriman in Persian lore. Set kills Osiris. Set throws him into the Nile which carries the body away. Isis searches for his body and finds it in Asia. She brings his body back to Egypt. Now Set cuts the body into fourteen parts. Isis buries these fourteen parts in various locations, so that they will belong to the earth for ever after.

Egyptian mystical wisdom "conceived of the connection between the powers of heaven and the powers of earth in a deeply meaningful way. On the one hand, Osiris is the representative of the powers of the sun. After having passed through death he is, in various places and simultaneously, the force that ripens everything that grows out of the earth. The ancient Egyptian sage imagines in a spirit-filled way how the powers which shine down from the sun, enter the earth and then become part of the earth, and how, as powers of the sun buried in the earth, they then hand over to the human being what matures out of the earth. The Egyptian myth is founded upon the story of Osiris — how he was killed, how his spouse Isis had to set out on her search for him, how she first brought him back to Egypt and how he then became active in another form, namely, from out of the earth."[234]

This Goddess of Wisdom, assisted by an archangel, bestowed the wisdom of the world to the Jesus of Luke's gospel when he was twelve. This wisdom had been developed and carried through many incarnations by the being who was born as the Jesus in Matthew's gospel. Of the four possible archangels of the four seasons: Uriel, Michael, Gabriel, and Raphael,[235] a strong case for each can be made. I was unable to reach a satisfactory conclusion about the archangel. I suspect that the presence of an archangel means that more than a guardian angel would be needed for the future merging of these two. An angel's capabilities are limited to guiding an individual. For a merging, it would take an archangel. Perhaps one day a student of this work will be able to say with certainty who this archangel is! For now, she remains a mystery.

Renaissance 2.0

With the words "To develop a complete mind: Study the science of art; Study the art of science. Learn how to see. Realize that everything connects to everything else"[236] Leonardo set the goal for the first Renaissance. Today we live in a time that calls for a new renaissance not only of knowledge but also of morality. As

---

[234] Rudolf Steiner, *Search for the New Isis, the Divine Sophia*, 24Dec1920, GA 202, Anthroposophic Press, 1988

[235] In the Dionysian model, a group of four archangels rotate leadership of the seasons. Another group of seven, which include these four, rotate leadership of cultural periods. These cultural periods last about 310 to 350 years. All seven would lead one period during the time it takes the sun to traverse a zodiac sign (about 2160 years).

[236] https://www.goodreads.com/quotes/1423493-to-develop-a-complete-mind-study-the-science-of-art

Gus Speth put it when discussing how to prevent climate change, "I used to think the top environmental problems were biodiversity loss, ecosystem collapse, and climate change. I thought that with 30 years of good science, we could address those problems. But I was wrong. The top environmental problems are selfishness, greed, and apathy. And to deal with those we need a spiritual and cultural transformation – and we scientists don't know how to do that."[237]

To begin with, our model of the human being has lost its spirit and, for most academics, its soul too. By the mid-twentieth century, following WW II, human consciousness was viewed as nothing more than a bio-chemical reaction to sensory stimuli. Free will was considered by academics as an illusion. Everything could be explained as the result of particles by science. Emotions were merely the effect from hormones. Such a philosophy for science and humanity, makes life meaningless. It naturally leads to a new Epicureanism where one aspires to a workless life while being continuously entertained by a flow of images on a screen.

Will our era have its own Leonardo to initiate a new Renaissance? Will there be a renewal of art-science-and-religion acting together for the progress of the cultural life? Will Knowledge of the human being as body, soul, and spirit arise again?

"Just as mankind has to do with the three realms of nature, he also has to do with three spiritual realms. Now you may say: It is of no consequence whether I believe it or not, for these three kingdoms are not visible, not perceptible. Yes, my friends, I have known people [1880s] to whom it had to be explained that air exists! They

---

[237] James Gustave Speth, 2007 Yale Forum on Religion and Ecology, quoted by Rev. Ken Wilson to the Miami Herald 18Feb2010, see
http://fore.yale.edu/files/2010_UNEP_emails.pdf

could not believe that there was something like air. When I say to such a person, this is a table – that he can believe, for when he goes to the table, he can knock on the table, and when he looks at it, he sees the table with his own eyes, but he cannot bump into the air. He looks around and says, there is nothing here. However, everyone nowadays admits the existence of air. The existence of air is simply accepted.

"In the same way, it will happen that people will come to admit the existence of a spiritual world. Today, people still say: The spiritual realm simply does not exist – in the same manner that the peasants used to say: There is no air. In my native village, the peasants used to say: there is no air at all, only the big-headed people from the city assert that because they want to give the impression that they are so clever; one can walk through it because there is nothing to walk through! – But that was long ago. Today [1924], farmers also accept that air exists. But even the smartest people still don't recognize that there are spiritual beings everywhere! They will, however, acknowledge it in due time, because otherwise certain things simply will be inexplicable, things that will need to be understood."[238]

Final Thoughts

Through Leonardo, Knowledge returned to its throne. Faith, who had ruled for a millennium, was overthrown. "For, verily, great love springs from great knowledge of the beloved object, and if you little know it, you will be able to love it only little or not at all."[239] Leonardo loved Sophia (wisdom).

---

[238] Rudolf Steiner, *Die Geschichte der Menschheit und die Weltanschauungen der Kulturvölker,* Dornach, 25Jun1924, GA 353, pg. 306
[239] https://www.leonardodavinci.net/quotes.jsp

"Learning acquired in youth arrests the evil of old age; and if you understand that old age has wisdom for its food, you will so conduct yourself in youth that your old age will not lack for nourishment."[240] Science has strong knowledge of the lifeless. If Leonardo could today, he would lead Science to rediscover the wisdom of the Human.

Although St. Paul described the human as a being of body, soul, and spirit,[241] over time the human constitution was reduced by dogma to body and soul. The eternal quality of spirit was deemed to be only attainable as a reward by the righteous on Judgment Day. In our time, it has become a form of scientific heresy for an educated person to speak about spirit or soul as realities. The concept "human" has been reduced today to body alone. With such a starved concept, no wonder today's Transhumanists can entertain images of future that no longer needs the human. No wonder it has become so difficult to conceive what Leonardo's painting the *Virgin of the Rocks* might actually depict!

Leonardo earned the title The Renaissance Man through his love of wisdom that united Art, Science, and Religion. Today we await the next Leonardo to take us into Renaissance 2.0. In Leonardo's time, wisdom was crippled by Church dogma. Today, wisdom is once again crippled, this time by the Church of Materialism. But the various scientific fields have reached the boundary of materialism. The next Leonardo will become a bridge to carry Art, Science, and Religion beyond the boundaries of materialism to the next spiritual and cultural Renaissance.

---

[240] https://www.leonardodavinci.net/quotes.jsp
[241] 1 Thessalonians 5:23, Paul refers to human nature as consisting of soma, psyche, and pneuma; that is body, soul, and spirit respectively.

Appendix A

Exploring the History Surrounding the Two Paintings

This sequence below is largely adapted from the online book, *Leonardo da Vinci and "The Virgin of the Rocks,"* by Tamsyn Taylor.[242] Her sequence aligns with other historical accounts. It is shown here to ground the reader in the historical sequence of events that pertain to the two paintings called *Virgin of the Rocks*. It is the contention of this book that the painting at the Louvre was begun by Leonardo while in Florence and completed in Milan while the second painting now in the National Gallery in London was begun in Milan to fulfill a commission.

1320. Dante Alighieri published *The Divine Comedy*.

1335. The Chapel of the Immaculate Conception was founded by Beatrice d'Este, wife of Galeazzo I, Duke of Milan apparently somewhat before 1335. The Chapel was attached to the church of San Francesco Grande, Milan.

1477. Pope Sixtus IV officially recognized the Doctrine of the Immaculate Conception and its feast day was set for the 8th of December. Bernardino de' Busti of the Confraternity of the Immaculate Conception wrote the commission.[243]

1479. The wealthy Confraternity of the Immaculate Conception contracted Francesco Zavattari and Giorgio della Chiesa to decorate the vault of the chapel.

---

[242] Tamsyn Taylor, Colchester Gallery, http://www.leonardodavincithevirginoftherocks.com/, 2011 (accessed 26Jan2018)

[243] James Kettlewell, *Leonardo da Vinci's Virgin Of The Rocks: The Subject Matter Explained*, http://www.jameskettlewell.com/virgin.html

1480. The Confraternity then contracted Giacomo del Maino to create a large wooden altarpiece with spaces for paintings and with carvings and decoration, to be placed above the altar of the chapel. Final payment was to be made on August 7, 1482.

1482. In the autumn, Leonardo da Vinci moved to Milan, to be employed by its Duke.

1483:

- **February**, Giacomo del Maino withdrew from fulfilling the requested paintings of the commission (apparently, he completed the carvings and frame). The bid is reopened.
- **April 25th**, Antonio de' Capitani, a notary, drew up a contract that listed Prior Bartolomeo Scorlione and the Confraternity as the client and listed Leonardo da Vinci, Ambrogio de Predis and his brother Evangelista de Predis as the painters. The whole altarpiece was stipulated with the subject to relate to the doctrine of the Immaculate Conception. The contract specified the sizes and subjects of three painted panels, a relief panel and several smaller panels. Even the colors of major areas and the use of gold leaf were specified. The work was to have been completed by the newly assigned Feast of the Conception, 8 December 1483.
- There was no contractual determination of which artist was to provide which part of the whole. They were commissioned as equals, except that Leonardo was accorded the title of "Master". However, Ambrogio de Predis was known as a painter and it is presumed that Evangelista was the gilder and paint mixer (Evangelista died in 1491).
- An example of what the Confraternity likely had in mind is shown in figure 88.
- The contract called for:

a) Virgin and Child in a crib
b) Two prophets who foresaw
c) Several delighted angels
d) Brightly colored background
e) Decorated "in the Byzantine manner"
f) Above: God the Father wearing robe of gold & ultramarine blue
g) Virgin Mary's garment was to be crimson and gold brocade and cloak of ultramarine
h) Two side panels with four angels playing instruments and singing

Figure 88 Albani Torlonia Altarpiece Perugino, Villa Torlonia, Rome, c. 1490

- **May,** Leonardo worked on the main painting while Ambrogio worked on the two side-panels. These paintings will eventually find their way to the National Gallery, London.

266

- **May 1**, an initial payment of 100 Lire was made. Thereafter, to ensure the work progressed, payments of 40 Lire per month were to be made starting July 1483 and monthly until December 1483 when the painting was to have been installed. This would total to 800 Lire. Another sum of money was to be negotiated upon completion and delivery of the work.
- **December 8th**. The painting was to be finished and installed by the Feast Day of the Immaculate Conception, the same year, 1483. Seven months was not enough for Leonardo and his team to complete the job.
- **Next 7 years**. Some suspect that the Confraternity was given (a mostly completed) painting (Louvre) until the other version (National Gallery) was completed. This would have required the original to have fit the frame or for the frame to have been completed to fit the painting.

1490-95. Ambrogio and Leonardo petition the Confraternity stating that they have completed the contracted work but that the centrepiece alone cost the whole 800 Lire and they ask for a further 1,200 Lire. But the Confraternity offered only 100 Lire as a result of this petition.

- Leonardo and Ambrogio then request Lodovico Sforza, the Duke of Milan, to intervene and persuade the Confraternity to pay them or else appoint two experts to represent the various parties, to evaluate the work. If payment agreement cannot be met, the painters seem to have requested permission to withdraw the work itself (this implies that a painting is in possession of the Confraternity).

1492. Leonardo begins planning for the work on the *Last Supper* mural (and Columbus sets sail).

1493. A portrait of Ludovico's niece, Bianca Maria, was painted by Ambrogio. He then accompanied her to Innsbruck after her wedding to Emperor Maximilian I in 1493. In 1494, he returned to Milan, where he designed coins for the mint, designed and supervised tapestry works, and prepared stage scenery. In 1502 he produced his only surviving signed and dated work, a portrait of the Emperor Maximilian.

1494. Charles VIII of France entered Italy with 25,000 men, stopping at Milan where its duke, Ludovico, encouraged him to attack Naples. They reached Naples on 22 February 1495 and expelled Alfonso with Charles being crowned King of Naples.

1495. Leonardo completes the *Last Supper* in the refectory of the Convent of Santa Maria della Grazie in Milan after three years of work.

1499. Louis XII of France invaded Lombardy. Leonardo fled Milan (with his key paintings).

1501. Fra Pietro da Novarella, after a visit to Leonardo in Florence, wrote to Isabella d'Este of Mantua that Leonardo was working on a Madonna for Louis XII's secretary, Robertet, and that he had an "obligation" to complete it for the King himself (some suggest this Madonna painting is the Louvre's *Virgin of the Rocks,* implying it was not the original).

1503. With the legal dispute now running 13 years, Ambrogio de Predi writes a further appeal for a settlement. Louis XII wrote to the commander of Milan on March 9, 1503 and requested he intervene on the king's behalf.

- **June 23.** The Confraternity set out a deed contesting De Predis' request for evaluation of the work or its return implying they, not the artists, are in possession of a painting.
- The petition states that, if settlement cannot be reached, the painting should be returned to the ownership of the painters. Likely this was a negotiation strategy. Besides, there is no evidence that a painting was returned or a swap took place.

1506. De Predis succeeded in re-opening the case that demanded expert valuators to be present. The meeting was called for April 4th but when one of the valuators did not show up, the case was adjourned.

- **April 27th.** An evaluation was made and it was judged that the work in the studio was still incomplete. Leonardo was requested to finish it, but he was still absent from Milan.

1507. August 7th, Ambrogio received a half payment of 100 Lire.

1508. August 18th, the painting (which has been further worked on, presumably by Ambrogio) is delivered and put into place.

- **October 23rd**, Ambrogio received a final payment of 100 Lire.
- Leonardo foregoes his share in favor of Ambrogio De Predis.

In 1524 and 1576. *The Virgin of the Rocks* in the Chapel of the Immaculate Conception was invoked against the plague.[244] [Wasserman p 110]

1576. The altarpiece containing the (London) *Virgin of the Rocks* was removed from the Chapel at the church of S. Francesco Grande in Milan before the chapel was demolished.

---

[244] Jack Wasserman, *Leonardo da Vinci*, Abrams, 1975

1625. *The Virgin of the Rocks* (Louvre) was inventoried by Cassiano dal Pozzo at Fontainebleau.

1785. June-July, Gavin Hamilton, a painter, purchased the (London) *Virgin of the Rocks* from Count Cicogna, administrator of Santa Catarina alla Ruota which succeeded the Confraternity of the Immaculate Conception. The Hamilton heirs later sold the painting to Lord Lansdown.

1880. The painting passed from the Earl of Suffolk to the National Gallery for 9,000 guineas. It was reported to be in a poor state of preservation. At the time, critics could not agree if the painter was by Leonardo or by Bernardino Luini.

2009-2011. the National Gallery's *Virgin of the Rocks* undergoes restoration and detailed examination using infrared reflectogram that reveal traces of an earlier composition beneath the present picture.

Appendix B

Merging of Zarathustra and Gautama Buddha

Lecture 3 of Rudolf Steiner's *Spiritual Guidance of Man and Humanity*[245] offers an even deeper look into what we've covered in the merging of the two Jesus boys. "Let us first consider Jesus of Nazareth. His conditions of existence were quite exceptional. At the beginning of our era two boys were born and named Jesus. The one came through the Nathan line of the house of David, [Luke III, 23–38.] the other through the Solomon line of the same house. [Matthew 1, 1–17. See also Appendix.] These two children were not born quite at the same time, but nearly so. In the Jesus descended from Solomon, described in the Gospel of St. Matthew, there was incarnated the same individuality who had formerly lived on the earth as Zarathustra, so that in this Child Jesus there appears the re-incarnated Zarathustra or Zoroaster. The individuality of Zarathustra grew up in this Child until, as St. Matthew says, His twelfth year. In that year, Zarathustra left the body of this Child and passed over into that of the other Child Jesus Whom the Gospel of St. Luke describes. In consequence of this the latter Child became suddenly quite different. The parents were astonished when they found Him in Jerusalem in the temple after the spirit of Zarathustra had entered into Him. This is intimated when it is said that the Child, after having been lost and found again in the temple, so spake that his parents did not recognize Him. They only knew Him, the Child descended from Nathan, as He had been up to this time. But when He began to reason with the doctors in the temple, it was possible for Him to speak as He did because the spirit of Zarathustra had come into Him. Until the

---

[245] Rudolf Steiner, *Spiritual Guidance of Man and Humanity*, lecture 3, 8Jun1911, Copenhagen, GA 15

thirtieth year did the spirit of Zarathustra live in the Jesus who was descended from the Nathan line of the house of David. In this body He ripened to a still higher perfection. The following remark must here be added: as regards this personality in which the spirit of Zarathustra now lived; an extraordinary feature was that into his astral body the Buddha rayed forth his impulses from the spiritual worlds.

The oriental tradition is correct which says that the Buddha was born as a "Bodhisattva" and only during his time on earth, in his twenty-ninth year, rose to the dignity of a Buddha. When the Gautama Buddha was a little child, the Indian sage Asita came weeping into the royal palace of his father, Suddhodana. He wept because, as a seer, he knew that this King's son would become the Buddha, and because as an old man, he felt that he would no longer be living to see that event take place. Now this sage was born again in the time of Jesus of Nazareth. It is he who is brought before us in the Gospel of St. Luke as the priest of the temple who saw the revelation of the Buddha in the Child Jesus descended from Nathan. And seeing this he was able to say: "Lord, now lettest Thou Thy servant depart in peace for I have seen my Master," What he had not been able to see previously in India, he saw through the astral body of the boy Jesus, who comes before us in St. Luke's Gospel: The Bodhisattva become Buddha.

All this was necessary in order that that body might be produced which received the baptism of St. John in the Jordan. At that moment the individuality of Zarathustra left the threefold body, the physical, the etheric and the astral body of that Jesus Who had grown up in so complicated a manner, in order that the spirit of Zarathustra might be able to dwell in Him. The reincarnated Zarathustra had to pass through two possibilities of development which were given in the two Jesus children. Thus, there stood before the Baptist the body of Jesus of Nazareth and in it from that time onwards there acted the cosmic individuality of the Christ."

Appendix C

Initiation in the New Testament

Based on John 11:5, the Beloved Disciple can be identified with Lazarus of Bethany, "Now Jesus loved Martha and her sister and Lazarus." This is confirmed by John 11:3, "Therefore his sisters sent unto him, saying, Lord, behold, he whom thou lovest is sick."

Ben Witherington III's[246] research showed that the character of the Beloved Disciple is not mentioned before the raising of Lazarus. Then, in the exact middle of the gospel, John 11, Lazarus is raised. Afterward, Lazarus is no longer mentioned while the Beloved Disciple is first mentioned in John 13 and thereafter.

Frederick Baltz[247] carries further the identification of Lazarus suggesting that the Beloved Disciple was a priest. Baltz, citing Josephus and rabbinic literature, concludes that the family of the children of Boethus is the same family we meet in John 11. Thus, Lazarus, Martha, and Mary of are members of this family that resides in Bethany. This is the beloved family mentioned in John 11:5. Thus, the historical Lazarus was Eleazar son of Boethus, who was once Israel's high priest.

and from a clan that produced several high priests. The Gospel's author, John, was not a member of the Twelve, but the son of Martha (Sukkah 52b). He closely matches the description given by Bishop Polycrates in his letter, a sacrificing priest who wore the petalon (i.e., emblem of the high priest). This John "the Elder" was a follower of Jesus referred to by Papias of Hierapolis, and an

---

[246] Ben Witherington III, *OneBook Daily-Weekly, The Gospel of John*, Seedbed Publishing, 2015
[247] Frederick Baltz, *The Mystery of the Beloved Disciple: New Evidence, Complete Answer*, Infinity Publishing, 2011

eyewitness to his ministry. He was the right age to have lived until the time of Trajan (according to Irenaeus). Baltz says John is probably the disciple ον ηγαπα ο Ιησους, and Eleazar is the disciple ον εφιλει ο Ιησους in the Gospel.

Initiation of Saul

"All talk of limits to human knowledge is a nonsense. One should rather ask: Is it not possible for the human being to rise to a higher level of knowledge? Are not what one calls the eyes and the ears of the spirit perhaps a reality? There have always been individuals who have worked on certain latent faculties and who can thus see more than others. Their testimony might be just as valid as the testimony of those who look through the microscope. How many people have actually seen what the scientific history of creation teaches? I would like to ask; how many people have seen what they talk about? How many, for example, have in actual fact, proof of the development of the human embryo? If they were to ask themselves such questions, they would see what a blind faith it is that governs them. And if it is a justified faith, then the faith based on the testimony of the Initiates who speak from their spiritual experiences is equally justified."[248]

---

[248] Rudolf Steiner, *Woman and Society*, Hamburg, 17Nov1906, GA 54

Appendix D

Modern Mysticism

Mysticism has existed, according to mystics, from the beginning of time. Throughout the times from Christ to the present, unbeknown to the general population and present in all cultures, mystics have lived and contributed to the evolution of humanity. Of this the German philosopher of Idealism, Johann Fichte, spoke, "Despite for the most part being misunderstood and persecuted by the established church, we assert that this knowledge, in all its integrity and purity, and which we are incapable of surpassing, has in every age and since the origin of Christianity still been able to prevail and flourish in secret here and there [...] though this doctrine may appear new and unprecedented in the present epoch, it is actually as old as the world, and it is especially the doctrine of Christianity that can be found in the most genuine and purest ancient document, in the Gospel of John, which up until this moment is present before our eyes; and this doctrine is even expounded there using exactly the same images and expressions that we employ."[249]

I was privileged to meet the scholar and author Marek Majorek during a sabbatical year (1978-79) of study I undertook at Emerson College in Sussex, England. We've lived on separate continents since then but kept in touch nonetheless. The following I include here, with permission and slightly edited, as a fitting description by a reviewer, Lorenzo Ravagli, of Marek's book on the new, modern mysticism, *Spiritual Science: Mythological Thinking or Science*.

---

[249] J.G. Fichte, *The Way towards the Blessed Life*, translated by David Wood, 1806.

"The second volume of Marek's encyclopaedic study lists in its first chapter about three hundred pages of scientists (mainly) of the twentieth century who can be regarded as witnesses of the metaphysics of materialism. Their biographies and key research findings are presented and discussed.

Emanuel Swedenborg, who was one of the most outstanding natural scientists of the eighteenth century and became a mystic towards the end of his life, opens the round. He is joined by "the Father of American Psychology," William James, who in his Gifford Lectures dealt with the diversity of religious experiences and professed the existence of a supernatural sphere of reality. He includes the leading figure of neo-vitalism Hans Driesch and the French philosopher Henri Bergson who spoke of a "creative development." Also, Marek mentions the English physicist Oliver Lodge, who published medially obtained messages from his deceased son. Marek includes the American philosopher Alfred North Whitehead, who spoke in his late work "*Process and Reality*" of transcendental entities that worked in nature.

Modern thinkers and scientists mentioned include

- Carl Gustav Jung, in whose mysterious "Red Book", the record of his mystical experiences, appeared long after his death,
- Aldous Huxley, who with the help of mescaline broadened the gates of perceptions,
- Alister Hardy, who pointed out the limits of the materialistic interpretation of evolution,
- Ian Stevenson, the author of "Cases of Reincarnation Memory",
- Celia Green with her exploration of out-of-body experiences,
- Psychologist Charles Tart exploring altered states of consciousness,

- Physicist Fritjof Capra exploring the coincidence of physical and mystical worldviews,
- Raymond Moody the pioneer of the well-known research into near-death experiences,
- Karl Popper who, in his book entitled "*The Self and His Brain*" written with John Eccles, coined the term, "promissory materialism" for a science that has not lived up to its promises for a hundred years, and who takes the mind to be an ontologically distinct and causally effective entity,
- The Swedish scientists who studied Christ's experiences of contemporaries in the 1970s,
- Other near-death researchers such as George Ritchie and Elisabeth Kübler-Ross,
- The physicists Barrow and Tipler, who considered the "anthropic principle" in cosmology,
- The authors of the 2005 Potsdam Manifesto, which advocated overcoming the mechanistic view of the world,
- Neurobiologist Eben Alexander, who himself had a near-death experience, argued that the universe must have spiritual qualities so that intelligent life can emerge at some point in its development.
- And many more for which it is not possible to name all of the listed natural scientists here.
- Only the last, to whom Majorek's special sympathies belong, Rupert Sheldrake, should at least be briefly mentioned here. The conclusion of this chapter [is hereby] quoted: "In view of the burden of proof presented in this chapter, especially empirical arguments against materialism, the claim seems justified that the visible, material world does not exhaust reality, but beyond that there is an invisible, non-material, spiritual world that manifests itself in many phenomena in the visible world and manifests its effectiveness in this world."

This claim "implies that today's science could be radically incomplete. Perhaps science has only dealt with the proverbial tip of the iceberg instead of the iceberg itself. Thus, today it is believed that the visible universe accounts for only 5% of the entire universe, if dark energy and dark matter are included in that universe. On the further assumption that this supersensible reality has not only, as the deists have suggested, set in motion the development of the material world, so as not to interfere with it any longer, but that it (in the manner of Sheldrake's morphogenetic fields or van Lommel's infinite consciousness) is constantly effective in it, the explanation of the phenomena of the sensory world without inclusion of the supersensible world cannot be complete. The share of the factors efficient in the world that we have come to know and explore in our contemporary natural science amounts to only about 5% of the totality of the forces manifesting themselves in the universe."[250]

"As the human being is prepared in the mother's body, so in the body of the great world mother — where we are while leading our physical life — is prepared what is necessary to make it possible for us to see and act in higher worlds. One is perfectly justified to speak of a higher world and to value it higher than our lower world, but we should only use these terms in a technical sense. All worlds are, basically, equally valid expressions of the highest principle, in different forms. We should not despise any world. In this way we learn to relate ourselves rightly towards both the

---

[250] Marek B. Majorek, *Rudolf Steiners Geisteswissenschaft: mythisches Denken oder
Wissenschaft* (Rudolf Steiner's Spiritual Science: Mythological Thinking or Science),
Narr/Francke/Attempo Verlag, Tübingen 2015, two volumes, 1586 pages, review by Lorenzo Ravagli

lower and the higher worlds." -- Source: Rudolf Steiner – GA 94 – The Gospel of St. John – Third Lecture – Berlin, 5th March 1906

In ancient times, the people of India and the Semites had fundamentally different dispositions of soul, of understanding, which is why they had different spiritual teachings. On the one hand you have reincarnation and karma (in Hinduism and Buddhism), and on the other hand you have monotheism with emphasis on morals. Although there is a clear thread, for instance, between Buddha's sermon at Benares and the Luke Gospel (the Bodhi tree becomes the fig tree etc.), but the Bible has never taught reincarnation any more than Buddhism has taught monotheism. – Rudolf Steiner, *Buddha and Christ, The Sphere of the Bodhisattvas*, 21Sep1911, Milan, GA 130
https://wn.rsarchive.org/Lectures/19110921p01.html

List of Figures

Figure 1 Virgin of the Rocks, LdV, Nat'l Gallery, London, close-up of child 10
Figure 2 Sideview of painting 11
Figure 3 Virgin of the Rocks with frame, LdV, National Gallery London.. 12
Figure 4 Virgin of the Rocks, LdV, Nat'l Gallery, London................ 13
Figure 5 Virgin of the Rocks, LdV, Louvre, Paris 15
Figure 6 Three Holy Children, Bernardino de Conti, private........... 19
Figure 7 from Zachariah in the Temple: Marsilio Ficino, Cristoforo Landino, Angelo Poliziano & Demetrios Chalkondyles, Domenico Ghirlandaio, Santa Maria Novella, Cappella Tornabuoni, Florence 23
Figure 8 Bust of Ficino by A.F. da Fiesole, Duomo, Florence 25
Figure 9 Bible Moralisee, 1220 AD, Osterreichische National Biblioteck, Vienna... 28
Figure 10 Adoration of the Magi, LdV, Uffizi, Florence, Italy, 1481 39
Figure 11 John the Baptist, LdV, Louvre, Paris 41
Figure 12 Leonardo's signature 44
Figure 13 Salvador Mundi, LdV, private 45
Figure 14 Erotic Lady in Red, Leonardo da Vinci, private collection 47
Figure 15 Third copy, Virgin of the Rocks, LdV et al, private collection 49
Figure 16 Anatomy Sketches from Leonardo's notebook................ 54
Figure 17 Human-powered helicopter, LdV 55
Figure 18 Baptism, Verrocchio with LdV, 1474 56
Figure 19 Comparing Virgin of the Rocks, Nat'l Gallery. London-Louvre, Paris 62
Figure 20 Clos Luce manor where Leonardo died........................... 73
Figure 21a Side Panel, Red Angel,   Figure 21b Side Panel, Green Angel,   79

Figure 22 Piero della Francesca, Madonna del Parto, Museo della Madonna del Parto of Monterchi 81
Figure 23 Madonna and Child Enthroned, Filippo Lippi, 1430 83
Figure 24 Coronation of the Virgin, Filippo Lippi, 1468 86
Figure 25 Madonna close-up, VoR, LdV, Louvre 88
Figure 26 Comparing Archangels, VoR, LdV, National Gallery and Louvre 89
Figure 27 Marsilio Ficino by Giovio de Como, 1520, Palazzo Volpi . 98
Figure 28 Plethon, Benozzo Gozzoli, Palazzo Medici Riccardi, Florence, Italy 102
Figure 29 Comparing VoR Nat'l Gallery, London to VoR Louvre, Paris 105
Figure 30 Burlington House Cartoon, LdV, National Gallery 108
Figure 31 Sketch of fetus, Leonardo's notebooks 112
Figure 32 Foreground and background of VoR LdV, Louvre 118
Figure 33 Greek Mystery Centers by Marsyas 131
Figure 34 Constantine and his mother Helena, Mosaic in Hosios Loukas, 11th C 135
Figure 35 Baptism, mosaic, Arian Hagia Anastasis, Ravenna 138
Figure 36 Transfiguration, Raphael, Vatican, 1520 140
Figure 37 Wall painting of Palm Sunday from a Nestorian church in Qocho, China, Ethnological Museum, Berlin, 7th Century 143
Figure 38 Hulagu Khan and his Christian wife Doquz Khatun depicted as the new "Constantine and Helen" in a Syrian Bible. .145
Figure 39 Saint Peter and Saint Paul, El Greco, Catalunya National Museum,Barcelona, 1590 151
Figure 40 Holy Infants Embracing, copy of lost work by LdV 154
Figure 41 Holy Infants Embracing, Luini? private collection, London 155
Figure 42 Thuelin Madonna, Marco d'Oggiono, Paris 156
Figure 43 Comparing the hands of VoR Louvre and Holy Family by B. Luini 158

Figure 44 Joos van Cleve, Private 159
Figure 45 Joos van Cleve, Art Institute Chicago 160
Figure 46 Joos van Cleve, Museo di Capodimonte 160
Figure 47 Joos van Cleve, Minerva Auction 161
Figure 48 Joos van Cleve, Private   Figure 49 Joos van Cleve, Private   162
Figure 50 Marco d'Oggiono, Royal Collection 162
Figure 51 Joos van Cleve, Museum Catharijneconvent 163
Figure 52 Detail of both boys, VoR, Louvre 167
Figure 53 Thuelin Madonna, Marco d'Oggiono, private, Paris 168
Figure 54: Madonna, Bernardino de Conti, private collection 169
Figure 55 Madonna, B. de Conti, private in comparison to the Virgin of the Rocks, Louvre 170
Figure 56 Three Holy Children, B. de Conti, private collection 171
Figure 57 Nursing Madonna, Bernardino de Conti, private collection 174
Figure 58 Jesus Among the Doctors, Bergognone, Saint Ambrogio Basilica, Milan 176
Figure 59 Jesus Among the Doctors, Pinturicchio, Bagloioni Chapel, Spello, Italy 178
Figure 60 Close-up of the feet, Jesus Among the Doctors, Pinturicchio 179
Figure 61 Comparison of feminine faces, Pinturicchio and Raphael's School of Athens 181
Figure 62 The Hierophant with his Four Assistants, Pinturicchio . 182
Figure 63 Jesus Among the Doctors, B. Luini, National Gallery, London 185
Figure 64 Jesus Among the Doctors, D. Ferrari, Staatsgalerie, Stuttgart 186
Figure 65 Sarcophagus, c.270, Baptism of Jesus by John (right), Santa Maria Antigua, Rome 188
Figure 66 Close-up of the background, VoR Louvre 189

Figure 67 Illustration by LdVinci in Pacioli's On Divine Proportions 196
Figure 68 Tetrahedron, Cube, Octahedron, Dodecahedron, Icosahedron 198
Figure 69 Original Virgin of the Rocks with isosceles triangle 200
Figure 70 Original Virgin of the Rocks with tetrahedron 202
Figure 71 Vitruvian Man from LdV notebook 204
Figure 72 Original Virgin of the Rocks, LdV, Louvre, Paris 206
Figure 73 The Virgin with St. Anne, LdV, National Gallery 209
Figure 74 VoR depiction of the Greek model of the human 210
Figure 75 VoR depiction of the heavenly hierarchies 210
Figure 76 Artemis of Ephesus, engraving   Figure 77 Zeus Labraunda, Robert Fleischer   218
Figure 78 Roman copy of Artemis of Ephesus 218
Figure 79 Awakening the Three Kings, Master Gislebertus, Cathedral of St. Lazarus, Autun, France 222
Figure 80 Sleeve as Stage Curtains, VoR National Gallery and VoR, Louvre 233
Figure 81 Close-up: Child with Staff, Same child from Virgin of the Rocks Paris 234
Figure 82 Madonna Terranuova, Raphael, c.1505 236
Figure 83 Madonna with Kissing Babes, Martino Piazza, Museum of Fine Arts (Budapest) 237
Figure 84 Saint John the Baptist In the Desert, Martino Piazza, National Gallery, London 239
Figure 85 The Bohdan And Varvara Khanenko Museum of Art, Kiev 240
Figure 86 Comparing Gabriel's Annunciation, Leonardo da Vinci, Uffizi to Archangel VoR, LdV, Louvre 242
Figure 87 Comparison of Virgin of the Rocks, LdV and Three Holy Children, B.de Conti 251

Figure 88 Albani Torlonia Altarpiece Perugino, Villa Torlonia, Rome, c. 1490 266

Bibliography

- Harold W. Attridge, *Eusebius, Early Christianity and Judaism*, Wayne State University Press, First Edition edition, 1992
- Carmen Bambach, *Leonardo da Vinci Rediscovered*, Yale University Press, 2019
- Nicola Barbatelli, Carlo Pedretti, *Leonardo a Donnaregina. I Salvator Mundi per Napoli*, Elio De Rosa Editore; CB Edizioni, 2017
- Richard Bauckham (Editor), Old Testament Pseudepigrapha: More Noncanonical Scriptures, Eerdmans, 2013
- Rachel Billinge, Luke Syson, and Marika Spring, 'Altered Angels: Two Panels from the Immaculate Conception Altarpiece once in San Francesco Grande, Milan'. National Gallery Technical Bulletin Vol 32, pp 57–77. http://www.nationalgallery.org.uk/technical-bulletin/billinge_syson_spring2011
- E. A. Wallis Budge, *Osiris and the Egyptian Resurrection*, P. L. Warner Books, 1911
- Tony Burke, *New Testament Apocrypha: More Noncanonical Scriptures*, Eerdmans, 2016
- Thomas Cahill, *Heretics and Heroes: How Renaissance Artists and Reformation Priests Created Our World*, Anchor Books, 2014
- James H. Charlesworth, *The Old Testament Pseudepigrapha* (2 Volume set), Hendrickson Publishers, 2010
- Angela Ottino della Chiesa, *The Complete Paintings of Leonardo da Vinci*, Penguin Classics, 1967
- Kenneth Clark and Martin Kemp, *Leonardo da Vinci*, The Folio Society, 2005

- April DeConick, *The Gnostic New Age: How a Countercultural Spirituality Revolutionized Religion from Antiquity to Today*, Columbia University Press, 2016
- Nicola Denzey Lewis, *Cosmology and Fate in Gnosticism and Graeco-Roman Antiquity: Under Pitiless Skies*, Brill, 2013
- Nicola Denzey Lewis, *Introduction to Gnosticism: Ancient Voices, Christian Worlds*, Oxford University Press, 2012
- Diogenes Laertius, *Lives of the Eminent Philosophers*, Oxford University Press, Oxford, 2018
- Bart Ehrman, *Jesus Before the Gospels. How the Earliest Christians Remembered, Changed, and Invented Stories of the Savior*, HarperOne, 2016
- Bart Ehrman, *The New Testament: A Historical Introduction to the Early Christian Writings*. Oxford University Press, 2015
- Bart D. Ehrman, *Lost Christianities: The Battles for Scripture and the Faiths We Never Knew*, Oxford University Press, New York, NY 2003
- Bart Ehrman, *The Orthodox Corruption of Scripture: The Effect of Early Christological Controversies on the Text of the New Testament*, Oxford University Press, 1996
- J. K. Elliott, *The Apocryphal New Testament: A Collection of Apocryphal Christian Literature*, Oxford University Press, 2005
- Paula Fredriksen, *From Jesus to Christ: The Origins of the New Testament Images of Jesus*, Yale University Press; 2nd edition, 2008
- Tom Harpur, *The Pagan Christ*, Thomas Allen Publishers, 2004
- M. R. James (Editor), *The New Testament Apocrypha*, Apocryphile Press, 2004
- Don Karr, *Esotericism and Christian Kabbalah: 1480-1520*, L'Époque de la Renaissance, John Benjamins B. V., 2017
- Rodolphe Kasser et al, *The Gospel of Judas*, Second Edition, National Geographic, 2008

- Martin Kemp, *Leonardo by Leonardo*, Callaway A&E, 2019
- Martin Kemp and Thereza Wells, *Leonardo Da Vinci's Madonna of the Yarnwinder, A Historical & Scientific Detective Story*, Artatk ePub, 2016
- Martin Kemp, *Leonardo da Vinci. The Marvellous Works of Nature and Man*, Oxford University Press, 2006
- Martin Kemp, *Leonardo*, Oxford University Press, 2004
- Helmut Koester, *Introduction to the New Testament, Vol. 2: History and Literature of Early Christianity*, de Gruyter, 2nd edition, 2000
- Oddbjørn Leirvik, *Images of Jesus Christ in Islam*: 2nd Edition, Bloomsbury Publishing, 2010
- Pieto Marani, *Leonardo Da Vinci: The Complete Paintings*, Abrams, 2003
- Marvin W. Meyer (Editor), *The Nag Hammadi Scriptures*, HarperOne, 2009
- Charles Nicholl, *Leonardo da Vinci: The Flights of the Mind*, Penguin, 2005
- Elaine Pagels, *The Gnostic Gospels*, Random House, 1979
- Carlo Pedretti, *Leonardo and the European Genius*, CB Edizioni, 2008
- Carlo Pedretti, *Leonardo Genius and Vision in the Land of Marches*, CB Edizioni, 2005
- Carlo Pedretti, *Leonardo da Vinci*, Taj Books, 2005
- E. Randolph Richards, *Paul and First-Century Letter-Writing: Secretaries, Composition and Collection*. Intervarsity Press, 2004
- Steven Runciman, *The Last Byzantine Renaissance*, Cambridge, 1970

- Wilhelm Schneemelcher, *New Testament Apocrypha, Vol. 2: Writings Relating to the Apostles Apocalypses and Related Subjects*, Westminster John Knox Press, 1992
- Wilhelm Schneemelcher, *New Testament Apocrypha, Vol. 1: Gospels and Related Writings Revised Edition*, Westminster John Knox Press, 1990
- Rudolf Steiner, *From Jesus to Christ*, Rudolf Steiner Press, 1973 (lectures from 1911)
- Rudolf Steiner, *Christianity as Mystical Fact*, Anthroposophic Press, 1972 (from 1910)
- Rudolf Steiner, *The Gospel of St. Luke*, Rudolf Steiner Publishing Co., 1946
- Rudolf Steiner lectures regarding the two Jesus boys:
    - 1909: *The Ego*, lecture 2, 7Dec1909, Munich, GA 117,
    - 1910: *The Gospel of St. Matthew*, lecture 6, 6Sep1910, Berne, GA 123
    - 1911: *Wonders of the World*: Lecture 9, 26Aug1911, Munich, GA 129; *Esoteric Christianity and the Mission of Christian Rosenkreutz*, 17Sep1911, Lugano, GA 130; *From Jesus to Christ*, lecture 8, 12Oct1911, Karlsruhe, GA 131
    - 1912: *Man in the Light of Occultism, Theosophy and Philosophy*, lecture 9, 11Jun1912, Christiania, GA 137; The Gospel of Mark: Lecture 2, 16Sep1912, Basel, GA 139
    - 1913: *The Bhagavad Gita and the Epistles of St. Paul*, 1Jan1913, Cologne, GA 142; The Occult Significance of the Bhagavad Gita, lecture 4, 31May1913, Helsingfors, GA 146; Christ and the Spiritual World, lecture 3, 30Dec1913, Leipzig, GA 149
    - 1914: *The Birth of Christ Within Us*, 27Dec1914, Berlin, GA 156

- 1915: *Occult Movement*, Lecture 5, 18Oct1915, Dornach, GA 254
  - 1916: *Universal Human*, lecture 4, 9Jan1916, Bern, GA 165, etc.
- Paul Strathern, *The Medici: Godfathers of the Renaissance*. London: Random House, 1993
- William Whiston (Editor), *The Works of Josephus*, Thomas Nelson, 2003
- Michael Williams, *Rethinking "Gnosticism": An Argument for Dismantling a Dubious Category*, Princeton University Press, 1996
- James VanderKam and Peter Flint, *The Meaning of the Dead Sea Scrolls*, HarperCollins, 2013
- Geza Vermes, *The Complete Dead Sea Scrolls in English*, Penguin Classics, 2012
- Giorgio Vasari (1568), *Lives of the Artists*. Penguin Classics, trans. George Bull 1965
- Sami Yli-Karjanmaa, *Reincarnation in Philo of Alexandria*, SBL Press, 2015
- Frank Zöllner, *Leonardo da Vinci. The Complete Paintings*, Taschen, 2018
- Center for the Study of New Testament Manuscripts, http://csntm.org/About
- Early Christian Writings, http://www.earlychristianwritings.com/
- Open Culture, Leonardo's Notebook Pages Online: http://www.openculture.com/2017/07/leonardo-da-vincis-visionary-notebooks-now-online-browse-570-digitized-pages.html

Index

Adam Kadmon, 120, 190, 193, 194, 200, 219, 220, 223, 242, 246, 254
Albigensian Crusade, 38
Alexander, 46, 122, 134, 135, 137, 277
Aquinas, 38
Aristotle, 100, 101, 103, 113, 131, 134
Arius, 138, 139, 140, 147
Athanasius, 139
Augustine, 18, 32, 33, 36, 37, 38, 103, 121, 133, 149
Bambach, 46, 285
Bergognone, 158, 174, 175, 176, 177, 183
Bruno, 109, 113
Cain, 190, 191, 192, 202, 214, 217, 222, 248, 251, 252, 255
Cathars, 239, 243, 253
Charlemagne, 103, 148
Clark, 65, 285
Confraternity of the Immaculate Conception, 14, 116, 256, 263, 268
Constantine, 31, 135, 136, 137, 152, 244
Council of Nicaea, 137, 138, 139
Cult of Mary, 84
Cyril of Alexandria, 142
d'Oggiono, 71, 157, 158, 167

Davies, 65
de Conti, 17, 50, 157, 171, 172, 174, 249
De Predis, 69, 268
Dead Sea Scroll, 187, 224, 225, 227, 231, 243, 246, 289
Dionysius the Areopagite, 106, 209, 240
Early Christianity, 18, 31, 33, 35, 39, 121, 130, 131, 248, 249, 285, 287
Ecumenical Council, 34, 39, 84, 245
Ehrman, 32, 42, 85, 124, 125, 138, 286
Ferrari, 184, 242
Ficino, 22, 25, 27, 53, 97, 98, 100, 101, 102, 195, 243
Filioque, 34
Gnostic, 33, 94, 163, 286, 287
Gnosticism, 59, 249, 286, 289
Great Schism, 34, 38, 98
hierophant, 23, 102, 125, 128, 182, 183, 209
Hippolytus of Rome, 132, 228
Hiram Abiff, 191, 202, 222, 223
Holy of the Holies, 125, 128, 176, 182, 244
Hulagu, 146
Irenaeus, 274
Justinian, 35, 148, 152, 244

Kabbala, 120, 187, 189, 190, 229, 243, 256
Kemp, 71, 285, 287
Kettlewell, 73, 74, 75, 94, 95, 108, 109, 263
Knights Templar, 38, 239, 243
Lippi, 59, 82, 87, 114
Louvre, 9, 16, 17, 40, 49, 51, 60, 62, 64, 65, 67, 69, 70, 71, 72, 73, 78, 96, 105, 106, 107, 233, 234, 248, 262, 265, 267, 268
Luini, 157, 158, 183, 268
Mani, 138
Manichaeism, 36
Melzi, 60, 61, 73
Mongol, 146
Nag Hammadi, 287
National Gallery, 9, 10, 11, 12, 17, 60, 62, 64, 65, 68, 70, 73, 78, 80, 89, 90, 91, 106, 107, 108, 116, 120, 154, 184, 188, 240, 263, 265, 266, 268, 269, 285
Neoplatonism, 21
Nestorius, 140, 142, 143, 144, 147
Origen, 35, 42, 94, 124, 147, 148
Ottino della Chiesa, 71, 76, 77, 107, 153, 285
Pacioli, 196, 197
Pedretti, 47, 48, 49, 285, 287
Philo, 32, 35, 37
Piazza, 236
Pinturicchio, 17, 179, 182, 248

Pistis Sophia, 163, 164, 165, 176, 244
Plato, 21, 22, 25, 27, 28, 29, 32, 35, 37, 100, 101, 103, 109, 121, 129, 131, 148, 195, 196, 211, 213, 243, 249
Platonic Academy, 103, 149, 195
Plethon, 22, 25, 28, 39, 53, 97, 98, 100, 101, 102, 103, 149, 163, 243, 244
Plotinus, 32, 35, 37, 101
Plutarch, 35, 37, 134, 135
Prester John, 144
Pythagoras, 196
Qumran, 224, 225, 228, 231
Raphael, 9, 21, 91, 157, 163, 181, 234, 235, 240, 258
Savonarola, 27, 195
Sforza, 55, 56, 57, 76, 116, 197, 266
Skaftnesmo, 6, 179
Steiner, 7, 9, 14, 15, 34, 128, 129, 130, 175, 176, 193, 202, 214, 215, 219, 221, 244, 254, 261, 270, 274, 278, 279, 288
Syson, 66, 285
Taylor, 65, 66, 68, 72, 81, 90, 91, 262
Theodosius II, 143
Theotokos, 84, 140
two messiahs, 20, 39, 224, 225, 226, 231, 246
van Cleve, 153, 159, 172

Vasari, 55, 56, 59, 82, 113, 195, 289
Verrocchio, 23, 52, 56, 57, 195, 241

Williams, 175
Zenale, 166, 174
Zoroaster, 101, 131, 221, 254, 270

www.ingramcontent.com/pod-product-compliance
Lightning Source LLC
Chambersburg PA
CBHW042055290426
44111CB00001B/8